Covenant Theology

Covenant Theology

A Reformed Baptist Perspective

Phillip D. R. Griffiths

WIPF & STOCK · Eugene, Oregon

Wipf & Stock
An Imprint of Wipf and Stock Publishers
199 W. 8th Ave., Suite 3
Eugene, OR 97401

www.wipfandstock.com

PAPERBACK ISBN: 978-1-4982-3482-5
HARDCOVER ISBN: 978-1-4982-3484-9
EBOOK ISBN: 978-1-4982-3483-2

06/20/18

I dedicate this work to my longsuffering wife Melody, and my two sons, Benjamin and Joseph.

For the Law was given by Moses, but grace
and truth came by Jesus Christ

(John 1:17)

Chapters

Preface

WHY AM I A BAPTIST? This is a question Baptists need to ask themselves. All too often, when they do, the answer many come up with appears to be something akin to a tinkered version of Presbyterianism; a reworked paedobaptist paradigm in which the various covenants are believed to be different administrations of the one covenant of grace.

This work completely rejects the paedobaptist paradigm. I have tried to explain the Reformed Baptist position in a manner that will make it easily accessible. In places I have repeated the essential elements. I make no apology for this because I believe repetition to be essential in enabling the reader to grasp the central principle, namely, that the only covenant of grace is the new covenant, and that none have been saved but by virtue of this covenant. One of the things I do, which may not be to everyone's liking, is to criticize the Reformed paedobaptist position. I do this because by understanding what something is not one can come to a better understanding of what it is. Wrong teaching acts as a foil that makes the truth explicit.

I hope by the end of the book the reader will come to see that this is the only covenant theology that is faithful to the teaching of Scripture. Understanding this will enable the reader to see how the Old and New Testaments relate to each other. Ultimately, it is hoped that it will assist the believer in coming to a greater appreciation of the riches that are his in Christ.

Introduction

Baptist Covenantal Theology

I DON'T THINK ANY would question that the church, particularly in the Western world, is going through difficult times. Times in which, to quote Ken Ham, "we are seeing before our very eyes the collapse of Christianity across Europe and North America."[1] There is, in the words of David Wells, "a yawning chasm between what evangelical faith was in the past and what it frequently is today, between the former spirituality and the contemporary emptiness and accommodation."[2] In many churches the great doctrines of the faith are not only neglected but are being substituted with a superficial hotchpotch of homemade theology. Don Haddleton, in a 2006 article entitled "Evangelical Superficiality," stated that in "Evangelicalism there is a growing trend toward frivolity and superficiality, affecting Christian life, prayer, witness, evangelism and worship. 'Easy-believism', 'user friendly-ism' and 'feel-goodism' are taking over the church's life and witness."[3] Increasingly, even in Reformed circles, Christians do not read in any depth the theology of their faith, and, unfortunately, one can but agree with Mohler that "the abdication of biblical faith is one of the hallmarks of our age."[4]

Affected, or should one say, infected, by this age's consumer culture, many Christians appear more concerned about where the next experience, or quick fix is to be found than about understanding the theology that undergirds their faith. The Jewish writer Dennis Prager made a telling observation about today's evangelicalism, "One thing I notice about Evangelicals is that they do not read. They do not read the Bible, they do not read the great

1. Ham, *Understanding the Times*, 2.
2. Wells, *No Place for Truth*, 135.
3. Haddleton, *Evangelical Superficiality*.
4. Mohler, *The Disappearance of God*, 8.

Christian thinkers, they have never heard of Aquinas ... I do not understand. I have bookcases of Christian books and I am a Jew. Why do I have more Christian books than 98 percent of Christians in America?"[5] One could argue that this is due to all the distractions of our modern age. Information is now available at one's fingertips. This has resulted in potential knowledge replacing actual knowledge. Whereas in times past Christians delved deep into God's word to glean truths applicable to themselves, now, this is believed to be the task of the minister or academic. According to Wells:

> Evangelicals today only have to believe that God can work dra-matically within a narrow fissure of internal experience; they have lost interest (or perhaps they can no longer sustain in in-terest) in what the doctrines of creation, common grace, and providence once meant for Christian believers, and even those doctrines that articulate Christ's death, such as justification, re-demption, propitiation and reconciliation. It is now enough for them to know that somehow Christ died for them.[6]

These comments, though harsh, appear to be a true representation of a growing number within the Western evangelical church.

Evangelical churches have been, to a greater or lesser degree, infected by our age's secular ethos, and one finds oneself having to agree with Blamires that, "the Christian mind has succumbed to the secular drift with a degree of weakness and nervousness unmatched in Christian history."[7] Evangelicalism has deteriorated to the point, to quote Carl Trueman, "where one can deny that God knows the future, one can deny that the Bible is inspired, one can deny that justification is by grace through faith, one can deny that Christ is the only way of salvation-one can do all these things and still remain a member in good standing of certain high-profile evangelical bodies."[8] Many evangelicals are more likely to listen to the unbiblical theology of men like Benny Hinn and Kenneth Copeland than sit under a ministry where the Word is system-atically expounded. They proudly display a false theology with stickers saying, "smile Jesus loves you," or "give your heart to Jesus," and all too many church ministers preach "peace, peace, when there is no peace" (Jer 8:11).

Theological illiteracy, coupled with an unmatched subjectivism, has opened the door to the postmodern mindset, one where relativism[9] has re-placed truth. Indeed, god can be whatever one wants him to be. The idea of

5. Prager, *Civilization that Believes in Nothing*, 15.

6. Wells, *No Place for Truth*, 131.

7. Blamires, *Recovery the Christian Mind*, 9.

8. Trueman, *Reformation*, 15.

9. Relativism is a position that rejects the idea of an objective truth.

an objective truth, of a God who alone is God and who sustains and determines all things, in a world where right and wrong exists, has become, to say the least, unfashionable. Evidence of the modern contagion is reflected in a generalized spiritual malaise, and even in many Reformed churches, where the gospel is evident in word, there nevertheless appears to be a deficiency in that assurance and power in the Holy Spirit of which the New Testament speaks (1 Thess 1:5).

Reformed Baptists have not been immune to the spirit of the age. We have moved away from our theological roots. As well as the negative influence of the prevalent worldview, there are a number of reasons that help to explain why a once thoroughly biblically grounded covenantal Baptist Church ended up losing its way.

In the nineteenth and for much of the twentieth century the church had to contend with attacks from without, in the form of Darwinian evolution and liberalism, and from within, with the rise of revivalism and dispensationalism. The revivalist phenomenon resulted in many turning from "a thoughtful and theological faith to an experience orientated belief."[10] This all too often led to feelings and experiences replacing intellectual rigor. Dispensationalism, associated with men like John Nelson Darby, and popularized in the *Scofield Reference Bible*, posited a view of Scripture that necessitated "discrete epochs in redemptive history, units of time with different standards and requirements."[11] Suffice it to say, it is a position diametrically opposed to the unity exhibited in Baptist covenantal theology. According to Richard Barcellos, it was dispensationalism that was the "most important factor in the demise of Baptist Covenantalism."[12]

The word "evangelical" has been denuded of its meaning, having undergone a death by association. Even in some Reformed churches, perhaps not intentionally, scriptural authority has been diluted by the zeitgeist of our modern culture. Writing about the twentieth, but, nevertheless, equally relevant to our century, James Hunter stated:

> This much is clear, however: Conservative Protestantism has changed in significant ways since the beginning of the century, and from all appearances, it is continuing to change . . . The most important case in point is the place of the Scriptures. When it is allowed, as it is increasingly so in Evangelicalism, to interpret the Bible subjectively, and to see portions of the Scripture as symbolic or non-binding, the Scriptures are divested of their

10. Renihan, "Introduction," 17.

11. Ibid., 17.

12. Ibid., 16.

authority to compel obedience. They may still inspire, but they are substantially disarmed.[13]

Baptist distinctiveness has come to be more associated with the mode of baptism, with the immersion verses sprinkling debate, than with its covenantal foundations. The old covenantalism has been neglected, with the resulting loss of our rightful Baptist heritage, as Richard Barcellos put it: "the beautiful system of faith has been exchanged for a novelty."[14] Reformed Baptists need to rediscover their rich heritage, one that will give them a deeper understanding of God's Word, and, hopefully, lead them into a closer walk with God.

Until relatively recently most of the books available were produced by paedobaptist publishers, and Baptists were essentially guilty of taking Presbyterian works and adjusting them to fit what they believed to be a Baptist framework. James Renihan goes so far as saying, "they produced works that look a lot like Presbyterian works, works that pretend to be Baptist and they are not."[15]

I was converted in 1978, and would describe myself as a conservative evangelical, although, as mentioned above, it is becoming increasingly difficult to define "evangelical." I have always been a "Reformed Baptist." Moreover, I am also an amillennialist, believing the thousand years referred to by John in his Apocalypse (Rev 20:4) to be symbolic of a long period of time, a time that the church is presently in.

In my early attempts to understand God's covenants, a large proportion of the books I read were written by paedobaptists. Try as I might, I could not come to terms with their understanding of the relationship between the covenants, especially the old and new covenants. Things just did not seem to fit. How is one to understand the references to the new covenant, for example, in Jeremiah 31 and Ezekiel 36? I was vexed by the paedobaptist contention that the new covenant only applied to God's people after Christ had completed his work; being just another administration of the covenant of grace. In Jeremiah God promises that he will put his law "within them, and will write it on their hearts" (Jere 31:33), and in Ezekiel, he speaks of the heart of stone being replaced with one of flesh (Ezek 36:27). When did these blessings occur? Paedobaptists, on the one hand, tell us that the new covenant came into force in regard to the application of its blessings only after Christ's work, whilst, on the other hand, they speak of believers under the old covenant being in

---

13. Hunter, *Evangelicalism,* 187.

14. Ibid., 17.

15. Renihan, 1689 *Federalism Compared.*

possession of these blessings. This for me made no sense because the Scriptures only associate these blessings with the new covenant.

Again, I could not accept the idea that the new covenant was simply another administration of the covenant of grace. From my understanding of Jeremiah, the new covenant seemed too radical to be just a fuller, broader manifestation of what was there before. It makes no sense to hold with the all too prevalent view that Old Testament saints were somehow excluded from these blessings. It is my understanding that whilst the new covenant was consummated or ratified in the death of Christ, the blessings secured by his redemptive work have been communicated to believers from the very beginning. In other words, all of God's people, from the first promise (Gen 3:3) have been in the new covenant in Christ and recipients of its blessings.

Understanding God's covenants, and how they relate to one another is essential for a correct understanding of the Scriptures, as Walter Chantry put it, "the doctrine of covenants is at the core of theology, and the health of any theological system depends on its understanding of this truth. It would be nearly impossible to overstate the central importance of the biblical teachings on covenants. Covenant theology is at the heart of biblical truth."[16] According to Rodney Petersen, "the first question in the interpretation of Scripture for the Christian after acknowledging the Lordship of Jesus Christ is how to relate the Hebrew Scriptures to the New Testament."[17] To misunderstand the relationship between the old and new covenants is not a minor issue. As we shall see, the Presbyterian/paedobaptist position not only misconstrues our Lord's command and instruction to the church, but results in a misunderstanding of elements of the gospel, particularly in regard to the beneficiaries of the new covenant and the nature of the church..

This work presents my understanding of this relationship. Those who grasp this important teaching can be compared to an explorer who, instead of having to find his bearings from a point on the ground, deep inside the jungle, has taken to a plane, having the entire landscape before his eyes. Understanding God's covenants will help one avoid getting lost in the detail, and will enable one to have a unified overview of God's redemptive schema.

The essential structure of the Scriptures is built around a covenantal scaffolding, which, to quote Michael Horton, provides "a matrix of beams and pillars that hold together the structure of biblical faith and practice. . . . It is not simply the concept of the covenant, but the concrete existence of God's covenantal dealings in our history that provides the context within which we

16. Chantry, *Covenants*.
17. Petersen, "Debate throughout Church History," 18.

recognize the unity of Scripture amid its remarkable variety."[18] As the skeleton gives the body form, so covenant theology gives form to the Scriptures.

Below is an example of some of the questions that particularly vexed me in my efforts to understand covenant theology:

- How were people saved before Christ came?
- Can Old Testament believers be said to be in the new covenant?
- Was the Abrahamic covenant one of grace or works?
- What is the role played by the covenant made with Moses?
- What has happened to all the promises made by the prophets regarding earthly blessings?
- What exactly is the new covenant, and how is it different from the old covenant?
- Should the children of Christian parents be baptized?

In what follows I hope to demonstrate that it is only Reformed Baptist covenant theology that is consistent in its understanding of Scripture, and that, to quote Barcellos, "a consistent adherence to covenant theology actually refutes all forms of infant baptism and upholds, even demands, the baptism of believers only."[19] It is important to point out that within the Reformed tradition, while there are significant differences regarding covenant theology, it is one of those issues on which, whilst being extremely important, after all is said and done, we can agree to disagree. I was converted under the ministry of the late Dr. Peter Trumper who was a Presbyterian. I still remember one occasion back in 1981 when I turned up at his home, armed with a number of Baptist arguments in the hope of turning him into a Baptist. Over cups of tea, we talked for a number of hours before we finally agreed to disagree. We did not fall out or take offense because we knew that first and foremost we were brothers in Christ. It is not my intention in this book to hurt or insult paedobaptists, but to, in grace, encourage them to, at the very least, rethink their position, and, maybe, even adopt the Reformed Baptist position. Of course, I may be wrong about some issues, but the purpose of this short book is to examine what is often considered to be a difficult topic and provide something that will encourage Christians to think about their faith. In an earlier edition of this work one reviewer criticized me because of my many allusions to the Reformed paedobaptist position. However, this made very little sense to me. One must bear in mind that the 1689 Baptist Confession is largely

18. Horton, *Covenant Theology*, 13.

19. Barcellos, *Paedoism or Credoism*, 2.

taken from the Westminster Confession of 1647, differing only in regard to covenant theology, baptism, and church government. Yes, I do make many allusions to those paedobaptist doctrines where there is disagreement. This needs to be done in order to show what the differences between us are, and to put across as unambiguously as possible exactly what Reformed Baptists believe. I have also sought to quote paedobaptist sources on some of the many points of agreement. I certainly do not, to use the old saying, want to throw the proverbial baby out with the bathwater.

One thing needs saying before we start. I have always been at a loss to understand why some of our paedobaptist brethren would view the title "Reformed Covenant Baptist" as being something of a misnomer, a contradiction-in-terms. We use the term "Reformed" because we accept the five *solas* of the Protestant Reformation, namely, *sola Scriptura, sola Gratia, sola fide, sola Christus* and *sola Deo Gloria*. We employ the word "Covenant" because we adhere to covenant theology. If this does not make us Reformed and covenantal I don't know what does. This work will hopefully, in the words of Ronald Miller, clearly demonstrate that we are "full blown adherents to covenant theology."[20] There are, of course, those who believe that to be Reformed one must accept everything Calvin said. In this sense I am certainly not Reformed, and then again, neither are so many of the giants from church history, men like John Owen, Charles Spurgeon, etc.

Although I am wholeheartedly of the opinion that the position put forward here is correct, I am not so naive as to think that perhaps the majority of readers will beg to differ with what I have to say. I am also aware that even among the ranks of Reformed Baptists there are significant differences regarding this doctrine. This is why I chose to call this book *A Reformed Baptist Covenant Theology*, and not *The Reformed Baptist Covenant Theology*. Any theological gaffs, and no doubt there are many, are mine, and mine alone.

20. Miller, *Covenant Theology*, 1–2.

2

What is a Covenant?

GOD'S RELATIONSHIP WITH HUMANITY has always been based upon a covenant. Apart from the covenant of redemption, there are only two, what might be called, primary covenants, namely, that made with the first Adam, and that made with Christ, the second Adam. All other covenants—for example, those made with Noah, Abraham and David etc.,—are subsidiary and are concerned with the application of the blessings that Christ secured in the second, or new, covenant.

A covenant is a relationship between two or more parties. It is usually entered into freely, with each party voluntarily working out and agreeing to abide by certain conditions. Examples of such covenants abound in everyday life, for example, between the husband and wife, employee and employer, etc. In this sense, a covenant is simply an agreement between two equal parties with each accepting that there will be in the terms of the agreement both duties and privileges attached. The covenant made between Abraham and Abimelech illustrates this kind of covenant (Gen 21:22–27, 31,32). Here each party agrees to the terms and conditions of the covenant; there is mutual agreement and consent, or what might be called "covenantal parity."

There is, however, a marked difference between the covenants made by sinful men and those covenants that God has condescended to enter into with man. Such covenants are not made between equal parties. God's covenants are imposed on an infinitely inferior party, where God has determined the covenantal conditions. In the Scriptures a covenant is essentially a conditional promise. It is a relatively simple concept. The essential meaning of a covenant was aptly put in the words of A.A. Hodge: "What is the essential nature of a covenant formed between a superior and an inferior but this—a conditional promise? The promise is a reward on the condition of obedience, associated with threatening of punishment on the condition of disobedience."[1]

1. Hodge, *Evangelical Theology*, 166.

According to the great puritan, John Owen:

> A covenant properly is a compact or agreement on certain terms mutually stipulated by two or more parties. As promises are the foundation and rise of it, as it is between God and man, so it comprises also of precepts, or laws of obedience, which are prescribed to man on his part to be observed.[2]

One could, however, argue that the covenant with Adam was not a mutual arrangement. Adam appears to have had no say in the covenant's nature. He simply had to accept the condition. Neither the covenant with Adam nor the revival of it under Abraham and its further elaboration under Moses, were, as Owen stated, "mutually stipulated." Peter Golding is perhaps more correct: "the covenant of grace is more like a one-sided grant than a two-sided pact, because it emanates entirely from God's side."[3] To again quote Golding, "there is not so much as a hint of bargaining involved. Rather, it is consistently characterized by unilateralism (on the part of God)."[4] In Exod 24:7 and Deut 5:1–3, the people of Israel had conditions imposed on them by God, their side of the covenant was the acceptance of these conditions. God's "law sprung from the divine sovereignty of God, who had a right to impose upon him whatsoever he thought fit; as it was a covenant, it was an act of condescension and goodness in God, to enter into it with man, his creature."[5]

The original covenant of works made with the first man differed from later covenants, not only in terms of blessings and curses but in the manner in which it was made. Whilst the consequences of being a covenant-breaker were plainly made known (Gen 3:3) in the making of it, there was no animal death symbolizing the consequences for breaking the covenant. This was simply because sin had not entered and, hence, there was no death.

In later covenants, both blood and death were always present in the covenant because they warned of possible consequences should the covenant be broken. For example, in God's covenant with Abraham in Genesis 15, Abraham was told to collect certain animals, kill and dismember them and then lay each half over the other. We then read that when the "sun had gone down, and it was dark, behold, a smoking fire pot and a flaming torch passed between the pieces. On that day the Lord made a covenant with Abram saying: 'To your offspring I will give this land, from the river of Egypt to the river Euphrates . . .

2. Owen, *Works*, 22, 135.

3. Golding, *Covenant Theology*, 89.

4. Ibid., 79.

5. Gill, *Body of Divinity*, 445.

"'(Gen 15:17–18). This was to cut the covenant. The animal-division symbolized, to quote O. Palmer Robinson, a "pledge to the death made at the point of covenant commitment. The dismembered animals represents the curse that the covenant-maker calls down on himself if he should violate the commitment which he has made."[6] For example, when Judah broke its covenant obligations, the prophet Jeremiah was called upon to inform the people, the covenant-breakers, about the consequences of their transgressions, "And the men who transgressed my covenant, and did not keep the terms of the covenant that they made before me. I will cut them like the calf that they cut in two and passed between the parts." (Jer 34:18).

In understanding the nature of the new covenant, it is important that one is aware of the difference that exists between a covenant and a testament. Confusion sometimes occurs between these two words because, to quote Robinson, "both a 'covenant' and a 'testament' relate to death."[7]

A testament is not synonymous with a covenant. In the case of a covenant, death is used symbolically, highlighting the fact that blood would be shed, that death would occur, should one party become a covenant-breaker, failing to abide by the covenant's conditions. This outcome, however, is not inevitable. The slain animal(s) served as a warning. If, however, one of the parties involved in the covenant had not broken one of its conditions, if there had been no violation, then there would be no necessity for blood to be shed.

This is not the case in regard to a testament, here death is inevitable for the testament or will to come into force. If I make a will that is to come into effect in the event of my death, then, unless I die, the will is to all intentions meaningless, as O. Palmer Robinson puts it, a death is necessary for "actualizing an inheritance."[8] Or as the writer to the Hebrews puts it, "for where a will is involved, the death of the one who made it, must be established" (Heb 9:16).

In the covenant of redemption, Christ agreed to become the testator for all those his Father had given to him. His legacy, that which is left in the testator's will, was to become the possession of his people as a result of the testator's death. Without the testator's death, all the blessings would be unavailable. Christ's death can then be viewed in two senses, he died in the place of another, the covenant-breaker, and he died so that his legacy as testator might become the possession of his people. As Robinson puts it, "Christ dies as a substitute for the covenant-breaker . . . Yet death in substitution for another has no place whatsoever in the making of a last will and

6. O Palmer Robertson, *Christ of the Covenants*, 10.

7. Ibid., 11.

8. Ibid., 11.

testament. The testator dies in his own place, not in the place of another. No other death may substitute for the death of the testator himself."[9] Jesus kept all of the conditions of the covenant, attaining a righteousness and taking his people's punishment by subjecting himself to his Father's wrath. Being the testator, his death has made it possible for his infinitely rich legacy to become theirs.

A question that naturally comes to mind is: if a testator's legacy can only be realized after the death of the testator, how then did those who lived before Jesus' death benefit from his legacy? Perhaps the best way to answer this is to quote John Gill:

> All the promises in covenant were on condition of Christ's making his soul as offering for sin, and of the pouring out of his soul unto death . . . all the blessings of grace bestowed on Old Testament saints, as they were legacies in this testament, so they were given forth in virtue of the blood of the covenant, which had *a virtue that reached backward.* . . . [10]

> For the first thoughts of God always remain, and that to all generations; his mind is never turned, his counsel is immutable, and so his covenant and testament founded thereon is unalterable; nor that the inheritance bequeathed in this will could not be enjoyed before the death of Christ; this indeed is the case with respect to the wills of men, the legacies are not payable, nor estates bequeathed enjoyed, until the testator dies; but such is not only the certainty of Christ's death, and which with God was as if it was, before it really was, *but such is the virtue and efficacy of it, that it reaches backward to the beginning of the world.*[11]

Although the legacy of Jesus, the testator, was enjoyed by the saints before his death, his death was necessary to confirm the testament, that the legatees might appear to have a legal right to what was bequeathed to them. This backward reaching efficacy of the new covenant, as we will see, lies at the heart of Baptist covenant theology.

The question has been raised as to whether what took place between God and Adam was a covenant of works. Attempts have been made to use Hosea 6:7 as evidence for the usage of the word in this context, but there are insurmountable problems with this. The *New International Version* translates the verse: "Like Adam, they have broken the covenant-they were unfaithful to me there." On the face of it, this appears clear-cut. The

9. Ibid., 12.
10. Gill, *Body of Divinity*, 348. Italics added for emphasis.
11. Ibid., 349. Italics added for emphasis.

Revised Standard Version, however, translates it thus: "But at Adam they transgressed the covenant; there they dealt faithlessly with me." It should also be borne in mind that Joshua refers to a place called "Adam" (Joshua 3:16). We can see then that the name Adam can be understood in two ways. It can either be taken to refer to the first man or a particular place. Because of the ambiguity, it is impossible to know exactly.

John Reisinger, an advocate of what has become known as New Covenant Theology, in his work *Abraham's Four Seeds*, commented that "covenant theology literally builds its whole system on two deliberate mistakes. It puts two covenants into Genesis 2 and 3, even though those chapters never mention either of the two covenants. The two unproven covenants then become the *foundation of the whole system of covenant theology*."[12]

One should, however, also consider those other portions of Scripture where the word covenant is initially absent, but later applied. For example, in God's dealings with David, it is only later that the word covenant is used (2 Sam 23:5, Ps 89:3). As Fesko informs us, "the absence of a particular term does not entail the absence of a particular concept."[13] We all know that the word trinity is found nowhere in Scripture, yet no true believer would doubt the presence of the concept. The question to ask, at least as far as this work is concerned is: does the covenant made with Adam exhibit the characteristics of a conditional arrangement? The answer must surely be yes. It was nothing less than a conditional promise made by a superior to an inferior. As John Owen put it:

> There was an original covenant made with Adam, and all mankind in him. The rule of obedience and reward that was between God and him was not expressly called a covenant, *but it contained the express nature of a covenant; for it was the agreement of God and man, concerning obedience and disobedience, rewards and punishments.*[14]

God pronounced the condition, Adam could only agree and accept it. This is essentially all one needs to bear in mind. And, ultimately, it matters not to me what it is called, the essential point is that it had the characteristics of a covenant, although not mutually agreed, God did impose a condition that Adam was to keep.

12. Reisinger, *Abraham's Four Seeds*, 135.

13. Fesko, "Calvin and Witsius on the Mosaic Covenant," 30.

14. Italics added for emphasis. Owen, *Works*, 6, 60.

3

Covenant of Redemption

THE NEW COVENANT IS essentially the outworking, or the putting into operation of that arrangement or covenant that was made between the three persons of the Godhead before the foundation of the world. Theologians have chosen to call this the covenant of redemption because it concerns decisions that took place between the persons of the Trinity for the accomplishment of man's redemption. Although Scripture does not specifically speak of the covenant one can, however, glean from what it does speak about that before this world was created, God decided to redeem a people and to do so in Trinity. The source of all redemptive history is to be found in the decisions made in this covenant, as Sinclair Ferguson put it, "the covenant of grace thus depends upon the covenant of redemption as its foundation, and for its saving power."[1]

Before the world was, the Son agreed to become man and perform all that was necessary to redeem those given to him by his Father. The 1689 Baptist Confession states that:

> It pleased God, in His eternal Purpose, to choose and ordain the Lord Jesus, His only begotten Son, in accordance with the covenant made between them both, to be the Mediator between God and man; to be Prophet, Priest and King, the Head and Savior of His Church, the Heir of all things, and the judge of all the world.[2]

In Christ, the second person of the Trinity would come to earth in a body prepared for him (Heb 10:5). In him, the whole fullness of deity would, and, indeed, still does, dwell bodily (Col 2:9). In becoming man he voluntarily placed himself under the original covenant of works, that he

---

1. Ferguson, *John Owen On The Christian Life*, 27.

2. *Baptist Confession of Faith* 1889, 8:1.

might be successful where the first Adam had failed. His redemptive work was two dimensional, consisting of both preceptive and penal obedience. Not only did he through his obedience secure a righteousness for his people (2 Cor 5:21), but he also took sin's penalty upon himself, "becoming obedient to the point of death, even death on a cross" (Phil 2:8). It was in this covenant that all the elect of God were given to the Son, as John Owen put it: "All the elect of God were, in his eternal purpose and design, and in the everlasting covenant between the Father and the Son, committed unto him, to be delivered from sin, the law, and death, and to be brought into the enjoyment of God"[3]

In the economy of salvation, Jesus, the Son, although co-equal and co-eternal, became subordinate to his Father. He came down from heaven not to do his own will but the will of his Father who sent him (John 6:38). It was because of his subordinate position, as the one who became flesh and dwelt amongst us (John 1:14), he could say that by himself he could do nothing (John 5:30), and say that "My Father is greater than I" (John 14:28). On earth Jesus, in his redemptive work, glorified his Father and accomplished all the work his Father had given him to do (John 17:4).

All too often we tend to read these texts without stopping to reflect on the incomprehensible condescension of the Son, who having all, agreed to set his glory aside for our salvation (Phil 2:6–7). One can do no better than quote the words of Thomas Boston:

> The eternal Word consented to be made flesh, that all flesh might not perish: he consented to become man, to take into a personal union with himself, a human nature, to wit, a true body and reasonable soul, according to the eternal destination of his Father. This was an instance of amazing condescension. The highest monarch's consent to lay aside his robes of majesty, to clothe himself with rags, and become a beggar, is not to be compared with. Nay, the highest angel's consent to become a worm, is not to be named in one day, with the eternal Son of God, the Father's equal, his consenting to become man: for the distance between the divine nature and the human is infinite; whereas the distance between the angelic nature, and the nature of worms of the earth, is but finite.[4]

It is the Father who chose a people and gave them to the Son to be redeemed. Paul tells us that "we were chosen in him before the foundation of the world" (Eph 1:4), and in John, we read that all those whom the Father

---

3. Owen, *Works*, 5, 180.

4. Boston, *Beauties of Boston*, 489.

has given to the Son will go unto him and be saved (John 6:37). The Father does the initial choosing, and he gives the people thus chosen to the Son, and it is the Father who sends the Son (John 3:16).

The Holy Spirit's role consists of applying Christ's redemptive work to sinners. He is the one who convicts the world of sin, righteousness, and judgment (John16:8). In other words, it is the Spirit's job to make the world aware of its need for a savior, to reveal the righteousness of Christ, and to point to the impending judgment for those who refuse it. It is the Spirit who gives life through the new birth (John 3:6), and it is the Spirit who guides the church and reveals to her the will of God, "When the Spirit of truth comes he will guide you into all truth, for he will not speak on his own authority, but whatever he hears he will speak, and he will declare to you the things that are to come" (John 16:13–14). All that Christ's work achieved becomes the believer's through the work of the Spirit. He places us into Christ, where we are forensically justified, and adopted into God's family, and, through his indwelling, he continues to apply Christ's redemptive blessings in our progressive sanctification. When Christ returns it will be the Spirit who will change our mortal bodies through the resurrection, so that they will resemble Christ's own glorified body.

4

The Plight of Man Under the First Adam

WHEN GOD FIRST CREATED Adam, he made him in his own image and after his own likeness (Gen 1:26). Adam was in possession of a will that was free, and the very laws of God were written upon his heart:

> The law given to him was both of a natural and positive kind. God who is the creator of all, Judge of all the earth, and King of the whole world, has the right to give what laws He likes to his creatures, and they are bound as creatures, and by ties of gratitude, to observe them. The natural law, or law of nature, given to Adam, was concreated with him, written on his heart, and engraved and imprinted in his nature from the beginning of his existence, by which he was acquainted with the will of his maker, and directed to observe it.[1]

In his state of original innocence God chose to test Adam's obedience by the imposition of a single precept. Why God chose this particular method lies outside of his revelation to us. The important point to grasp is that God was testing Adam's faithfulness and presenting him with the possibility of eternal life for both himself and his posterity on the condition of his obedience.

In his original righteousness, the law of God written upon Adam's heart assured him that all was well. It was a law unto life. This law was "the reflection of God's own moral character, which he was determined to share analogically with his human partner."[2] The law served to vouchsafe to Adam that all was well in his relationship with God. Should he, however, fall short of the law's requirements by failing to abide by God's condition, he would find that the law which pronounced life would become an agent of condemnation. To quote Buchanan, "The law provided for the justification of

1. Gill, *Body of Divinity*, 444.
2. Horton, *Introducing Covenant Theology*, 84.

the righteous only. It was evidently adapted to the case of man while he was yet, not only innocent and sinless, but possessed of original righteousness, enjoying the favour of God, which is life, and retaining the divine image in which he was created."[3]

Adam was essentially on probation under the terms of the covenant of works. Life was promised to Adam and all of his posterity, should he but fulfill the condition. This was the basis of the covenant. God commanded Adam saying, "You are free to eat from any tree in the garden; but you must not eat from the tree of the knowledge of good and evil, for when you eat of it you will surely die" (Gen 2:16,17). Adam failed to abide by the condition, and subsequently, he incurred the wrath of God, dying spiritually, and, eventually, physically. The righteousness in which he was created was forfeited, and the law became, not a law unto righteousness for the righteous, but, rather, a law unto death for the guilty. The law that was written upon Adam's heart now served only to condemned him.

In his failure to keep the condition Adam did not only bring spiritual death, that death which entails separation from God, upon himself alone, but also upon his posterity. In his sinful partaking of the forbidden fruit Adam committed an act in which we all shared, "The law was Adam's lease when God made him tenant; the conditions of which bond he kept not, he forfeited himself and all of us."[4]

Man now had to live with the consequences of sin. One should bear in mind that "Original sin does not refer to the first sin but, rather, to its consequences. Original sin describes our fallen sinful condition, out of which actual sins occur."[5] It may be asked in what sense was Adam the head of humanity? What was the peculiar relationship that existed between the first man and woman and their posterity? The 1689 Baptist Confession tells us that:

> They being the root, and by God's appointment, standing in the room and stead of all mankind, the guilt of sin was imputed, and their corrupted natures conveyed, to all their posterity descending from them by ordinary generation. Their descendents are therefore conceived in sin, and are by nature the children of wrath and all other miseries, spiritual, temporal, and eternal, unless the Lord Jesus sets them free.[6]

Here we see two effects, not only is Adam's posterity polluted by sin, having "corrupted natures," but the "guilt of sin" is imputed to them. The first might

3. Buchanan, *Doctrine of Justification*, 22.

4. Fisher, *Marrow of Modern Divinity*, 38.

5. Sproul, *Everyone's A Theologian*, 108.

6. 1689 *Baptist Confession of Faith*, 6:3.

be called the "realistic union" with the second, the imputation of sin, often referred to as the "federal" or "representational union."

Regarding the realistic union, to quote Martyn Lloyd-Jones: "Adam was the totality of human nature. In that one Adam was the whole of human nature. He was the father of all mankind. In him, therefore, according to this view, resided the whole of human nature and, the human nature of every person who has been born."[7] Perhaps the best way of explaining this is to make reference to an incident that occurs in Hebrews 7:9–10. In this text the writer is referring to an event that occurred in the fourteenth chapter of Genesis where Abraham paid a tenth of his spoils to the mysterious Melchizedek. Although the writer's purpose here is to prove the superiority of the Melchizedek priesthood, and hence Christ's superiority because he was a priest after the order of Melchizedek, this concept can be applied to the "realistic union" of humanity's relationship with Adam. Melchizedek met Abraham "returning from the slaughter of the kings and blessed him" (Heb 7:1). Abraham paid a tenth of his spoils to him. The lesser is giving to the greater (v7). Then the writer comes to the heart of the matter by stating that Levi, the one from whom the Levites came, gave a tenth of the spoils to Melchizedek, "for he was still in the loins of his ancestor when Melchizedek met him" (v10). The point here is that Levi, although he was the grandson of Abraham, is said to have paid a tenth in virtue of his being in the body or loins of his grandfather. The same principle can be applied to humanity's position in Adam. When Adam sinned, we sinned in him in the same way that Levi paid tithes through Abraham. As Sproul put it, we can say, "from a genetic standpoint that our great-grandchildren are already present in our bodies, but we do not mean that those actual children are present in us."[8] Whichever way it is communicated, something of the consequences of the first sin can be found in our genetic makeup. Our genes became reprogrammed. We are often told that death is as natural as being born, this, however, is not the case. Our genes have been programmed for us to die, with death being the result of God's curse.

The "realistic union" concerns our being made sinners intrinsically, with the pollution of our natures, whereas the federal or representational union is extrinsic and concerns the imputation of Adam's sin to all of humanity. This was the "only time, apart from the cross, in all human history when we were perfectly represented."[9] Because Adam was "the federal representative of the race, his disobedience affected all of his descendants, as Paul tells us, 'by one man's disobedience many were made sinners" (Rom

---

7. Lloyd-Jones, *Romans 5, Assurance*, 213.

8. Sproul, *Everyone's A Theologian*, 117.

9. Ibid., 118.

5:19). In his righteous judgment God imputed the guilt of the first sin committed by the head of the covenant to all those that are federally related to him."[10] Having made Adam, to quote Lloyd-Jones, God:

> said to him in effect: "Adam, I regard you as not only the first of a series, not merely in the natural sense of all who are going to come out of you, I constitute you the representative head, the federal head of all humanity; I am going to make a covenant with you, and I am going to deal with you as the representative head of the entire human race of which you will be the progenitor. I intend to make a covenant with you to this effect that every benefit you enjoy will pass upon your progeny."[11]

When Adam sinned we all became guilty because he was our federal head before God. His sin became our sin because of our relationship with him. It is a guilt by association. We will see later that the same applies to Christ, the second Adam, in regard to his righteousness.

About Adam's fall Arthur Pink comments:

> Man's defection from his primordial state was purely voluntary and from the unconstrained choice of his own mutable and self-determining will. Adam was "without excuse." By eating of the forbidden fruit, he broke, first, the law of his very being, violating his own nature, which bound him unto lowing allegiance to his maker: self now took the place of God. Second, he flouted the law of God, which requires perfect and unremitting obedience to the moral Governor of the world: self had now usurped the throne of God in his heart. Third, in trampling upon the positive ordinance under which he was placed he broke the covenant, preferring to take his stance alongside his fallen wife.[12]

God's holiness is such that he cannot so much as look upon sin (Hab 1:13). It is a holiness which, because of its nature, demands that all sin be punished. Setting his wrath against sin, in the words of Hugh Martin, is "the necessary aspect or expression of the Divine nature and perfections . . . It originates not in the will of God; for in that case, the same will of God might set it aside or depart from it without satisfaction or pacification—without appeasement or atonement at all. But it originates from the Divine nature, and that necessarily."[13]

---

10. Berkhof, *Systematic Theology*, 242.

11. Lloyd-Jones, *Romans, 5, Assurance*, 215.

12. Pink, *Divine Covenants*, 40.

13. Martin, *The Atonement*.

This punishment is essentially separation from God. It is seen in the way God has barred the way back to him. Following Adam's expulsion from the garden God placed a "cherubim and a flaming sword that turned every way to guard the way to the tree of life" (Gen.3:24). Because of humanity's relationship with Adam we are all, from birth, estranged and alienated from God. Without the intervention of another party, there can be no hope of a reconciliation.

The apostle, writing under divine inspiration, states that "Sin entered the world through one man, and death through sin, and in this way, death came to all men, because all sinned" (Rom 5:12). We are all by nature "children of wrath" (Eph 2:3). "The very truth is, Adam by his fall threw down our whole nature headlong into the same destruction, and drowned his whole offspring in the same gulf of misery."[14]

Nehemiah Coxe gives a graphic description of man's sinful condition:

> He sinned and fell short of the glory of God (Rom.3:23). And now instead of that original righteousness with which he was first beatified, there was nothing to be found in him but abominable filthiness and horrid deformity. His mind was covered over, even possessed with hellish darkness. Hatred of God reigned in his heart and his affections were no longer subject to right reason but became vile and rebellious.[15]

Or as Walter Chantry put it, "From our mother's womb we have been corrupted, from the time of our conception, death stalks us with the awful assurance that we are his, and all because of that one act of the one man."[16]

In regard to doing anything good i.e., acceptable to God, man is now like the Ethiopian, unable to change his skin, or the leopard his spots (Jer.13:33). He is "dead in sins and transgressions" (Eph.2:1). The awful thing is that not only can man of his own do absolutely nothing to rectify matters, in his sinful state he does not want to do anything, as Thomas Watson put it: "When Adam lost his righteousness, he lost his anchor of hope and his crown, there was no way for relief, unless God would find out such a way as neither man not angel could devise."[17]

Man had been made in God's image and after his likeness (Gen 1:26). Regarding this, we can distinguish between the natural and the moral image. According to the former man can be said to have been created spiritual, rational, moral, and immortal. This has been severely marred on account of

---

14. Fisher, *Marrow of Modern Divinity*, 34.

15. Coxe, "Discourse of the Covenants," 51.

16. Chantry, "Imputation of Righteousness," 116.

17. Watson, *A Body of Divinity*, 130.

the Fall but not entirely removed. As for the moral image, man was created like God in true righteousness and holiness, and this was almost, if not entirely expunged. Man still, however, has some memory of his previous state, knowing the difference between right and wrong, and it is this that serves to condemn our wrong acts. It is essentially what we refer to as conscience.

One can reasonably assume that should Adam have partaken of the tree of life, instead of the tree of the knowledge of good and evil, he would have secured eternal bliss for both himself and his posterity. Although one can but speculate on this issue, it would appear, especially in light of the fact that it was the tree of life that was guarded (Gen 3:24), that eating from this tree would have secured Adam's relationship with God. This assumption appears to make sense when one considers that one of the great promises reserved by God for those who overcome, by virtue of their relationship with Christ, will be the right to eat from the tree of life (Rev 2:7). Eating from this tree, according to Buchanan, would secure "not merely the continuance of temporal life, nor even a state of immortal existence, but the perpetuity of that holy blessedness which consisted in the favor and fellowship with God; for the life which was promised was the counterpart to the death which was threatened."[18]

The important point for us is that Adam did not make the right choice and we are all suffering the consequences. We are all polluted and guilty. We have "all sinned and are falling short of the glory of God" (Rom 3:23) "None is righteous, no, not one; no one understands; no one seeks for God" (Rom 3:10).

The original covenant of works that the first man was under has not gone away. It is very much still in force. It still demands not only perfect righteousness but death for any transgression. Humanity is now helpless, standing under the curse, deserving only condemnation. The covenant of works has, to quote John Owen, "not been abolished or abrogated by an act of God as a law, but only made weak and insufficient unto its first end as a covenant."[19]

> Though the Lord be free from performing his condition, that is from giving man eternal life, yet so is not man from his part; no, though strength to obey be lost it is by his own default, the obligation to obedience still remains; so that Adam and his off-spring are no more discharged of their duties, because they have no strength to obey them, than a debtor is acquitted of his bond, because he wants the money to pay it.[20]

18. Buchanan, *Doctrine of Justification*, 21.

19. Owen, *Works*, 6, 61.

20. Fisher, *Marrow of Modern Divinity*, 39.

This then is the awful plight of man in sin. He is in the kingdom of sin and darkness and owes God a debt that he is incapable of paying. God will not reduce the bill, he still demands full payment, i.e., perfect righteousness and the punishment of sin. God always demands one hundred percent effort, yet man, because of what he has become, is incapable of giving even one percent. He is rotten by nature and no amount of reformation will change his position before God.

The law shows no mercy. It can but pronounce judgment, John Bunyan, a Baptist who suffered much for his faith, about whom John Owen said that he would gladly relinquish his learning if he could but have the kind of walk with God that Bunyan, a tinker from Bedford, appears to have had, perfectly expressed the place of the law broken by man:

> The law, as it is a covenant of works, doth not allow for any repentance unto life, to those that live and die under it. For the law being once broken by thee, never speaks good unto thee, neither doth God at all regard thee. If thou be under that covenant, not withstanding, all thy repentings, and also thy promise to do so no more, "No," saith the law, "thou hath sinned, therefore I must curse thee, for it is my nature even, and I can do nothing else but curse, every one that doth in any point transgress against me." Gal. iii:10. "they break my covenant and I regarded them not, saith the Lord." Heb. viii. "Let them cry, I will not regard them; let them repent, I will not regard them; they have broken my covenant, and done that in which I delighted not; therefore by that covenant I do curse, and not bless; damn, and not save; frown and not smile; reject, and not embrace; charge sin, and not forgive it.[21]

Without Christ man goes about his business unaware that the Sword of Damocles is suspended above his head. He can only hold his hands up and plead for mercy. This is not a matter of giving one's heart to Jesus, as some believe, for man in sin has nothing to give. What is needed is a new creation. For fallen humanity this is tantamount to a camel going through the eye of a needle, it is, however, something that God has made possible by sending his Son, the second Adam, into this kingdom of darkness so that those who believe might be translated into the kingdom of God.

---

21. Bunyan, *Doctrine of Law and Grace Unfolded*, 502–3.

5

The Work of the Second Adam

The New Covenant

MAN IS, BECAUSE OF sin, both separated from God and at enmity with him. He is now deserving only of God's wrath. God has, however, intervened on man's behalf in the person of his own Son Jesus Christ to provide salvation for his people. This truth is eloquently put in what is probably the best-known verse in the whole of Scripture, "For God so loved the world that he gave his only son, that whoever believes in him should not perish but have eternal-life" (John 3:16). In Christ, we see God from heaven to earth come down to take upon himself a humanity, so that in that humanity he might vicariously work out salvation for his people. Whereas in the first Adam there came sin, death, and condemnation, in Christ, the second Adam, there is righteousness, justification, and life. Christ, the lion from the tribe of Judah triumphantly succeeded where the first man had so miserably failed.

The establishment of this work in time and space is called the new covenant. Throughout the Old Testament this work of Christ was promised, however, it was not formally established and consummated until the shedding of Christ's blood. Jesus Christ took Adam's place under the covenant of works, and all that he did, in both his life and death, he did in order to fully honor the covenantal requirements, to quote Thomas Boston:

> Howbeit, as the first Adam, standing as the head and representative of all his natural seed, entered into the first covenant with God, accepting the promise thereof, upon the terms and conditions therein promised, which he engaged to fulfil: so our Lord Jesus, standing as the second Adam, head and representative of the particular persons of lost mankind, by name elected to life, and given to him as his spiritual seed, entered into the second

covenant with his Father, accepting the promises thereof; con-
senting and engaging to fulfil them.[1]

The covenant Christ voluntarily placed himself under was the same
covenant that the first man broke, as Edward Fisher put it:

> Jesus Christ, the second Adam, entered into the same covenant
> that the first Adam did, so by him was done whatsoever the first
> Adam had undone. So the case stands thus,-that as whatsoever
> the first Adam did, or befel (sic) him, was reckoned as done by
> all mankind, and to have befallen them. So that as sin cometh
> from Adam alone to all mankind, as he in whom all have sinned.
> So from Jesus Christ alone cometh righteousness unto all that
> are in him, as he in whom they all have satisfied the justice of
> God; for as being in Adam, and one with him, all did in him
> and with him, transgress the commandment of God; even so,
> in respect of faith, whereby believers are ingrafted into Christ,
> and spiritually made one with him, they did all, in him and with
> him, satisfy the justice of God in his death and sufferings.[2]

There has only ever been two heads of humanity, the first Adam who
brought us into a state of bondage and the second Adam who brings his
people into righteousness and everlasting life. The apostle Paul brings out
the federal, representative headship of the two Adams in Romans 5:12–19
where he compares and contrasts them. In regard to covenantal similarities,
"both were appointed by God; each was the head of a race; each was the
head of a covenant; each represented his seed; each passed onto his seed the
effects and fruits of his own work."[3]

The differences between the two are profound. The grace which comes
through the Lord Jesus Christ undoes the consequences of the one man's
offence and also provides for his people a righteousness, "For as by the one
man's disobedience the many were made sinners, so, by the one man's obedience will the many be made righteous" (Rom 5:19). All of humanity can
be put into two groups, one either stands in a condemned position under
the headship of the first Adam or one stands under the second Adam, being
both forgiven and clothed in the righteousness he procured. If one is in
Christ one is, as I hope to show, in the new covenant, where one's heart of
stone has been replaced with a heart of flesh; a heart that is being recreated
into the very image of God's own Son.

1. Boston, *Beauties of Boston*, 493.
2. Fisher, *Marrow of Modern Divinity*, 106.
3. Lloyd-Jones, *Romans*, 5, Assurance, 226.

In his role as his people's representative, Christ became their mediator. The "Greek word for mediator signifies a middle person, one that makes up the breach between two disagreeing parties. He came to make at-one-ment. God and we were at variance by sin, now Christ becomes umpire between us."[4] Christ's redemptive work secured peace and reconciliation between God and the people he represented. He honored the law of God both in its penal and preceptive requirements, in other words, Christ both suffered the punishment due to us for breaking the law, thereby bringing forgiveness, and he perfectly kept the law's precepts, thereby obtaining a righteousness for his people. Fallen man in his sin is effectively bankrupt, yet Christ has voluntarily made himself his people's surety or sponsor (Heb 7:22) for all their debts, and, in the words of Thomas Watson, he is "the great restorer of mankind."[5]

Christ's Threefold Offices

In Christ's redemptive work it is usual to refer to his three offices, namely prophet, priest, and king. In his role of mediator Jesus as prophet represents God before fallen man, in his priesthood he represents man before God and in his kingship he holds all things in his sway, exercising all power and dominion in working his purposes out. These offices are, to quote A. A. Hodge, "like several functions of the one living human body-as of the lungs in inhalation, as of the heart in blood circulation, and as of the brain and spinal column in innervation; they are functionally distinct, yet interdependent, and together they constitute one life. So the functions of prophet, priest, and king mutually imply one another: Christ is always a royal Priest and a priestly King, and together they accomplish one redemption, to which all are equally essential."[6] It is in these three offices that the Old Testament types of kingship, prophet and priest come to fruition. To sum up, in the words of Hodge, "Christ is always a prophetical Priest and a priestly prophet, and he is always a royal Priest and a Priestly King, and together they accomplish one redemption, to which they are equally essential."[7]

---

4. Watson, *Body of Divinity*, 162.

5. Ibid., 161.

6. Hodge, *Evangelical Theology*, 202.

7. Ibid., 202.

Christ the Prophet

A prophet is one who speaks on behalf of God, he is God's mouthpiece revealing God's will to men. Throughout the period preceding Christ's advent God revealed himself to his people in a number of ways, but, to quote the writer of Hebrews, God has "in these last days spoken to us by his Son, whom he appointed heir of all things, through whom he made the universe"(Heb 1:2). Christ referred to himself as a prophet (Luke 13:33), and his prophetic role is clearly seen in the way he spoke to men on behalf of his Father (John 12:49,50, 14:10–24). All that Jesus said and communicated to men was exactly what the father had taught him (John 8:27). He was the very Word of God (John 1:1). It was this Word of God who "became flesh and dwelt among us" (John 1:14). The God who dwells in unapproachable light, whom no man has ever seen, has revealed himself in the person of his Son. This is what John was referring to when he stated that "no one has ever seen God; the only God, who is at the Father's side, has made him known" (John 1:18). In the Old Testament the prophets of God would receive revelation at particular times, Christ is, however, different in that he is the revelation of God. Old Testament prophets bore witness to another, whereas Christ bears witness to himself and his work, to quote Bavinck, "the preaching of Christ was therefore in the profoundest sense self-revelation. It was a proclaiming of His own person and work."[8]

After death, resurrection, and ascension Christ remains a prophet. It was the Spirit of Christ that communicated himself through the apostles, their various letters contained not their own words, but the very words of Christ. The apostle Paul could state that the gospel he preached was not something he had made up, and neither did he receive it from any man, rather, he had received it from a direct revelation of Jesus himself (Gal 1:12).

I remember talking to a minister of the gospel who informed me that he found the gospels to be more important than the New Testament letters. He wore a band around his wrist on which was written: "What would Jesus do?" To answer this he only went to the gospels. He was, however, making a fundamental error. The gospels and the rest of Scripture must be viewed equally as the Word of God. In all Scripture, the Spirit reveals God's plan of salvation in Christ to humanity. This is why in Luke 24:27 the resurrected Christ, beginning with Moses, showed the two disciples that the whole of Old Testament Scripture spoke of him.

---

8. Bavinck, *Our Reasonable Faith*, 314.

Christ the Priest

In his priestly role, Christ became, and continues to be, man's representative before God: "A priest is a man divinely chosen, qualified and authorized to appear before God and act on behalf of men."[9] Man, in his sinful state is incapable of bringing any acceptable gift before the throne of God, and he neither has the right or inclination to enter into the presence of God. Christ, however, is one who, "acting on man's behalf, undertakes to restore harmonious relations between God and man."[10] In the Mosaic covenant, there was given an elaborate system of regulations which were performed by the priests in the administration of bloody sacrifices. These priests and the sacrifices they offered were a type and shadow of the work of the true priest, namely, Christ himself.

In his priestly work, the second Adam secured not only the forgiveness of sins but also a positive righteousness. It is therefore usual to refer to his passive and active obedience. "The real purpose of the formula is to empha-size the two distinct aspects of our Lord's vicarious obedience. The truth expressed rests upon the recognition that the law of God has both penal sanctions and positive demands. It demands not only the full discharge of its precepts but also the infliction for all infractions and shortcomings."[11] Christ's active obedience is concerned with the way he perfectly kept all of the law's requirements in his earthly life, whilst his passive obedience refers to his having taken upon himself his people's punishment due to their sins. About this twofold aspect of Christ's work Calvin states that "Our Lord came forth as a true man and took the person and name of Adam to take Adam's place in obeying the Father to present our flesh as the price of satisfaction to God's righteous judgment, and, in the same flesh, to pay the penalty that we had deserved."[12] Through his active obedience Christ rendered unto his Father a perfect satisfaction of the preceptive requirements of the law, whilst in his passive obedience he paid the penalty merited by our sin, satisfying the law's penal requirements.

There is in today's church a tendency to emphasize Christ's passive obedience at the expense of his active obedience. Indeed, in some quar-ters Christ's active obedience is even denied, to quote Boettner, "Through-out the history of the Church most theological discussions have stressed Christ's passive obedience . . . but have had very little to say about His active

9. Hodge, *Evangelical Theology*, 208.
10. Boettner, *Studies in Theology*, 244.
11. Murray, *Redemption Accomplished and Applied*, 21.
12. Calvin, *Institutes*, II, XII, 3.

obedience . . . They seem altogether unaware of the fact that the holy, sinless life which He lived was also a vicarious work on their behalf, wrought out by Him in His representative capacity and securing for them title to eternal life."[13] Without Christ's obedience to God's law his entire redemptive work would have been of no effect. If Christ's redemptive work had consisted only in the payment of our debt, in regard to punishment, we would all still be without hope. This is because, as well as the punishment of sin, God demands a perfect righteousness.

Arguably the most poignant description we have in Scripture of Christ, the second Adam, is found in Isaiah's suffering servant. The Ethiopian labored over this prophecy, (Acts 8:27–34), without understanding the one to whom it referred. Philip was at hand to explain to him that the passage referred to Jesus Christ. The subject of the prophecy was one about whom people were deeply ashamed: "He had no beauty or majesty to attract him, nothing in his appearance that we should desire him", "he had no form or majesty that we should look at him, and no beauty that we should desire him" (Isa 53:2). Rather than bow at his feet in acknowledgment of his true personage, men despised and rejected him, hiding their faces from him (v3). "He was in the world, and though the world was made through him, the world did not recognize him. He came to that which was his own, but his own did not receive him" (John 1:10–11). He took upon himself his people's infirmities and carried their sorrows. When he was pierced and crushed under the wrath of his own father, it was only for his people, to bring them to God; by his wounds we are healed (Isa 53:4–5).

When John the Baptist saw Jesus approaching him near the banks of the Jordan he knew that here was one who had a redemptive work to accomplish. John declared Jesus to be none other than the "lamb of God who takes away the sins of the world" (John 1:29). In ages past people would have offered up bloody sacrifices. These in themselves had no real efficacy in the removal of sin, and any efficacy they did possess served as a temporal type of the eternal blessings available in the sacrifice of Christ, the antitype. For example, at the exodus the Israelites were instructed by God to sacrifice a paschal lamb, an animal free from any taint or blemish. They were instructed to smear the blood on the doorposts of their houses so that the Angel of the Lord, sent to administer the wrath of God, on seeing the blood, would pass over (Exod 12:13). This was foreshadowing Christ's shed blood in the establishment of the new covenant, for Jesus is the true Passover (1 Cor 5:7). He was the one who whilst being the very Son of God, was voluntarily led to the slaughter (Isa 53:7). God made him who was perfect and without

---

13. Boettner, *Studies in Theology*, 299.

sin, a lamb without blemish (Heb.9:14) "to be sin for us" (2 Cor 5:21). He was subjected to the curse of the law in his people's stead, "He redeemed us from the curse of the law by becoming a curse for us" (Gal 3:13). In him we see the innocent dying the death of the transgressor that the transgressor might be spared. In Christ's death, God declared to the world that he is the just and the justifier (Rom 3:26). He is just in that divine justice is satisfied; his justice being exhibited in the open and public punishment of sin in the body of Christ. He is the justifier in that in his own son he has provided a righteousness and a propitiatory sacrifice.

In the procurement of a salvation for his people, a price was paid. The word 'ransom' means to buy back, to purchase. The word "redeem" is closely related and means to deliver through the payment of a ransom price. Christ is both the ransom and redeemer; the deliverer of his people (Matt 20:28, Mark 10:28). Jesus offered up to his Father a full and definitive payment for the sins of his people, to quote John Owen: "Jesus Christ paid into his Father's hands a valuable price and ransom for our sins, as our surety, so discharging the debt we lay under, that we might go free, then did he bear the punishment due to our sins, and make satisfaction to the justice of God for them (for to pay such ransom is to make such satisfaction); but Jesus Christ paid such a price and ransom, as our surety, into his Father's hands."[14] With his blood, Christ has "ransomed a people for God from every tribe and language and people and nation" (Rev 6:9). The payment was of infinite value. It was of such value because of the nature of his person. He was very God of very God; the offended party to earth come down to offer himself to his father as a "fragrant offering and sacrifice to God" (Eph 5:2). Nothing else would do, we have been saved "not with perishable things such as silver or gold, but with the precious blood of Christ, like that of a lamb without blemish or spot" (1 Pet 1:19,20).

All of Christ's work would have counted for nothing if God, the offended party, had not accepted it. God did accept the work of Christ and he declared this to the world by raising him up on the third day. The fact of the resurrection is at the center of Christianity. God was declaring to the world that Christ had been successful in completing the work of salvation. Had he not been raised we would be without hope, still estranged from God and still dead in our sins, to quote the apostle, "If Christ has not been raised, your faith is futile; you are still in your sins" (1 Cor 15:17). Christians can, however, rejoice because Jesus "was delivered up for our trespasses and raised for our justification" (Rom 4:25). As Berkhof commented, "In the resurrection of Jesus Christ from the dead the father publically declared

14. Owen, *Works*, 10, 281.

that all the requirements of the law were met for all the elect."[15] Not only did Christ rise from the dead, but he ascended to the right hand of God where he forever lives to make intercession for his people. He is our great high priest who is in heaven to vouchsafe his people's salvation and "he is able to save to the uttermost those who draw near to God through him, since he always lives to make intercession for them" (Heb 7:25).

Christ the King

In regard to his deity, Christ has always been King, ruling over and sustaining all of his creation. Here brief mention will be made to Christ's Kingly office within the economy of redemption. Here one is effectively referring to his mediatorial kingship. This may be defined as "his official power to rule all things in heaven and on earth, for the glory of God, and for the execution of God's purpose in salvation."[16] In this role, Christ has been given both a universal and spiritual kingship. In his universal kingship, he rules the universe. It was to this Jesus referred when he told his disciples that "all authority in heaven and on earth has been given to me" (Matt 28:18). God placed "all things under his feet and gave him as head over all things to the church" (Eph 1:22) (1 Cor 15:27). In this role "as mediator He now guides the destiny of individuals and nations, controls the life of the world and makes it subservient to His redemptive purpose, and protects His Church against the dangers to which it is exposed in the world."[17] Christ's spiritual kingship is concerned with his rule over his church, where his kingship is acknowledged in the life of believers who have set him aside in their hearts as lord (1Pet 3:15). His reign in the hearts of his people continues to grow through the preaching of the gospel. On hearing this people believe, acknowledging and submitting to Christ's reign, and doing his will "on earth as it is in heaven" (Matt, 6:10).

There is a day approaching when all will bow at his name and acknowledge his supremacy, to quote the apostle, "at the name of Jesus every knee should bow, in heaven and on earth, and every tongue confess that Jesus in Lord" (Phil 2:10,11). Believers will do so with joy, thanking the Lord for the salvation he has bestowed upon them, unbelievers, those still under the first covenant of works, being still in the first Adam, will bow the knee with hearts filled with terror, wishing that the very mountains and rocks would

15. Berkhof, *Systematic Theology*, 519.

16. Ibid., 406.

17. Bavinck, *Our Reasonable Faith*, 101.

fall upon them to hide their faces "from the face of him who is seated on the throne, and from the wrath of the lamb" (Rev 6:16).

6

Two Kingdoms

THE TWO HEADS OF humanity, Adam, and Christ, each found themselves under the covenant of works, however, where Adam failed Christ has succeeded. The covenant of grace or new covenant is the result of Christ having kept the original covenant of works. As for us, born under the covenant of works, entrance into the new covenant is unconditional, this being the case because Christ has kept all of its conditions on our behalf. All we need to do is believe, and, it should be remembered, even faith itself is a gift from God (Eph 2:8). A gift that was earned by the work of Christ on our behalf. To be in the new covenant, or to put it another way, to be a participator in the covenant kept by Christ, is to be in the kingdom of God, to be outside of this kingdom is to be in the kingdom of the devil. There is no in-between, we are all in one or the other.

A kingdom is essentially a place, a territory that is ruled over by a king. When we speak of the kingdom of Christ we mean the place in which Christ reigns, where his rule and kingship is acknowledged by his people. So to be in the kingdom of God is to acknowledge in your heart the lordship of Christ, to "honor Christ the Lord as holy"(1 Pet 3:15).

The kingdom of God was a major theme in Jesus' teaching. Prior to Jesus' baptism, John the Baptist prepared the way of the king, telling the people to repent because the kingdom of God was at hand (Mark 1:15). John was not suggesting that the kingdom was non-existent prior to this time, but was declaring the arrival of the king himself. The one whom the prophets spoke about but did not see in the flesh (Matt 13:16) had now come to work out salvation for his people.

The kingdom of God can be said to be here, now, and can also be spoken of as both a past and a future reality. When Jesus walked the earth in his flesh, the kingdom was close to the people, the kingdom of God was indeed at hand in the very person of the king himself (Luke 11:20, Matt

12:28). When describing the kingdom to his disciples Jesus, according to the King James Bible, told them that "the kingdom of God is within you" (Luke 17:21). Perhaps a better translation of this verse would be that "the kingdom of God is in the midst of you." In the very person of the king himself, the kingdom was "among" them, it was physically present in the person of Christ.

In today's church, the kingdom is a present reality because Jesus reigns as king in the hearts of his people. In the Old Testament, all those who believed in the promises of the coming Messiah were also in the kingdom. For example, when Abraham saw Christ's day and rejoiced (John 8:56), or when Isaiah saw his glory (John 12:41), they set their hearts on the promise and honored him as king. The Christian knows that there is a day approaching when there will be a new earth and a new heavens (Rev 21:1). A world where the believer will reign with Christ, having a body like his post-resurrection body. Presently, one can say that the believer has been redeemed and is yet to be redeemed, as Paul tells us, "if Christ is in you, although your body is dead because of sin, the spirit is life because of righteousness" (Rom 8:10). This is the result of the believer presently living in a mortal body that has yet to be redeemed. He is aware of a warfare being waged between his resurrected redeemed spirit and his unredeemed body. This is why Paul says that "we ourselves, who have the firstfruits of the Spirit, groan inwardly as we wait eagerly for adoption as sons, the redemption of our bodies"(Rom 8:23). Not only our spirits, but, but creation itself is like one groaning in labor pains (Rom 8:22), eagerly awaiting for the time when it too "will be set free from its bondage to corruption and obtain the freedom of the glory of the children of God" (Rom 8:21).

There appears to be some confusion among many evangelicals concerning the position of Old Testament saints in regard to the kingdom of God. Walter Chantry states, in regard to John the Baptist, "John will be there too, though in his life on earth he never entered that stage of redemptive history which was called 'the kingdom of God', to distinguish it from the law and the prophets. Old Testament believers and those who enter the kingdom of God share a common salvation through faith in Jesus the Lord."[1] One would wholeheartedly concur with what Chantry says about salvation through faith in Christ, however, he appears mistaken in excluding Old Testament believers from the kingdom of God.

There is a tendency among many to equate the kingdom in the Old Testament with the nation of Israel. Chantry tells us that "Old Testament Israelites had expectations which were territorial and spatial. Conquering

---

1. Chantry, *God's Righteous Kingdom*, 47.

the promised land to expel oppressive Gentiles was a firm hope."[2] He tells us that the people "were looking for external purification of a literal Israel, for renovation of rulers, temple, and customs."[3] It is a position that fails to distinguish between Israel after the flesh and the true spiritual Israel. Whilst what Chantry says may well have been the case for carnal Israel, it was not so for the true Israelite, one who like Abraham, believed in the promise concerning the coming Christ. One must remember when speaking of Israel that "not all who are descended from Israel belong to Israel" (Rom 9:6). About the true Israelite we can say that he would have been born of the Spirit and translated from his position in Adam into a new position in Christ. He would have been, like his New Testament brothers, in the kingdom of God. All Old Testament saints possessed new hearts, and a new hope, and, as the writer to the Hebrews tells us, they "all died in faith not having received the things promised, but having seen them and greeted them from afar, and having acknowledged that they were strangers and exiles on earth" (Heb 11:13).

Possessing such faith, it is unlikely that these would have looked for spiritual fulfillment in the things of this world. Chantry is right when he contrasts the true kingdom with the outward formal religion displayed in the national Israel, "Christ's kingdom is inward. It comes mightily but secretly in the hearts of men."[4] He is, however, wrong in suggesting that this inward kingdom was not possessed by Old Testament believers. We must distinguish between the letter that kills and the Spirit who gives life. National Israel was carnal, standing condemned before the law, whereas spiritual Israel was in Christ in heavenly places.

As I hope to show, there is, however, a difference between the saints who lived in Old Testament times from those living after Christ. This difference does not concern their position or standing in Christ, for both Old and New Testament saints were together in Christ and in possession of all that he achieved. The difference is to be found in their subjective understanding of exactly what was theirs in Christ. This, however, in no way affected the fact that they were in the kingdom of God. Imagine a child born in the UK. The child, although not understanding the implications of his citizenship, is nevertheless, in the kingdom of Great Britain. Now think of this child reaching the age of eighteen and meeting the king in person. Now, although he will have a much greater understanding of what it means to be in the kingdom, his actual position in the kingdom will be the same. This is

2. Ibid., 51.

3. Ibid., 50.

4. Ibid., 51.

similar to what occurred when Jesus, the king, appeared in the flesh, dwelling among us. The believer would have gleaned a much greater appreciation of what it means to be in the kingdom, a citizen of heaven. As we will see later, it was the believer's appreciation of his position in Christ that lay at the heart of what occurred on the day of Pentecost.

In Matthew 11 John the Baptist sent some disciples to Jesus to enquire whether he was indeed the one. Jesus, after telling the disciples to go back to John reporting the miracles he was doing, miracles that declared him to be the Messiah, told his disciples something that many have found somewhat perplexing, and it's often used in the claim that Old Testament saints were outside of the kingdom. Jesus said that "among those born of woman there has arisen no one greater than John the Baptist. Yet the one who is least in the kingdom is greater than he" (Matt 11:11). What could he possibly mean by this? Should we conclude that John was not in the kingdom of God? If true, this conclusion would severely undermine Baptist covenant theology, or, at least, that put forward here. If John was not in the kingdom then it could be deduced that Old Testament believers were also not in God's kingdom. Should this be the case, one is left with more questions than answers. As already said, there are only the two kingdoms, if John is not in the kingdom of God, then where are we to place him? In the first Adam and in the kingdom of the devil?

Jesus often made comparisons using rhetorical hyperbole. On one occasion Jesus said to the crowd that was following him, "If anyone comes to me and does not hate his own father and mother and wife and children and brothers and sisters, yes, even his own life, he cannot be my disciple" (Luke 14:26). Obviously, Jesus did not mean this literally, rather, he was speaking of a comparative love, emphasizing the extent to which one must put him first in all things. Not even those closest to us must be allowed to stand in the way of obedience to Christ. The same principle can be applied here. Jesus was not saying that John was outside of the kingdom, but, rather, that John's position, when compared with those who now found themselves in the physical presence of the king, was relatively speaking, not to be compared. Also, of course, Jesus, in these words, may have been referring to John's immediate circumstances which found him in prison, comparing his plight with those disciples who were privileged enough to sit at Jesus' feet, and follow him in his earthly ministry. These disciples were in the immediate presence of Jesus the king. John was considered to be a prophet of God and was therefore highly esteemed, yet he did not understand the details of the kingdom in the way they were to be explained to those in Jesus' presence, nor was John a witness to the miracles that Jesus performed, hence, even the least in that company was greater than John. When John asked the question as to whether Jesus was the Christ, he was speaking as one who saw Jesus from afar, through a mist as it were, possessing an element of uncertainty.

Again, it is plausible that Jesus is here contrasting his people before and after Pentecost. As we will see later, when the Spirit manifested himself to the church in the Pentecostal dimension he communicated to the believer the true nature of his position in Christ, and in his kingdom. The believer will, after Pentecost, come to a realization of his place in the kingdom that was not available to Old Testament believers, even though they were in the kingdom. Compared to the kingdom blessings after the Spirit had come, John, and, indeed, all those who lived before Pentecost could be considered "least in the kingdom," at least from a subjective perspective during their time upon earth because, although being in possession of all, they had not subjectively entered into the blessings that are theirs in Christ.

In the gospels Jesus alludes to the kingdom of heaven or the kingdom of God, while the apostle Paul emphasizes one's being "in Christ." In his letters, he employs the expression "in Christ" and "in the Lord," or "in him no fewer than one hundred and sixty-four times. Being in the kingdom of God is synonymous with being "in Christ." The apostle is speaking from the perspective of one who has entered into a new understanding of what it means to be in God's kingdom. Paul is like all those who have been baptized with the Spirit, one to whom God has made known the mystery of his will in Christ. He can, therefore, speak as one who has received the Spirit of sonship, enabling him to enter into his inheritance in a manner that was not available prior to Pentecost. In speaking from this vantage point then, he can understandably use the expression "in Christ."

For the person outside of Christ, the things of God are dead to him. They relate to a realm of which he has no conception. To enter into God's kingdom one must be made spiritually alive. This occurs when the Holy Spirit brings about what might be called a spiritual resurrection, the new birth (John 3:3). Obviously, this entails not simply a reformation of one's behavior, but something far more radical. Christians are often ill-informed about the radical nature of the change that that occurs when one to becomes a Christian, a member of God's kingdom. It is a change as radical as going into a cemetery and commanding the dead to rise. Spiritually, one is born dead. A Christian is one who has experienced a miracle where he/she has been resurrected spiritually, and has been translated from the kingdom of darkness into the kingdom of Christ, "For he has rescued us from the dominion of darkness and brought us into the kingdom of the Son he loves" (Col 1:13).

Perhaps the greatest spur for sanctification in a Christian's life is a realization of just what he/she has become in Christ. Yes, we were at one time in Adam, however, having believed, we have been placed into Christ and made to share in all that his work secured. The Christian needs to live in the realization of this miraculous fact.

7

The Application of Blessings Secured
by the Second Adam

Pre-Abrahamic

FOR ADAM AND HIS posterity, the punishment for sin was, and still is, death. In the midst of pronouncing the curse, God in his mercy, intimated his sovereign purpose to act as fallen man's friend in and through the woman's seed. Whilst spiritual death followed immediately on the heels of the first sin, God, in his mercy, postponed man's physical death and revealed a work of grace in which he would put enmity between the woman's seed and the devil, and though the woman's seed would suffer a bruised heel, he would nevertheless crush the devil's head (Gen 3:15). This is the first reference to the gospel or good news in the Scriptures. God was declaring that what Adam had failed to do, he was somehow going to do on fallen man's behalf.

Although the promise is somewhat obscure, it did "contain enough to lay a solid foundation for faith and hope toward God, and it was the first beam of gospel light to fall on a fallen world."[1] God had revealed himself as the lawgiver and judge, he was now revealing himself as the "just and the justifier" (Rom 3:26). What will become clear as we examine the application of redemption is that the "New Covenant in its preexistent state reaches back, stretching its wings over the Old and New Testament people of God."[2]

In those early days the message of the gospel, be it ever so faint, was apprehended in faith. We see evidence of this in the Lord's acceptance of Abel's offering. About this, we read that the "Lord had regard for Abel and his offering, but for Cain and his offering he had no regard" (Gen 4:4–5). We can only suppose that this was because Abel, with an eye of faith fixed firmly on what God had promised, saw the need for God to provide a propitiatory

1. Buchanan, *Doctrine of Justification*, 27.

2. Vos, *Redemptive History*, 99.

sacrifice. He acknowledged this by offering, in thanksgiving for what God would do, the firstborn of his flock (Gen 4:4), a bloody token offering. Gill tells us that "Abel's 'sacrifice was a more excellent one; not only as to its kind, being a lamb, and so typical of the lamb of God; but as to the manner in which it was offered, by faith in the view of a better sacrifice than that, even the sacrifice of Christ, by which transgression is finished, sin made an end of reconciliation for it made, and an everlasting righteousness brought in."[3] By accepting the offering God gave Abel a commendation that he was indeed righteous in his eyes (Heb 11:4). The righteousness he received was nothing less than that righteousness secured by Christ, hence, "he is called righteous Abel, not by his own righteousness, but by the righteousness of faith, the righteousness of Christ, received by faith, for he had the grace of faith, which is the covenant of grace bestowed on him."[4]

In the prediluvian age, God communicated to his prophet Moses and spoke of a coming catastrophe, saying that he was to withdraw his Spirit from humanity (Gen 6:3). God's revelation to man is progressive, and it is only when we come to the New Testament we grasp something of the verse's meaning. In 1 Pet 3:18–21 we are told that the Holy Spirit that raised Jesus from the dead was also in Noah, causing him to preach to the lost souls in the time preceding God's impending judgment in the flood.

These people were under the covenant of works, lost in the prison-house of sin. Noah, under the Spirit's influence and guidance, pointed to the promise of God that would be realized at some time in the future. In 1 Pet 1:11, the Holy Spirit is referred to as the "Spirit of Christ." It was this Spirit who was in the Old Testament prophets as they enquired into "what person or time the Spirit of Christ in them was indicating when he predicted the sufferings of Christ and the subsequent glories." It was under the Spirit of Christ that Noah warned the people of his day. The term "Spirit of Christ" suggests that Noah's message pointed to a savior who was to appear in the distant future, one who would take away sin. Noah, like all believers in those days, would have believed the promise becoming a recipient of new covenant blessings.

In these pre-Mosaic times, although the law of God was not explicitly revealed, it was nevertheless a reality, people knew the difference between right and wrong, demonstrating that "the work of the law is written on their hearts" (Rom 2:15). In reference to God's law in the time of Noah, Anthony Burgess writes:

---

3. Gill, *Body of Divinity*, 496.
4. Ibid., 496.

He that should think that this Law was not in the Church of
God before Moses, his administration of it, should greatly erre
[sic] . . . And when we say, the Law was before Moses, I do not
mean only, that it was written in the hearts of men, but it was
publikely preached in the ministry that the Church did then enjoy, as appeareth by Noah's preaching . . . So that we may say, the
Decalogue is Adams and Abrahams, Noahs, and Christs,(sic)
and the Apostles, as well as Moses[5]

We see the grace of God in the ark that Noah was instructed to build. The ark
was a type of Christ, all those who took refuge in it would survive the wrath
of God. The ark "may be considered an emblem of the church of God, which
is to be formed in all things, according to the pattern given by God himself,
as that was; and which weathers the storms and tempests. and beatings of the
waters of affliction and persecution, as that it did in a literal sense."[6]

In these pre-Abrahamic times, the promises of God were universal in
nature. There was no division between Jew and Gentile. When God set apart
the Jewish nation, these universal promises were still in effect, they did not
go away and could still be embraced in faith. Therefore, although Israel was
to be given special blessings, one should not think that there was not the
possibility of salvation for those who became known as Gentiles.

The Central Principle of Covenant Theology

Before examining particular covenants, one needs to realize that the essential nature of God's covenants is a relatively easy principle to grasp. All too
often, people get befuddled when they examine the details of the various
covenants and they end up missing the woods for the trees. There are essentially two primary covenants made in time: that made with the first Adam
and the new covenant made with Christ, the second Adam. Those who lived
before Christ looked forward to the ratification or the formal establishment of the new covenant in the shedding of Christ's blood. In believing
the promise they became recipients of what Christ was to achieve. Even
though the work that this covenant necessitated had not yet been worked
out, believers still became members of it, beneficiaries of its blessings.

For a moment try to imagine that the covenants with Abraham, Moses,
and David had not been made. There are only the two primary covenants,
that made with Adam, and that made with Christ. We are all by nature in
the first Adam, born dead in sin and estranged from God, or else we have

5. Burgess, *Vindiciae Legis*, 150.
6. Gill, *Body of Divinity*, 498.

been made alive by the Spirit, and through faith in Christ, have been translated into the kingdom of his Son. We are all then either united to the first
Adam or else we are united to the second Adam. This is the essential thing
one needs to keep in mind when reading the Scriptures. Unless one grasps
this, reading about the other covenants can serve to confuse matters. One
must remember that these other covenants do not change this essential fact.
They are all subservient to the covenant made with Christ. About salvation
bestowed on Old Testament saints, John Owen states:

> The church of old had the promises of Christ, Rom IX:4, Gen
> 3:15, XII:3; were justified by faith Gen XXV:6, Rom iV, Gal 3;
> obtained mercy for their sins and were justified in the Lord Isa
> XLV, 24,25; had the Spirit for conversion, regeneration, and
> sanctification Ex Xi, 19, 36; 26, expected and obtained salvation
> by Jesus Christ, things as remote from the covenant of works as
> the east is from the west . . . the covenant of grace which they
> lived under was dark, legal and low in comparison of that which
> we now are admitted into since the coming of Christ in the flesh;
> but the covenant wherein they walked with God and wherein we
> find acceptance is the same.[7]

"The covenant wherein they walked with God and wherein we find
acceptance" is nothing less than the new covenant.

The Abrahamic and Mosaic covenants did not change this. They were
conditional, with the promise of worldly blessings that served only a subservient role in order to make the promise more prominent. They should
be viewed as having come in alongside the promise in order to make the
promise more manifest. Before Christ's appearance salvation was through
believing that which was promised, after Christ, it is about believing in him
who is a fulfillment of the promise. If the Abrahamic covenant etc., had not
been made God could have continued to save people as he did in the case of
Abel, Noah. However, in his mercy he chose to channel the promise through
the conduit of subsidiary covenants, in order to safeguard and, as I have
said, highlight the promise.

Some allow themselves to become muddled because of the word 'new'
in new covenant. Sometimes, the Old Testament does make it seem that the
benefits of this covenant are only for a future time, for example, (Jere 31,
Ezek 36). One simply needs to keep in mind that these texts allude, not to
the application of the blessings, but, rather, to the formal establishment of
the new covenant in Christ's work. One objection frequently raised when
one speaks of new covenant blessings being available before the covenant's

---

7. Owen, *Works*, 12, 369.

ratification concerns the words uttered by Jeremiah when he alludes to the covenant that will be made in the future, being "after those days" (Isa 31:31; Heb 8:10). For clearly, if it was futuristic and "after those days" how could the fruits thereof be available to those who lived before "those days"? Understanding the answer to this question is vital for understanding the unity that exists in Scripture concerning the way of salvation. The word "new" is used because the covenant in Christ, the new covenant, is usually set against the backcloth of the broken covenant, and especially with its reiteration in the Old Testament in the form of the conditional Mosaic covenant. The Puritan, John Owen is arguably the greatest theologian the English speaking world has ever produced. He was only too aware that many were misunderstanding the nature of the "newness" of the new covenant. He addresses this in the form of a question and answer:

> First, 'this covenant is promised as that which is future, to be brought in as a certain time, "after those days," as has been declared. But it is certain that the things here mentioned, the grace and mercy expressed, were really communicated unto many both before and after the giving of the law, long ere this covenant was made; for all who truly believed and feared God had these things effected in them by grace: wherefore their effectual communication cannot be esteemed a property of this covenant which was afterwards made.
>
> Ans. This objection was sufficiently prevented in what we have already discoursed concerning the efficacy of the grace of this covenant before it was solemnly consummated. For all things of this nature that belong unto it do arise and spring from the mediation of Christ, or his interposition on behalf of sinners. Wherefore this took place from the giving of the first promise; the administration of the grace of this covenant did therein and then take its date. Howbeit the Lord had not yet done that whereby it was solemnly to be confirmed, and that whereon all the virtue of it did depend.[8]

Essentially, the new covenant was before the old. Regarding Old Testament believers, Woolsey's comment is worth quoting, "Christ was their Mediator too. Though his incarnation had not yet happened, the fruits of it still availed for the fathers. Christ was their head . . . So the men of God in the Old Testament were shown to be heirs of the new. The new covenant was actually more ancient than the old, though it was subsequently revealed. It was 'hidden in the prophetic ciphers' until the time of revelation

---

8. Owen, *Works* 22, 147.

in Christ."[9] Colin Hamer states that "the covenant starts not in the desert of Sinai, or even with the promise to Abraham, but in the garden of Eden."[10] The writer to the Hebrews tells us that "Christ has obtained a ministry that is as much more excellent than the old as the covenant he mediates is better, since it is enacted on better promises" (Heb 8:6), and that, "In speaking of a new covenant, he makes the first one obsolete" (Heb 8:13). This superior ministry of Jesus did not start following his incarnation, rather it started in the covenant of redemption, and its communication to sinners with the first promise in Genesis 3:15. The writer of Hebrews is here considering the new covenant's consummation and not its beginning, as Owen reminds us in his examination of Hebrews 8:8–12, "he treated of such an establishment of the new covenant as wherewith the old covenant made at Sinai was absolutely inconsistent . . . wherefore he considers here as it was actually completed, so as to bring with it all the ordinances of worship which are proper unto it."[11] By ordinances he means the Lord's Supper and baptism which were peculiar to the time after Christ's completed work. As I shall keep emphasizing, to be a recipient of these "better promises" one must be in that covenant of which Jesus is the mediator, and Scripture knows of no covenant other than the new covenant of which this is the case. This is why the people of God have always been members of the new covenant in Christ.

God's Covenant with Abraham

The Abrahamic covenant represented a major turning point in God's dealings with humanity. From this point on God was to reveal himself to a particular people, namely, the Jews. They received a special manifestation of the purposes of God unto salvation, and it was from this people that Christ according to the flesh was to come forth. Particularization starts with Abraham, and, as we will see, becomes more pronounced under Moses 430 year later.

It is with the appearance of the Abrahamic and Mosaic covenants, especially the latter, that many Christians become confused, and it is perhaps an understatement to say that from the time of the Protestant Reformation in the 16th century, this has been the source of much controversy. Indeed, the essential source of the division between Reformed Baptists and paedobaptists can be traced back to a different understanding of the covenant made with Abraham. The point to keep in mind is what we saw above,

9. Woolsey, The Covenant in the Church Fathers, 42–43.

10. Hamer, The Bridegroom Messiah, 39.

11. Owen, Works, 6, 60.

namely, that *the way of salvation does not change*. The goal of these covenants is to encourage people to realize the nature of their position under
the broken covenant of works, and to look to the one who is promised, that
they might believe in him and be saved.

A Brief View of the Paedobaptist Position

Before we examine a Reformed Baptist view of God's covenants I want to
briefly examine what it is that the Reformed paedobaptists believe. Later I
hope to show why I believe it to be a position that has served to obfuscate
our understanding of the true nature of covenantal unity. It should be noted
that there are a number of different nuances of interpretation within the
paedobaptist camp. Here I seek to provide a general synopsis of Reformed
paedobaptism.

Although, of course, covenant theology is a very important biblical
doctrine, it only became an important article of faith from the time of the
Protestant Reformation. According to Schrenk, it was the Anabaptists who
first drew attention to the covenant:

> The Anabaptists called themselves by the nickname of "cov-
> enanters" and saw themselves as those sealed with the covenant
> sign. Baptism to them was a covenant. Therefore it is highly
> probable, that the Zurich reformers owing to this opposition
> to their emphasis made use of the covenant sealing of God in
> infant baptism. So we will hardly go wrong in taking the view
> that it was the Anabaptists who first hurled covenant thought
> into the Reformation movement. Thus it is that the Zurichers
> as well as Bucer converted the movement idea, especially in the
> doctrine of the sacraments, in order to expound the signs of the
> covenant in their importance.[12]

The Reformers struggle with the Anabaptists was instrumental in that
they felt compelled to generate a detailed response to Anabaptist thinking.
David Wright informs us that:

> The 16th century Reformers . . . were confronted with the ur-
> gency of justifying [infant baptist] in the face of Anabaptist pro-
> tests which took sola Scriptura more strictly than did the likes of
> Luther, Calvin and company. [Supposed] covenantal parallelism
> [between the covenant with Abraham and the new covenant]
> proved the most sophisticated and durable of their [attempted]

12. Schrenk, *Gottesreich und Bund*, 37.

defences, which in turn made the assumption of universal infant baptism (made legally binding in some Reformation strongholds, such as Geneva) a factor in the rise of covenantal theology to prominence in the later 16th and 17th centuries.[13]

So covenant theology arose because the Reformers were faced with the problem of having to defend their practice of infant baptism against what they considered to be Anabaptist heresy. Wright quotes John W. Riggs,

> From a historical perspective, the Reformed use of covenant to interpret Christian baptism first arose, almost always, when arguing for infant baptism. In other words, its origin was not in theological or exegetical reflection on baptism as such, but as a specific response to the [Anabaptist] challenge to a long-held practice of infant baptism.[14]

Many of the ideas employed by the Reformers in their attempt to refute Anabaptist thinking were essentially what they had inherited, and it is perhaps no exaggeration, to quote David H. Gay, that, "the Reformers began with a practice they had inherited from Rome, and went looking for a theology to support it."[15]

Zwingli's case is interesting simply because it appears he nearly sided with the Anabaptists. He believed the true church to consist only of regenerate believers; those who have made a profession of faith. This being the case there could be no room for infant baptism. He is believed to have said, "Nothing grieves me more than that at the present I have to baptize children."[16] Later, however, Zwingli changed his mind, no doubt because of what he believed to have been the excesses of the Anabaptists. In 1525 he published *On Baptism: Anabaptism and Infant Baptism*. This was essentially a denunciation of the Anabaptist views of men like Balthasar and Hubmair. The latter responded to Zwingli in a work entitled *The Christian Baptism of Believers*. Zwingli likewise responded with *An Answer*, where he sought to counter Anabaptist views. According to Bierma, "Zwingli defended the practice of paedobaptism on the grounds that there has been one covenant of grace between God and his people from the time of Adam to the present . . . Upon this foundation-the continuity of the history of salvation and

---

13. Wright, "Christian Baptism," 28.

14. Riggs, *Baptism in the Reformed Tradition*, 122.

15. Gay, *New Covenant Articles*, 3, 239.

16. Long, *New Covenant Theology*, 27.

the unity of the covenant of grace-Zwingli goes on to make his case for infant baptism."[17]

It was Zwingli's response to Hubmair that initiated Covenant Theology, to quote Long:

> In this response Zwingli held baptism to be a covenant sign under the new covenant like circumcision had been a sign under the Abrahamic covenant. What Zwingli initiated laid the basis for the one covenant of grace—different administrations teaching of Reformed Theology, holding that the church is generically one in both the Old Testament and New Testament and that the covenant made with Abraham in Genesis 17, with its sign and seal of circumcision is fulfilled in the New Covenant with its sign and seal of baptism.[18]

Again Gay was, I believe, correct in asserting that if only the Reformers "had taken Scripture as seriously as did the Anabaptists, they would have started with Scripture, tested their practice against it, and come to the right way to baptise."[19] Unfortunately, however, this is what they didn't do, rather, they developed a convoluted theology of the covenant that is a distortion of the otherwise simplicity that has been revealed in Scripture. The position they adopted was essentially a throwback to Roman Catholicism.

The first Reformers, men like Luther, Zwingli, and Calvin etc., are often referred to as magisterial Reformers. This is because of the way they understood the church's relationship with the state. It was an understanding based upon a particular view of God's covenant with Abraham. This helps to explain the somewhat bizarre relationship within Presbyterianism between the church and the state where the secular authorities are accorded a degree of jurisdiction in the church of Christ.

In Calvin's Geneva "every member of the church and citizen of the community was required to profess his faith in Christ, and all the children of those who made such a profession were to be baptized."[20] These children grew up and exercised power in the state, a state that was seen as being another arm of the church's spiritual authority. In regard to Luther and Zwingli, the relationship between church and state was such that "the church was in practice largely controlled by the civil powers and was practically regarded as a phase of the state."[21] To quote Zwingli, "it was the state that organized

17. Ibid., 30.

18. Ibid., 29–30.

19. Gay, *New Covenant Articles*, 3, 139.

20. Schenck, *Presbyterian Doctrine of the Children in the Covenant*, 4.

21. Ibid., 5.

everything in the church, yet a state that was not an ordinary state, but a Christian state."[22] It was again expected that all infants be baptized, and, of course, all were treated from infancy as being Christian. This served to encourage a nominal Christianity. There was the presumption of regeneration rather than a personal encounter with the risen Christ. It is this that lies behind the Westminster Confession's insistence that secular authorities should have jurisdiction in church matters.[23]

Paedobaptists display a remarkable confidence in what they believe, and they are not reticent in criticizing the Reformed Baptist position. According to Andy Booth, "only the Reformed and covenantal view of the Scriptures does justice to God's redemptive revelation."[24] Beeke and Lanning go further, maintaining that "Baptists are not faithful to the Scriptures, nor to the Reformers who clearly and unanimously understood infant baptism in the covenantal terms of Acts 2:39."[25]

Beeke and Lanning are right in what they say about the Reformers, but wrong in their assertion that Baptists are not faithful to the Scriptures, rather, quite the opposite is the case. Concerning the Reformers, one must not forget that, like us all, those men possessed feet of clay. Yes, they repudiated the false teachings of Rome, and they rediscovered essential doctrine, for example, Justification by faith, they also, however, like all mortal men, were fallible and made mistakes, one being their belief that circumcision was replaced by baptism, and that the new covenant is simply the last installment of a series of administrations of the covenant of grace.

The Scriptures and not the Reformers or the various confessions of faith must be our ultimate guide. I can't help feeling that when paedobaptists criticize the Baptist paradigm, which they appear all too willing to do, they are, to use the metaphor, "pulling at the tiger's tail." We will see that it is the paedobaptist who is on the back foot, putting forth a view of the covenants that is anything but scriptural. For reasons that will become clear later, one might go so far as to regard it as dangerous.

At the heart of the paedobaptist position is the idea that the covenants made with Abraham, Moses, and David were different administrations of the one covenant of grace. The Abrahamic covenant was the first formal establishment of the covenant of grace, the first of a number of administrations of this covenant, with the new covenant being the last. According to Booth:

22. Schulthess-Rechberg, *Luther, Zwingli and Calvin*, 179–82.

23. Schaff, *Creeds Of the Evangelical Protestant Churches*, 653.

24. Booth, *Children of Promise*, 78.

25. Beeke and Lanning, "Unto You and Your Children," 61.

The Covenant of Grace is like a constitution, in that it must be administered. There is one covenant (or constitution), but there are various administrations over time. Covenant administrations are similar to the various presidential administrations in the United States, each of which administers the one US constitution. Although certain amendments may lawfully be made to the constitution under a particular administration, the one constitution remains in place.[26]

Jonty Rhodes employs up-to-date computer speak to describe the covenant's administrations:

It's a bit like when you download the new editions of the latest software for your smartphone. Is the update the same or different from its predecessor? Well, both really. It's the same fundamental package: a program to make calls, send texts, access the internet, and all the rest. But the later edition is a better version of the earlier one: it's a step forward, while maintaining the fundamental continuity with the original package. So too the covenant of grace. There are various editions: with Adam, Abraham, Moses, David, and the church. Each sees progression and expansion on the last one. But underneath they are the same deal, the same covenant.[27]

Within each administration there exists covenant duality in terms of its internal and external aspects, comprising of the visible and invisible church. Only those Israelites who were the elect of God were believed to be members of the internal covenant and the invisible church. All others, the vast majority, whilst they were clearly participators in the covenant of grace, belonged only to the external visible church. In other words, they were participants in the covenant's external administration but did not participate in the substance of the covenant. Whilst, as with all the administrations of the covenant, the circumstantial aspects changed, but the substance remains the same.

According to Robertson this "identity of substance between the Old and New Covenants constituted the theological foundation of Paedobaptism."[28] In spite of these different administrations of the covenant, whether the Israelite participated in the external elements only or both the external and internal aspects, he was nevertheless deemed to be in the covenant of grace. This then serves to maintain the essential oneness of the covenant. It is believed that "The cumulative evidence of the Scriptures points definitively

26. Booth, *Children of Promise*, 34.

27. Rhodes, *Covenants Made Simple*, 64–65.

28. Denault, "By Further Steps," 77.

toward the unitary character of the biblical covenants. God's multiple bonds with his people ultimately unit into a single relationship."[29]

The sign that one was in the covenant was circumcision. It is important to distinguish between circumcision in the flesh and circumcision of the heart. Those who participated in the internal substance, the church invisible, would have experienced circumcision of the heart, others, the participators in the external circumstantial visible church, would only have experienced the physical circumcision.

It is essential to keep in mind that all Israelite children became members of the covenant of grace by circumcision. The paedobaptist position maintains that because non-believers were in the Abrahamic covenant, an administration of the one covenant of grace, so, likewise, children of believers, through baptism, are to be included in the new covenant, which, it is believed, is the final administration of the covenant of grace. One can go so far as to say that the children under both covenants were in the covenant from birth, and their circumcision or baptism is deemed to demonstrate this fact. It was a mixed church in the Old Testament and it is a mixed church in the New Testament. God has not abrogated this principle, as Warfield put it, "The argument, in a nutshell, is simply this: God established His Church in the days of Abraham and put children into it. They must remain there until He puts them out. He has nowhere put them out. They are still then members of His Church and as such entitled to its ordinances."[30] According to Charles Hodge:

> The status, therefore, of baptized children is not a vague or uncertain one, according to the doctrine of the Reformed Churches. They are members of the Church; they are professing Christians; they belong presumptively to the number of the elect. These propositions are true of them in the same sense in which they are true of adult professing Christians. Both are included in the general class of persons whom God requires his Church to regard and treat as within her pale, and under her watch and care.[31]

Children of believers in today's church are then considered to be in the covenant of grace and therefore are to undergo the covenantal rite of baptism, a rite that has replaced circumcision.

Paedobaptists believe they are simply perpetuating the principle of Genesis 17:7, where God said: "And I will establish my covenant between

29. Robertson, *Christ of the Covenants*, 28.
30. Warfield, "Polemics of Infant Baptism," 9.408.
31. Hodge, "Church Membership of Infants," 389.

me and you and your offspring after you throughout their generations for an everlasting covenant, to be God to you and to your offspring after you."

To quote Denault, the paedobaptists, "by making the distinction between the substance and the administration . . . justified a legitimate place for them."[32] So, as the unregenerate Israelite would have undergone the rite of physical circumcision, so in the new covenant, the children of believing parent(s) are to undergo the rite of water baptism.

Much is made of Peter's statement on the day of Pentecost when he alluded to the fulfillment of God's promise in the sending of his Spirit, "For the promise is for you and for your children and for all who are far off, everyone whom the Lord our God calls to himself" (Acts 2:39). It is believed that, to quote Booth, "since God has not changed the terms of church membership, new covenant believers and their children are likewise included in the church."[33]

Paedobaptists try not to let the word "new" deter them from their contention that the new covenant is not really new. About the newness of the new covenant Rhodes tells us:

> The word "new" can be a bit misleading. Take two examples: "I'm going to build a new house," and "He's become a new man since he married." In the first example, new means 'never existed before." In the second, it has more in the sense of renewed" or "dramatically changed for the better." It is in this second sense that the new covenant is "new." It is not a completely new creation unrelated to what came before.[34]

It should also be noted, and this is very important, the new covenant, being another administration of the covenant of grace, only came into operation with the advent of Christ.

The above is a brief synopsis of the paedobaptist paradigm. It is a position I shall continue to make reference to as I seek to show that it is unbiblical and, dare I say, damaging to individuals and the propagation of the gospel.

A Reformed Baptist View

How then does the Reformed Baptist position put forward here differ from that of the Reformed Presbyterians or paedobaptists? As I hope to show,

---

32. Denault, *Distinctiveness of Baptist Covenant Theology*, 48.

33. Booth, *Children of Promise*, 73.

34. Rhodes, *Covenants Made Simple*, 95.

the essential difference lies in the way the Abrahamic covenant is viewed. The Reformed Baptist position makes a distinction between the covenant of grace, or what I would prefer to call, the new covenant that was revealed to Abraham and the later covenant that was established with him. This latter covenant was made with Abraham's physical seeds (plural) and was conditional. However, the promise of the new covenant which Abraham believed and by which Christ's righteousness was imputed to him, occurred twenty-five or so years before any conditional covenant was madewith him.

A number of years before the conditional covenant was established with Abraham in respect to his physical offspring, he had believed God in his promise. This promise alluded to Abraham's seed (singular), i.e., the Christ, and was unconditional. It was through this seed "which is Christ" (Gal 3:16) rather than through his seeds (plural) that the true children of Abraham would come forth. This is why Scripture tells us that it is "those of faith who are the sons of Abraham" (Gal 3:7). About this promise, Nehemiah Coxe states:

> The sum of all gospel blessings is comprised in this promise. Therefore it will follow that the proper heirs of this blessing of Abraham have a right (not only in some, but) in all the promises of the new covenant. This is true not in the limited sense, suspended on uncertain conditions, but in the full sense and secured by the infinite grace, wisdom, power, and faithfulness of God. Accordingly they are in time made good to them all . . . All the blessings of this covenant redound on believers by means of their union and communion with the Lord Jesus Christ, who is both the Head and Root of the new covenant, and the Fountain from which all its blessings are derived to us.[35]

Although the new covenant would not be formally ratified for another two thousand years in the completed work of Christ, it was, nevertheless retrospective in regard to its benefits, hence, one could become a beneficiary of its blessings by believing in the promise, just like Abraham had done. To quote Herman Bavinck:

> For though God communicates his revelation successively and historically makes it progressively richer and fuller, and humankind therefore advances in the knowledge, possession and enjoyment of that revelation, God is and remains the same . . . Although Christ completed his work on earth only in the midst of history and although the Holy Spirit was not poured out till the day of Pentecost, God nevertheless was able, ready in the

35. Coxe, "Discourse of the Covenants," 81.

days of the Old Testament believers who were saved in no other way than we. There is one, one faith, one Mediator, one of salvation, and one covenant of grace.[36]

While the Reformed Baptist would not see eye-to-eye with Bavinck concerning the administration of the one covenant of grace, we can not but agree with these words. What he refers to as the covenant of grace is nothing other than the new covenant. So whilst covenant duality for paedobaptists is found to exist within the one covenant of grace itself, the Reformed Baptist position put forward here sees any duality resulting from there being two separate covenants, one revealed to Abraham in the promise and the other formally made with him a number of years later.

The first promise given to Abraham contained the "sum and Substance of all spiritual and eternal blessings."[37] About God's promise to the patriarch "I will bless you and make your name great, so that you will be a blessing" (Gen 12:2), Coxe states, "The grace and blessings of the new covenant were given and ensured to Abraham for himself. What is more, this honor was conferred on him that he should be the head of covenant blessings as the father of all true believers." We read in Genesis 15:6, that "Abram believed the LORD, and this was credited to him as righteousness."[38] Against all expectations, because of her being well beyond child-bearing age, God promised Abraham that his wife Sarah would be with child. Abraham believed in the humanly impossible, resting entirely in the belief that God would do as he had promised (Gen 15:5). By exercising faith, the righteousness of God, procured by Christ, was then credited to him.

The covenant that was later made with Abraham in no way shape or form changed the essential fact that salvation was patterned on what happened in the case of Abraham believing the promise. Salvation, throughout the Old Testament was always a matter of believing the promise concerning the Messiah and becoming a recipient of new covenant blessings. John Spilsbury, one of the first Particular Baptists, commented:

> Again, its called a promise and not the Covenant, and we know that every promise is not a covenant: there being a large difference between a promise and a covenant. And now let it be well considered what is here meant by the promise, and that is Gods sending the Messais [sic], or the seed in whom the Nations should be blessed.[39]

36. Bavinck, *Reformed Dogmatics*, 3, 214–15.

37. Coxe, "Discourse of the Covenants," 75.

38. Ibid., 75.

39. Spilsbury, *Treatise Concerning the Lawful Subject of Baptisme*, 26.

In the time of Christ's earthly ministry the Jews believed salvation was theirs simply because they were Abraham's physical offspring. In this they made their boast (John 8:33). They put great faith in the rite of circumcision, seeing it as a prerequisite for salvation. To quote Owen:

> Herein lay the great mistake of the Jews of old wherein they are followed by their posterity to this day. They thought no more was needful to interest them in the covenant of Abraham but that they were his seed according to the flesh; and they constantly pleaded the latter privilege as the ground and reason of the former. It is true that they were the children of Abraham according to the flesh: but on that account they can have no other privilege than that he should be set apart as a special channel through whose loins God would derive the promise.[40]

The apostle Paul clearly shows that Abraham was justified by faith before circumcision, "Under what circumstances was it credited? Was it after he was circumcised or before? It was not after, but before!" (Rom 4:10). The Jews put their confidence in the rite rather than the promise, but Abraham possessed Christ's righteousness because he was in union with Christ. About this righteousness John Owen could write:

> The righteousness of Christ (in his obedience and suffering for us) imputed unto believers, as they are united unto him by his Spirit, is that righteousness whereupon they are justified before God, on account whereof their sins are pardoned, and a right is granted them unto the heavenly inheritance.[41]

The apostle tells us that Abraham "received the sign of circumcision as a seal of the righteousness that he had by faith while he was yet uncircumcised. The purpose was to make him the father of all who believe without being circumcised so that the righteousness would be counted to them as well" (Rom 4:11). Whatever later appeared, nothing altered the fact that, to quote Owen: "The way of reconciliation with God, of justification and salvation, was always one and the same; and that from the giving of the first promise none was ever justified or saved but by the new covenant and Jesus Christ, the mediator thereof."[42]

The entire paedobaptist edifice is built upon the idea that the promises were for Abraham's physical descendants, his seed in the plural. This is then carried over to the New Testament and applied to the children of believers.

40. Owen, *Works*, 16, 122.
41. Owen, *Works*, 5, 208.
42. Owen, *Works*, 6, 71.

This, however, is not what the Scriptures tell us. As Paul states: "Now the promises were made to Abraham and his offspring. It does not say, 'And to offsprings,' referring to many, but referring to one" (Gal 3:16). When the covenant was made with Abraham's seeds (plural), about twenty-five years after the promise, and whilst it was conditional, and separate from the promised covenant, it did, nevertheless, point toward it. It was essentially typological, serving Abraham's seed (singular), namely the Christ, who would establish the new covenant. Abraham's true children are those who believed the promise, thereby becoming children of God with a heavenly inheritance. Those without faith, on the other hand, knew only the conditional covenant that spoke of mundane blessings, and which could only lead to condemnation. Again, the apostle leaves us in no doubt about who the children of Abraham are: "Know then that it is those of faith who are the sons of Abraham" (Gal 3:7).

The conditional Abrahamic covenant did not constitute the covenant of grace, it was an entirely separate covenant, with a number of conditions attached to it. God said to Abraham:

> And I will make thee exceedingly fruitful, and I will make nations of thee, and kings shall come out of thee. And I will establish my covenant between me and thee and thy seed after thee in their generations for an everlasting covenant, to be a God unto thee, and thy seed after thee. And I will give unto thee, and they seed after thee, the land wherein thou art a stranger, for an everlasting possession; and I will be their God. And God said unto Abraham, Thou shalt keep my covenant therefore, thou and thy seed after thee in their generations. This is my covenant which ye shall keep, between me and you and thy seed after the; Every man child among you shall be circumcised. (Gen 17:7–10)

All Israelites by virtue of birth were members of the covenant made with Abraham, whilst only those who exercised faith in the promise belonged to the new covenant in Christ. So we have two posterities, one physical, the other spiritual. The covenant concluded with him applied to his physical posterity, and its promises were of a mundane nature, for example, the land of Canaan as an everlasting possession (Gen 17:8). Whilst this covenant established with Abraham, and later elaborated under Moses was not a covenant of grace, it was, nevertheless, the result of God's grace simply because the nation received blessings that were undeserved, as Coxe put it:

> This was a covenant of grace and mercy, originating from the mere goodness and underserved favour of God toward Israel . . .

In it many excellent privileges were given to them which no other nation under heaven had a right in except themselves. These were conferred on them in pursuit of the great design of God's grace in the covenant of redemption by Christ. Yet it was not that covenant of grace which God made with Abraham for all his spiritual seed, which was earlier confirmed by God in Christ, and through which all nations (that is, true believers in every nation) have been ever since, now are, and will be, blessed with the spiritual and eternal blessing of Abraham.[43]

The paedobaptists believe that the everlasting covenant referred to in Genesis 17 refers to the covenant of grace. This, however, was not so. God said to Abraham, "my covenant shall be in your flesh an everlasting covenant"(Gen 17:13). If this was indeed the case, if it constituted the covenant of grace, then we would expect God to have kept his promise. But this is not what we see. What has become of circumcision? If it was to be an everlasting sign surely we would expect it to be a requirement for all believers throughout time. We would also expect to see the fulfillment of the promise, "I will give to you and your offspring after you the land of your sojournings, all the land of Canaan, for an everlasting possession"(Gen 17:8). We don't see this because the covenant was not of grace, but of works, "walk before me, and be blameless"(Gen 17:2). The Mosaic covenant did not change this, it was essentially the same covenant, only considerably more detailed. These earthly promises did not come to fruition because they were conditional not on Christ's obedience but that of the nation that consisted of a sinful people.

Of course, paedobaptists would have us believe that the essence of this covenant is still in force, only now circumcision has given way to infant baptism. The apostle, however, tells us that once a covenant has been confirmed or ratified it cannot then be added to or pronounced void or of no effect (Gal 3:15). Obviously, if the covenant of grace was established with Abraham, as we read of in Genesis 17, then it must have been changed because circumcision was replaced with baptism, the very thing Paul informs us cannot happen. When the apostle refers to the promise in Galatians he does not have in mind the Abrahamic or Mosaic covenants, but what was said to Abraham that caused him to believe and to receive the righteousness of Christ. It was the promise of the new covenant that lay in the distant future. This is the promise that runs through the entire Old Testament, and whilst it is served by the conditional covenants, it was not dependent on them.

When examining the promises made to Abraham it can be difficult to ascertain whether they apply to his natural or his spiritual posterity, or,

---

43. Coxe, "Discourse of the Covenants," 116.

indeed both. Intermingled with the mundane promises that were dependent for their fulfillment upon the obedience of Abraham's posterity "seeds" after the flesh, there were also promises that applied to only his spiritual children, who would, like Abraham, exercise faith in his "seed." About this covenant's different ends, John Owen commented:

> Unto this twofold end of the separation of Abraham, there was a double seed allocated to him;-a seed according to the flesh, separated to the bringing forth of the Messiah according unto the flesh; and a seed according to the promise, that is, such, as by faith, should have an interest in the promise, or all the elect of God. Nor that these two seeds were always subjectively diverse, so that the seed separated to the bringing forth of the Messiah in the flesh should neither in whole nor in part be also the seed according to the promise; or, on the contrary, that the seed according to the promise should none of it be his seed after the flesh. But sometimes the same seed came under diverse considerations, being the seed of Abraham both according to the flesh and according to the promise; and sometimes the seed itself was diverse, those according to the flesh being not of the promise, and so on the contrary. Thus Isaac and Jacob were the seed of Abraham according to the flesh, because they were his carnal posterity; and they were also of the seed of the promise, because by their own personal faith, they were interested in the covenant of Abraham their father.[44]

At the heart of the Abrahamic covenant is God's promise that he would be a father to his people. Not only did God promise the land as an everlasting possession, but he promised that the covenant would be everlasting, but only if the people were faithful to the Lord. This was the covenant of circumcision that was concluded with Abraham. Abraham and his posterity would find themselves having to keep conditions they found impossible. This is why the "everlasting" aspect could never be fulfilled in Abraham's carnal seed. There was one, however, who was to come forth from the loins of Abraham who would keep the original covenant of works that the Abrahamic and Mosaic covenants were but a type. Abraham, in faith, embraced the promise concerning this seed, the one to come, and consequently, through looking forward he became a member of the new covenant; the only truly everlasting covenant.

So we have two separate yet related covenants, namely, that made with Abraham's carnal "seeds," the Jews, and the promise of the new covenant, that would be ratified in his "seed," the Messiah. About these two covenants,

---

44. Owen, *Works*, 16, 121–22.

Denault tells us, "the covenant of grace was revealed to Abraham, but the formal covenant that God concluded with him was not the covenant of grace . . . the Abrahamic covenant did include the physical posterity of Abraham, but it was not the covenant of grace, even if it was in a covenant that revealed the grace of God by way of a promise."[45]

One was not deemed to be a true Israelite or Jew simply because one was born to certain parents and had undergone the fleshly rite of circumcision, in the words of the apostle, "For no one is a Jew who is merely one outwardly, nor is circumcision outward and physical. But a Jew is one inwardly, and circumcision is a matter of the heart, by the Spirit, not by the letter" (Rom 2:28–29). About Abraham's two seeds Nehemiah Coxe commented:

> Abraham is to be considered in a double capacity: he is the father of all true believers and the father and root of the Israelite nation. God entered into a covenant with him for both of these seeds and since they are formally distinguished from one another, their covenant interest must necessarily be different and fall under a distinct consideration. The blessings appropriate to either must be conveyed in a way agreeable to their respective covenant interest. And these two things may not be confounded without a manifest hazard to the most important articles of the Christian religion.[46]

To quote Henry Lawrence, what we have is: "a begetting Abraham, and a believing Abraham, and also two seeds, the children of the flesh, that is by carnal generation only, and the children of the promise."[47] It is only those from the physical stock of Abraham who believe the promise who are to be considered as the true Israel of God. This is why the apostle could say, "For not all who are descended from Israel belong to Israel, and not all are children of Abraham because they are his offspring . . . it is not the children of the flesh who are the children of God, but the children of promise are considered his offspring" (Rom 9:6–8).

Even though an Israelite found himself in this world to be subject to the physical requirements of the conditional aspects of the Abrahamic, and later the Mosaic covenant, if he believed, like Abraham, he would also have been a member of the new covenant. For example, Isaac was the seed of Abraham according to the flesh, yet at the same time, he was his seed according to the promise because of his faith in the promise. Such a person would have found himself under the Abrahamic and later the Mosaic covenant because

45. Denault, *Distinctiveness of Baptist Covenant Theology*, 116.

46. Coxe, "Discourse of the Covenants," 73.

47. Lawrence, *Of Baptism*, 90.

of his birth, while being at the same time, because of his faith in the promise, a participator in the new covenant in Christ. John Owen aptly describes the nature of what one might call a double entry, where one can be in the covenant formalized in Abraham, and also in that covenant that was to be formalized in the Christ:

> Not that these two seeds were always subjectively diverse, so that the seed separated to the bringing forth of the Messiah in the flesh should neither in whole nor in part be also the seed according to the promise; or, on the contrary, that the seed according to the promise should none of it be his seed after the flesh . . . But sometimes the same seed came under diverse considerations, being the seed of Abraham both according to the flesh and according to the promise; and sometimes the seed itself was diverse, those according to the flesh being not of the promise, and so on the contrary. Thus Isaac and Jacob were the seed of Abraham according to the flesh, separated unto the bringing forth of the Messiah after the flesh because they were his carnal posterity; and they were also of the seed of the promise, because, by their own personal faith they were interested in the covenant of Abraham their Father. Multitudes afterwards were of the carnal seed of Abraham, and of the number of the people separated to bring forth the Messiah in the flesh, and yet were not of the seed according to the promise, nor interested in the spiritual blessings of the covenant; because they did not personally believe . . . And many, afterwards, who were not of the *carnal seed* of Abraham, nor interested in the privilege of bringing forth the Messiah in the flesh, were yet designed to be made his *spiritual seed* by faith; that in them he might become "heir of the world" and all nations of the earth be blessed in him.[48]

All those Israelites who believed, like their spiritual father, Abraham, were "seed of the promise" and were incorporated into Christ on the basis of his future salvific work. To quote the 1689 Baptist Confession of Faith:

> Although the price of redemption was not actually paid by Christ until after His incarnation, yet the virtue, efficacy (the certain effect or result) and benefit arising from His payment were communicated to the elect in all ages from the beginning of the world through the promises types and sacrifices in which He was revealed and signified (pictured and expressed), as the seed which should bruise the serpent's head.[49]

48. Owen, *Works*, 16, 122.
49. *The Baptist Confession of Faith of* 1689, 8:6.

The paedobaptist hermeneutic, and, it must be said, that of a number of Reformed Baptists, makes the mistake of confounding these two covenants. While acknowledging two posterities, they fail to acknowledge two covenants. It is a position that fails to see that the new covenant is not just another administration of the covenant of grace, but is itself the only covenant of grace. It is the paedobaptist failure to recognize this that causes them to talk about a mixed church, with all being members of the covenant of grace, only with some belonging to the internal aspects of the covenant and others to the external administration, as Wellum puts it:

> OT Israel and the NT church may include within them the elect and the non-elect' believers and unbelievers, that is, those who by receiving the covenant sign (circumcision or baptism) are externally brought into covenant membership but who may never exercise saving faith. Given this situation, so the paedobaptist argues, there is nothing objectionable in applying the covenant sign of baptism in infants and viewing them as full members of the church apart from explicit faith in Christ.[50]

Robert Booth, in his book, *Children of Promise*, implies that the Reformed Baptists are guilty of cutting God's child into pieces. He states that "The Reformed and covenantal understanding of God's dealings with his people throughout the ages, instead of cutting God's child (i.e. the church) into separate pieces, recognizes that God has had one people throughout the ages."[51] I would rather suggest that it is only the Reformed Baptist position put forward here that is consistent in its understanding concerning the one people of God throughout all of redemptive history. We believe that God's people have been one in Christ since the first person believed the promise. Moreover, Reformed Baptists are, in fact, more consistent in their understanding of the one church, the one true people of God, because we do not presume infants to be members of the church when they are not.[52]

Booth, as with other paedobaptists, appears to be making the mistake of seeing the physical nation of Israel as God's true people, whereas we make the same distinction as did the apostle, namely, insisting not "all descended from Israel belong to Israel" (Rom 9:6). All of Abraham's offspring were circumcised and were members of the conditional covenant, this, however, did not place them in the covenant of grace, the new covenant. This is something only a new birth in Christ can accomplish. Another who charges us

50. Wellum, "Baptism and the Relationship between the Covenants," 115–16.

51. Booth, *Children of the Promise*, 73.

52. This is not to say infants cannot be saved by God's regenerating grace. Scripture tells us little about this.

with dividing the Abrahamic covenant is Pierre Marcel, "the device whereby an attempt is made to divide the Abrahamic covenant into two or three covenants distinct from each other in order that, to suit the convenience of certain people, a carnal element may be inserted into it, has no justification when the Bible refers to the covenant with Abraham it always speaks of it in the singular and says covenant and not covenants."[53] In the words of David Kingdon, "this is a gross misrepresentation."[54] We divide not the Abrahamic covenant, this is one undivided conditional covenant, we do, however, as we have seen, draw a distinction between it and the covenant of grace or the new covenant that Abraham entered some time prior to a covenant being made with him. It is staggering that the paedobaptist cannot see that within the literal Israel there was another Israel, and one could be in the literal Israel without being in the covenant of grace and a member of the true, spiritual Israel. Throughout the ages God has only had one people, a people united to Christ, beneficiaries of his saving work, and it is only this recreated humanity, this new race, that that belong to the new covenant.

The paedobaptist paradigm gets into difficulty because it is forced into making an unwarranted distinction between Old and New Testament believers. This is because many of the blessings that have always been true of believers seem to apply to only the new covenant, which, according to them, was not itself applicable until after Christ's death. For example, can it possibly be the case that Old Testament believers did not possess the heart of flesh referred to by Ezekiel (Ezek 36:36)? Or that they did not have the laws of God within them, written upon their hearts (Jer 31:33)? A consistent reading of the paedobaptist position leads one to conclude that Old Testament saints lacked these blessings. One can conclude that if the new covenant in regard to its unique blessings only became operative after Christ's redemptive work then it is the paedobaptists who cut God's child into pieces.

Paedobaptist, David Gibson is of the opinion that the Reformed Baptist understanding of the covenant fails to begin at the beginning, that somehow our theology has had something of a late start:

> I wish to suggest that the covenant of grace is a story with a beginning that credobaptists have failed to start: it is founded on Christ before it ever progresses to Christ. The credobaptist traces a line from Abraham to Christ, but in reality the line to be traced is from Christ to Abraham to Christ again. Abraham is Christ's seed, before Christ is ever Abraham's seed.[55]

---

53. Marcel, *Biblical Doctrine of Infant Baptism*, 191.

54. Kingdon, *Children of Abraham*, 32.

55. Gibson, "Fathers of Faith," 19.

Our paradigm, however, does not start with Abraham, but in the covenant of redemption before the foundation of this world. In its application the new covenant has been operative since the first promise in Genesis 3:15. The covenant made later with Abraham did not change the promise. While the promise itself did not change, a conditional aspect came in alongside it. The promise was channeled through a particular people because its ratification would entail the work of one who, according to his human nature, would be Abraham's seed. He was the same seed that Abraham himself looked to in faith some eighteen hundred years before the seed became flesh. It was the righteousness obtained by this seed that was credited to him. Whilst the genealogical principle never saved anyone, the people of Israel were placed in a unique position because it was to them that the promise was explicitly revealed. Gibson's criticism appears to make no sense whatsoever. It appears to be another straw man; just another obtuse attempt to undermine the Baptism position.

8

The Meaning of Circumcision

THE JEWS PLACED GREAT importance on the rite of circumcision, as Johnson informs us, "It gave them entrance into the covenant. It gave them citizenship and legal status within the nation of Israel. It profited them in that it separated them from the heathen barbarians, and the unclean and filthy Gentiles."[1] None could enter the covenant unless they underwent circumcision. Indeed, the penalty for the uncircumcised was to be cut off from the people, in other words, death: "Any uncircumcised male who is not circumcised in the flesh of his foreskin shall be cut off from his people; he has broken my covenant" (Gen 17:14).

Circumcision was both a seal and symbol for Abraham and a symbol only for all others. This rite was to be applied to all of his posterity, and, also, to any outsider who became a Jew. What exactly then was the meaning behind this physical act?

In the case of Abraham, circumcision was a seal of a salvation received. He is the only person for whom the act of circumcision post-dated justification by faith. He is the only one for whom the rite was a seal, as Pink informs us, "nowhere does Scripture say that circumcision was a seal to anyone but to Abraham himself."[2] As we have seen, Abraham was in fact justified about twenty-five years prior to the establishment of the covenant of circumcision. The act was a seal in his body that a change had already taken place. The foreskin of his heart had been removed, in other words, he had been made alive to God, having been translated from his position of condemnation in the first Adam, into the glorious light of the promised Christ. According to John Murray, "if circumcision signified faith, the faith must be conceived as existing prior to the signification given, and, in a way, still more apparent, a seal or authentification presupposes the existence of the thing sealed and

1. Johnson, *Fatal Flaw*, 189.
2. Pink, *Divine Covenants*, 96.

the seal does not add the content to the thing sealed."[3] It is somewhat ironic because Murray was a paedobaptist, and his words here serve to exclude infants, unless, of course, they have faith prior to their baptism.

For Abraham's posterity, unlike in the case of Abraham, the rite would precede any change of heart. The rite was a symbol rather than a seal, denoting the fact that their forefather had undergone a profound change of heart, and that it was through the promise concerning the one who would come forth from his seed that such a change was made possible, "to Abraham's male seed, circumcision presented the gospel message, their need for a circumcised heart."[4]

Circumcision looked backward to the faith of Abraham, the one to whom the Lord had credited righteousness, and it also looked forward to the work of one in whom the righteousness credited was made possible. It pointed to the possibility of a spiritual circumcision for those who would believe. It signalled that God would demand the cutting away of something intimate. Physical circumcision can be seen as a type of the antitype, where the external fleshly act points to the internal spiritual reality that is available through faith alone.

Jeffrey Johnson tells us that "Covenantal Presbyterians are correct . . . when they press for the importance of the spiritual and inward significance of circumcision. Circumcision meant more than an outward act of obedience; it also signified the cutting away of the old fleshly nature and loving God with a renewed heart (Col 2:11–12)."[5] Johnson quotes G.K. Beale, who stated that circumcision, "represented . . . the "cutting off of the flesh' to designate that the sinful flesh around the heart was cut off, signifying the regeneration of the heart and the setting apart of the person for the Lord."[6] The rite then "functioned at two levels, one corresponding to the people of God in their physical descent as the ethnic and national people of Israel, and the other corresponding to the spiritual Israel, as those who had circumcised hearts before God."[7]

According to David Kingdom, "Circumcision as a covenant sign in the flesh of all male Israelites, was a sign and pledge that God would be as faithful with respect to the earthly elements of the covenant promise as he would be to the heavenly and spiritual."[8] If Israel had kept the covenantal

---

3. Murray, *Epistle to the Romans*, 137.

4. Crampton, *Paedobaptism to Credobaptism*, 33.

5. Johnson, *Fatal Flaw*, quoted in *Recovering A Baptist Covenantal Heritage*, 289.

6. Beale, *New Testament Biblical Theology*, 812.

7. Ware, "Believer's Baptism," 45.

8. Kingdon, *Children of Abraham*, 31.

conditions, God would have, as he had promised, blessed it with land, peace, longevity etc. It was all designed to highlight Israel's inadequacy; God's way of showing that one must not rely on one's own righteousness, but the righteousness of another. It was not the promise of God that failed in the case of Israel, but, rather, her refusal to, like Abraham, believe in the promise.

The problem for many Jews was their reliance on the external rite rather than what it symbolized. They ascribed or credited the act with an efficacy it never possessed. They boasted in the fact that they were the physical seed of Abraham (John 8:39), believing themselves to be the true people of God. In Romans chapter two the apostle shows the sheer stupidity of their false hopes. When Adam was on probation in Eden, God gave him one command, however, the one command or condition essentially encompassed the entire moral law. In failing to adhere to the condition Adam broke the entire law (James 2:10). Jeffrey Johnson tells us that, "in the same way, keeping the condition of circumcision implied more than the simple act of external obedience . . . it symbolized full obedience of the law from the heart Deut 30:6."[9] Paul wanted these Jews to realize that their dependence on the rite was misplaced, "For circumcision indeed is of value if you obey the law, but if you break the law, your circumcision becomes uncircumcision" (Rom 2:25). According to Lloyd-Jones, "what Paul is saying here is that it is true that circumcision is of great value but it has not intrinsic and inherent value in and of itself . . . it proclaims that you are God's people—yes, but only on the condition that you really are one of God's people in the true and vital sense—namely that you are a holy people, for God is a holy God."[10] God's true children are viewed by God as having kept the law because they are 'in Christ', the one who kept it for them. The problem with the Jews is that they tried to keep the law off their own backs rather than putting their faith in the one who kept it for them. This is not to say that they considered themselves to be without sin, but that they performed the sacrifices, attributing to them an efficacy they never possessed, they believed that such sacrifices could remove their sin. Their essential problem was that they considered themselves to be God's true people because they were in possession of the law.

The apostle supports his argument with a hypothetical example: "So if a man who is uncircumcised keeps the precepts of the law, will not his uncircumcision be regarded as circumcision?" (Rom 2:26). The Gentiles were uncircumcised, however, imagine it possible that one of them kept God's law, would it matter that he had not been cut in his flesh? Of course not. Why? because God wants a holy people. Keeping the law is the thing the rite

9. Johnson, *Fatal Flaw*, 238.

10. Lloyd-Jones, *Romans*, 2:1—3:20, 153.

pointed to, so the physical act makes no difference if one can keep the very thing the physical act typified. Paul presses home his argument in demonstration of the folly of those Jews who put faith in the external rite, "Then he who is physically uncircumcised but keeps the law will condemn you who have who have the written code and circumcision but break the law" (v.27). So, if hypothetically, the non-Jew, he who is uncircumcised, keeps the law, he would condemn those Jews who relied on the things of the flesh, who put their faith in both the external written law of Moses and the rite of circumcision that came down from Abraham. Paul's entire argument about circumcision is summed up in the two following verses, "For no one is a Jew who is merely one outwardly, nor is circumcision outward and physical. But a Jew is one inwardly, and circumcision is a matter of the heart, by the Spirit, not of the letter" (Rom 2:28,29).

Also, it should be borne in mind that, to quote Gary Crampton, "the fact that the covenant sign was administered to the male organ of generation shows that the covenant status 'in the land' passes from generation to generation merely due to physical birth. This is further suggested by the stipulation that a man who suffered damage to his sexual organs was not allowed to join the congregation of Israel (Deut 23:1)."[11] In all, the rite was a blessing bestowed on Abraham's offspring that served as a symbol of what happened to him spiritually, and it also pointed to this as a possibility for others should they, like Abraham, put their faith in his seed, the Christ.

One more thing is worth mentioning. Not only did the rite mark the Jews as a people separate from surrounding peoples, but it also afforded some protection against certain diseases. I remember reading (I forget where) about research that was conducted to determine if circumcision made any difference in the contraction of diseases. The men from two tribes, one circumcised and the other uncircumcised, on a regular basis frequented a local town's prostitutes. It was found that the men from the circumcised tribe had a far less incidence of Aids, suggesting that circumcision provided them with a degree of protection. In Israel one can conclude that the rite served to ensure the relative health of the people in that it afforded a degree of protection against sexually transmitted diseases.

11. Crampton, *Paedobaptism to Credobaptism*, 31.

9

Was Circumcision Replaced by Baptism?

FOR THE PAEDOBAPTIST THERE exists a parity between circumcision and baptism. Just as the Israelite was in the covenant of grace in virtue of his birth and therefore underwent circumcision, so the same status should be accorded to children of believing parents in the new administration of this covenant; thus they should be baptized. For them, "the covenant of the Old Testament, sealed with circumcision, and the covenant of the New Testament, sealed by baptism, are one and the same."[1] Charles Hodge tells us that "baptism has taken precisely the same place as circumcision."[2] And, according to Berkhof, "If children received the sign and seal of the covenant in the old dispensation, the presumption is that they surely have a right to receive it in the new."[3] In answer to question 74, "Should infants, too, be baptized?" the Heidelberg Catechism states:

> A. Yes, for since they as well as the adult are included in the covenant and church of God; and since redemption from sin by the blood of Christ, and Holy Spirit, the author of faith, is promised to them no less than to the adult; they must, therefore, by baptism, as a sign of the covenant, be also admitted into the Christian Church, and be distinguished from the children of infidels, as was done in the old covenant or testament by circumcision, instead of which baptism was instituted in the new covenant.[4]

The Westminster Confession of Faith is essentially the same, concerning the recipients of baptism, the answer to question 166 of the Larger Catechism states:

1. Schenck, *Presbyterian Doctrine of Children In The Covenant*, 7.
2. Ursinus, *Heidelberg Catechism*, 368.
3. Berkhof, *Systematic Theology*, 634,
4. Ursinus, *Heidelberg Catechism*, 365.

Baptism is not to be administered to any that are out of the visible church, and so strangers from the covenant of promise, till they profess their faith in Christ, and obedience to Him (Acts 8:36–38), but infants descending from parents, either both, or but one of them, professing faith in Christ, and obedience to Him, are in that respect within the covenant, and to be baptized . . . [5]

According to John Calvin, infants "are to be baptized into future repentance and faith, for though these graces have not yet been formed in them, nevertheless, by secret operation the Spirit, the seed of both lies hidden within them by the secret work of the Spirit."[6] Calvin also considered infants to be the recipients of the very thing that circumcision and baptism symbolized:

The Lord did not deign to have them circumcised without making them participants in all those things which were then signified by circumcision (Gen.17:12). Otherwise he would have mocked his people with mere trickery if he had nursed them on meaningless symbols, which is a dreadful thing even to hear of it. For he expressly declares that the circumcision of the tiny infant will be in lieu of the seal to certify the promise of the covenant. But if the covenant still remains firm and steadfast, it applies not less today to the children of Christians than under the Old Testament it pertained to infants of the Jews. Yet if they are participants in the things signified, why shall they be debarred from the sign?[7]

About such infants, Charles Hodge could write: "They are members of the Church; they are professing Christians; they belong presumptively to the number of the elect. These promises are true of them in the same sense in which they are true of adult professing Christians."[8] According to Douglas Wilson the "children of believers are members of Christ's Kingdom. Little children and infants of believers are expressly included by Christ in the Kingdom of God."[9] Robert Reymond went so far as to state that: "parents are also to recognize that to deny their children these God-ordained rights," by rites he means baptism, "is virtually to deny that they possess the status in the kingdom of God which God himself guarantees to them, and is to

5. Westminster Confession of Faith, Larger Catechism, Q&A, 166.

6. Calvin, *Institutes,* IV, XV, 20.

7. Ibid., 1328.

8. Hodge, *Church Membership of Infants,* 389.

9. Wilson, *To A Thousand Generations,* 16.

commit 'great sin' against God."[10] Likewise, Charles Hodge considers it a great sin not to have one's children baptized: "Those parents sin grievously against the souls of their children who neglect to consecrate them to God in the ordinance of baptism."[11] Randy Booth sees no problem in replacing circumcision with baptism. He tells us that "this clear connection between the two covenant signs of circumcision and baptism creates a difficult problem for the opponents of infant baptism, for any argument against infant baptism is necessarily an argument against infant circumcision."[12]

What stands out immediately from a careful reading of the two Testaments is that circumcision, for all except Abraham, was before the fact, while baptism is after the fact. By this I mean the rite of circumcision was performed on all male Israelites before they could make any profession of faith. Baptism, on the other hand, is only to be administered on profession of faith. So circumcision can at best represent what may occur at some future time while baptism looks back to what has occurred. Clearly, this suggests that these rites did not signify the same thing.

Circumcision is a sign that marks one as belonging to Abraham's physical seed. The only prerequisite was for one to be born to the right parents. Parents had their children circumcised simply because it was obligatory. Indeed, it would not be an exaggeration to say that the vast majority of parents whose children were circumcised were unbelievers, as James White commented, "for every David there were a dozen Ahabs; for every Josiah a legion of Manassehs. Unfaithfulness, the flaunting of God's law, the rejection of the role of truly being God's people, the rejection of His knowledge, and the experience of His wrath, were the nominative experiences seen in the Old Covenant."[13] The sons of Israel were not required to make a profession of faith before receiving the sign. "The emphasis is entirely on this outward relationship, with no hint that one might be disqualified to receive the rite who did not personally show the faith of the patriarch."[14] Baptism, on the other hand, is both a sign and a seal, marking one as belonging to the spiritual seed of Abraham; sealing the fact that he is united to Christ. The one prerequisite for baptism is that the individual repent and believe. These different criteria hardly suggests parity between these two rites.

Genesis 17:10–14 tells us that all Abraham's seed, including those purchased as slaves, are to be circumcised. There were no males belonging to

---

10. Reymond, *New Systematic Theology,* 937.

11. Hodge, *Systematic Theology,* Vol. 3, 399.

12. Booth, *Children of Promise,* 109.

13. White, "Newness of the New Covenant," 88.

14. Jewett, *Infant Baptism,* 98.

Abraham's household who were not to have the rite performed on them. It was, in other words, performed by compulsion, with the only alternative being to be cut off from the nation, i.e., put to death. As Pink put it, "circumcision was not submitted to voluntarily, nor given by reference to faith, it was compulsory, and that in every instance . . . How vastly different was that from Christian baptism."[15] Birth, or ownership, rather then faith was the criterion. This is in marked contrast with baptism where there must be a personal profession of faith, a conscious decision on the part of the recipient. As to the idea that those circumcised inherited the promises, the case of Ishmael proves quite the opposite. As Paul tells us in Galatians 4, Ishmael was the son of the "slave woman." Unlike Isaac, he did not inherit the promises (Gen 21:10–12). If the mysteries represented by circumcision are, as Calvin tells us, the same as those represented by baptism, then why on earth was Ishmael circumcised? He was not an heir to the promises, indeed, he and his mother were cast out. There is nothing that remotely corresponds to this in baptism. Not only was the criterion required for the two rites different, but they did not always signify the same thing for their respective recipients, for surely Calvin would not have us believe circumcision signified the same for Ishmael as it did for his half-brother Isaac.

Marcel asks why it was necessary for Abraham to believe before circumcision took place, whereas his son Isaac received circumcision before it was possible for him to believe and repent? Marcel answers under two rules:

> It is because the adult who is not a member of the covenant must *first of all* know what it is in order to enter into it and receive its sign and seal: *this is the first rule.* But the child whom he begets, being an *heir of the covenant* according to the promise made by God to his father, is fitted to receive its sign and seal before it is possible for him to understand what it is: *this is the second rule.* Through the goodwill and promise of God the believer's child, who participates in the covenant without having the slightest subjective consciousness of it, in the thing itself, can and ought, without understanding and without previous knowledge to receive the sign and seal which assures him that God declares Himself to be his father. The children of believers are begotten by God.[16]

The assumption that the children of believers are begotten by God is rather worrying because it depicts God as one who makes promises that turn out to be false. For example, Calvin tells us that "the Lord did not deign

---

15. Pink, *Divine Covenants*, 97.
16. Marcel, *Biblical Doctrine of Infant Baptism*, 210–11.

to have them circumcised without making them participants in all those things which were then signified by circumcision."[17] This suggests that all those who received the sign are to be considered as certainly participating in the things signified. This, however, is blatantly untrue, for we know that carnal Israel did not follow the Lord. Why would God tell the believer that his physical offspring are in his covenant of grace, and even begotten of him, when the truth is, rather, that they are dead in their trespasses and sins, and at enmity with him? God has nowhere made such a promise. The external rite of circumcision signified, or pointed toward the possibility of a circumcised heart. Calvin seems to suggest that all those who underwent the rite would have experienced this inward change. Israel after the flesh, however, never did become the true children of God because of disobedience. It mattered not who one's natural parents were or what they believed. Rather, all that mattered was whether one followed Abraham's example by exercising faith in God's promises. As Paul told the Galatians, "Know then that it is those of faith who are the sons of Abraham" Gal 3:7), and, only "those who are of faith are blessed along with Abraham, the man of faith" (v.9).

John Murray tells us:

> It is a grave mistake to think of circumcision as a sign and seal of merely external blessings and privileges. Circumcision is a sign and seal of the covenant itself in its deepest and richest significance, and it is the sign of external privileges only as these are the fruits of the spiritual blessings it signifies . . . What then is the highest reaches of its meaning? Undeniably and simply, "I will be your God and ye shall be my people" . . . In a word it is union and communion with Jehovah, the God of Israel. It was this blessing circumcision signified and sealed.[18]

As with Marcel, Murray wrongly assumes that circumcision was a seal, when for the majority of Israelites it was not. It can only be a seal for something that has already taken place. Indeed, Murray himself tells us what a seal is:

> It is usual [right and essential] to discover a distinction between a sign and a seal; a sign points to the existence of that which it signifies, whereas a seal authenticates, confirms, and guarantees the genuineness of that which is signified . . . The seal is more than definitive of that in which the sign consisted; it adds the thought of authentication. And the seal is that which God himself appended to assure Abraham that the faith he exercised in

17. Calvin, *Institutes*, IV, XVI, 5.
18. Murray, *Christian Baptism*, 47.

> God's promise was accepted by God to the end of fulfilling to Abraham the promise which he believed.[19]

Surely Murray is not suggesting that Israel after the flesh received circumcision as a seal? Yes, it confirmed or sealed "to Abraham the promise which he believed," what however, did it seal to his natural descendants? In the case of Abraham, it was indeed a seal of the fact that he was in possession of a circumcised heart. The great promise, "I will be your God and you shall be my people" was only true for such as believed in the promise. In the same way, baptism is a seal, sealing what has already happened. About such as these the apostle tells us they were, "circumcised with the circumcision made without hands, by putting off the body of sins of the flesh, by the circumcision of Christ" (Col 2:11). Paul emphasizes "without hands" to distance this from physical circumcision. No Baptist would disagree that this spiritual circumcision and the thing water baptism symbolizes and seals are not similar. And, if there is an identity between the Old and the New Testament church, then it lies here. Consisting of the people of God who share in new covenant blessings, who having believed in Abraham's "seed," experienced a rebirth, being in possession of new circumcised hearts of flesh, upon which God's law is being written. For the majority, Abraham's "seeds," however, whilst they were circumcised in their flesh they remained uncircumcised in their hearts. Although they had the sign of circumcision they did not share in the thing to which it pointed, namely a circumcised heart

Murray comments that, "the sign of external privileges only as these are the fruits of the spiritual blessings it signifies" appears to, as with Calvin's comments alluded to earlier, suggest that any physical, external blessings signified by circumcision are the result of what has already taken place in its recipients "union and communion with Jehovah." Is he saying that the circumcised Israelite was in receipt of spiritual blessings in the same way as one who is baptized? This will have far reaching theological consequences, because he is effectively assuming circumcision of the heart, and applying to the infant what can only be true of those who are truly in Christ. As with other paedobaptists, Murray does not adequately distinguish between carnal and spiritual Israel. He makes the classic paedobaptist mistake of assuming that all old covenant children were in the covenant of grace when they were not, and he therefore wrongly infers that the children of believers in the new covenant are likewise in the covenant of grace.

Such assumptions made about the infants' of believing parent(s) causes one to wonder what has happened to the doctrines of total depravity

---

19. Murray, *Epistle to the Romans*, 138.

and justification by faith alone. Can there be such a thing, as Calvin would have us believe, as a latent seed in one who is dead in trespasses and sins? Man's position in Adam seems to have been side-stepped. It is presumptive salvation; a Christianity by physical birth and upbringing. Such infants will presume themselves to be Christian, wrongly believing regeneration to be something that must have occurred at some time or other. John Murray is willing to accord to infants everything accorded to confessing adults, "If it is proper to administer baptism to infants, then the import of baptism must be the same for infants as for adults . . . Baptism is a sign and seal of member-ship in Christ's body."[20]

Charles Hodge even went so far as to speak about the names of bap-tized infants residing in the Lamb's book of life: "Do not the little ones have their names written in the lamb's book of life, even if they afterwards choose to erase them; being thus enrolled may be the means of their salvation."[21] This is somewhat presumptive. Not only is it not taught in the Scriptures, but it appears illogical, denying total depravity and placing persons in Christ before they can exercise faith and repent. Martyn Lloyd-Jones holds no punches on what has been the legacy of this position:

> Nothing is so fatal as the notion that because we were born of Christian parents, and were christened when we were infants, and have been brought up in the Church, and "received in mem-bership," therefore we are Christian. Nothing has done so much harm to true Christianity as just that teaching, and everything that encouraged such error.[22]

It is believed that these baptized infants can at a later stage choose to exercise faith and continue in the kingdom, or deny the faith and find themselves outside of the kingdom. If they choose to deny the Faith we are told that they were never actually regenerate, although they were, nevertheless, for a time, in the kingdom. Scripture, however, tells us that the kingdom of God can only be entered by a new birth, by being born of the Spirit (John.3:3), and not on the basis of what one's parents may happen to believe. Yes, all Israelites were in the conditional covenant made with Abraham, but they were not all in the covenant of grace, the new covenant. None but the saved can be in the new covenant and Christ's kingdom, and if one is in the king-dom one cannot then at a later stage find oneself outside of it. One cannot reverse the new birth. According to John Murray:

20. Murray, *Christian Baptism*, 43.

21. Hodge, *Systematic Theology*, 3, 388.

22. Lloyd-Jones, *Romans*, 8, 8:17–39, 306.

[There are] certain principles which lie close to the argument for infant baptism and without which the ordinance of infant baptism would be meaningless . . . These principles are: (1) that little children, even infants are among Christ's people and are members of His body; (2) that they are members of His kingdom and therefore have been regenerated; (3) that they belong to the church, in that they are received as belonging to Christ, that is to say, received into the fellowship of the saints.[23]

From what Murray says here it would appear that nothing else is necessary. Murray is implying that entrance into God's kingdom is by natural birth, rather than by a supernatural new birth. The infant appears to be complete in Christ simply on the basis of what its parents believe. I say complete in Christ because if the infant is truly in the kingdom of God, then it is in Christ, and to be in Christ is to be complete, possessing what he secured in his redemptive work. I know of no half-way position. Murray appears to be advocating salvation by proxy. This whole teaching encourages a kind of hypocrisy in that it informs the young of a falsehood. It tells the child that he/she is a Christian, that they have been regenerated and are now in God's kingdom. Surely this amounts to providing the unregenerate with a false hope.

Earlier I said infant baptism is a dangerous teaching. This is because these infants are to be told that they are in the covenant of grace, that they are Christians when they are not. A Presbyterian minister, in a letter to the New York Times in March 1845 wrote, "But O how we neglect that ordinance! Treating children in the Church, just as if they were out of it. Ought we not daily to say (in its spirit) to our children, 'You are Christian children, you are Christ's, you ought to think and feel and act as such.'"[24] It should also be borne in mind that this quote is not exceptional, look at what Hodge had to say:

When the child is taught and trained under the regimen of his baptism—taught from the first to recognize himself as a child of God, with all its privileges and duties; trained to think, feel, and act as a child of God, to exercise filial love, to render filial obedience—the benefit to the child directly is obvious and immeasurable. He has invaluable birthright privileges, and corresponding obligations and responsibilities.[25]

In reality we are told that it is perfectly legitimate to take a child who is dead in trespasses and sins, at enmity with God and under his wrath, and

23. Murray, *Christian Baptism*, 62.
24. Lyman, "Children of the Covenant," 622.
25. Hodge, "Baptism."

try to convince him that all is well. It is effectively to cry peace, peace when there is no peace (Jer. 8:11). It constitutes a dereliction of the Christian's duty to preach the gospel to the lost.

The entire paedobaptist paradigm is built upon a false syllogism.

Premise 1: There is harmony between the old and new covenants.

Premise 2: Circumcision in the old covenant is parallel to baptism in the new covenant.

Premise 3: Infants of believers were circumcised in the old covenant.

Conclusion: Infants of believers should be baptized in the new covenant.[26]

Of course, if the premises are faulty so is the conclusion. The fundamental weakness is the underlying presumption that both covenants are of grace, only different administrations of the same covenant. This, however, is not the case, for how can the old covenant that Paul calls "a ministry of death" be the same as "the ministry of the Spirit" (2 Cor 3:7)? To suggest that those circumcised had believing parents is rather presumptive considering that the majority within the nation were unfaithful. Just this fact alone demonstrates that there is no parallel between the two rites. All Israelites were circumcised, even if their parents were unbelievers, whereas it is only those infants whose parents are believers who are deemed suitable candidates for baptism.

According to Daniel McManigal, "our Baptist friends first must produce a text that commands children be removed from the covenant. Since children have been included in the covenant for thousands of years."[27] Baptists, however, do not need to find such a text because children were never in the covenant of grace. Children only belonged to the conditional part of the Abrahamic and Mosaic covenant, therefore, when the Messiah came, this covenant came to an end. The paedobaptist assumption that they are comparing two administrations of the one covenant of grace, comparing like with like, is their fundamental mistake. On the contrary, they are comparing a conditional covenant whose mediator was Moses with the unconditional new covenant, the only covenant of which Christ is mediator. Is it then any wonder that the conclusions they arrive at are false?

According to Charles Hodge: "If the Church is one under both dispensations; if infants were members of the Church under the theocracy, then they are members of the Church now, unless the contrary is proved."[28] He is

---

26. Chantry, "Baptism and Covenant Theology," 128.

27. McManigal, *Encountering Christ in the Covenants*, 132.

28. Hodge, *Systematic Theology*, 3, 555.

assuming that because the infant belonged to the physical Israel it belonged to the church, it did not. The infant belonged only to that covenant which was a "ministration of death." All Israelites belonged to this. The church, however, consisted only of those who looked to Christ with the eye of faith. The true church of God consisted of an Israel within Israel. (Rom 9:7). Hodge is again not comparing like with like. The paedobaptist position takes a principle that applied only to Abraham's physical seed, namely physical circumcision, and, wrongly, applies it to today's infants in the rite of baptism. Or it, anachronistically, reads truths that pertain only to baptism and applies them to circumcision. There is a failure to appreciate the newness of the new covenant. Paedobaptists are, as already said, drawing certain deductions by looking for duality within the covenant of grace itself, rather than distinguishing between the covenant established with Abraham and the new covenant whose formal establishment he anticipated.

Philip Mauro brings out something of the relationship between circumcision of the flesh and baptism:

> The analogy between circumcision and baptism is plain. Infants were eligible for the former because every one of the children of Israel was, by his natural birth, within the terms of God's promise to Abraham, Isaac and Jacob. No work of God in an Israelite was needed to make him one of the natural seed of Abraham. Natural birth made him an Israelite, and hence the proper subject for circumcision. But, to bring a sinner within the scope of the new covenant, ratified in the blood of Christ, a work of God in the heart is needed. He must be born from above; and then immediately, but not before, can he be "buried with Christ" in baptism, and assume to walk in newness of life. Spiritual birth is required to make an individual a proper subject of baptism. The analogy is so plain I wonder any can fail to see it.[29]

For the Israelite no change of heart was required for him to be in the Abrahamic and Mosaic covenant. Being of the natural seed did not place him in the covenant of grace. Yes, he may have received a sign in his flesh, nevertheless, he remained of the flesh unless he believed the promise. Entrance into the covenant of grace requires a miraculous intervention by God in the form of a new heart, a new creation. If one is in this covenant, be it from the earliest times, starting with Adam, (if he believed the promise), one is in Christ and his kingdom. Such teaching cannot be applied to an infant of believing parents, or an Israelite because he was circumcised in his flesh. When old enough the child may repent and believe, as a result of the

---

29. Mauro, "Baptism," 98.

new birth, this, however, is the Lord's doing. The only entrance is through faith in Christ, he alone is "the way and the truth and the life," and no one can go to the Father except through him (John 14:6.).

Many of the children who have been baptized end up falling away, and even renouncing the Faith. This either makes the assumption made concerning their salvation false, or as we have seen, it implies the possibility of one being in the new covenant/covenant of grace and then, at a later stage, out of it. It is then somewhat difficult to reconcile this with the security in Christ that belongs to every true believer. Indeed, it is a view more in keeping with the teachings of Jacob Arminius.

One senses that Hodge is somewhat ambivalent about the issue. On the one hand he can see from Scripture that there are no grounds for infant baptism, yet on the other he is determined to find some way to justify the rite:

> The difficulty on this subject is that baptism from its very nature involves a profession of faith; it is the way in which by the ordinance of Christ, He is to be confessed before men; but infants are incapable of making such confession; therefore they are not the proper subjects of baptism. Or, to state the matter in another form: the sacraments belong to them as members of the Church; but the Church is the company of believers; infants cannot exercise faith, therefore they are not members of the Church, and consequently ought not to be baptized. In order to justify the baptism of infants, we must attain and authenticate such an idea of Church as that it shall include the children of believing parents.[30]

Hodge the theologian knows that what the Scriptures teach about salvation rules out infant baptism, yet Hodge the paedobaptist feels himself constrained to find a way whereby he can interpret Scripture to make it fit with his paedobaptist paradigm. He never seems to be comfortable with the stance he feels compelled to take. One wonders if perhaps sentimentality has a part to play. I feel compelled to agree with David Kingdon, in that "paedobaptist writings so often range between high and abstruse theology and the most maudlin sentimentality."[31] To demonstrate this Kingdon quoted Douglas Bannerman's words about the mother who has lost her child, "it is an unspeakable consolation for her to know that the little one, whom she took from off her breast to lay in the tomb was indeed signed with the sign of Christian baptism."[32] Such sentiments are not isolated. In a recent magazine article, David Gibson referred to Marilynne Robinson's novel, *Gilead*

---

30. Hodge, *Systematic Theology*, 3, 546–47.

31. Kingdon, *Children of Abraham*, 64.

32. Ibid., 64.

and the character of the Rev. John Ames, who in old age was writing down the things he would not be able to tell his young son. Gibson tells us:

> The novel has some charming cameos on baptism. When Ames says in a description of infant baptism, "That feeling of a baby's brow against the palm of your hand-how I have loved this life, but how I have loved this life," he is not talking about the ministerial life, or church life, but simply *life*. He is talking about the sheer blessing of the genealogical principle, physically and spiritually, and what it feels like to be a human being in deep bonded relationship to another human being. So conceived, baptism is not itself the gospel, but its function as sign and seal of the gospel is being enacted within the created order. Indeed, in *Lila*, the third of Robinson's Gilead vignettes, Lila's first encounter with the gospel is when she gatecrashes a baptism. In an achingly beautiful moment, her own lost and destitute childhood, spent as a wandering outcast, stands in stark opposition to a world of tender inclusion and adopting grace. In seeing more than she understands, Lila speaks better than she knows: "He was going on about baptism. A birth and a death and a marriage, he said. A touch of water and these children are given the whole of life."[33]

This sounds like sheer emotionalism and sentimentality. Yes, it is indeed the case that God brought forth his Son into the world through a particular people whose children he blessed with greater exposure to his promise. However, in regard to the individual soul's salvation God has never worked through families and the genealogical principle, but through the Holy Spirit. All parents would like to believe that their children are "given the whole of life," however, this is not what the Scriptures teach. One must question whether the kind of intransigence one encounters in the paedobaptist position is more the result of sentimentalism than sound doctrine.

One of the major differences between circumcision and baptism concerns the gender of those for whom the rite is performed. Circumcision was only to be carried out on the male reproductive organ. Baptism, on the other hand, is to be performed on all those who exercise faith, both male and female. This seems to undermine the parity accorded to these rites by the paedobaptists.

Not only are the paedobaptists wrong in believing baptism as being essentially the same as circumcision, but they err in giving these rites an efficacy they have never possessed. The only circumcision that is of spiritually significance is that performed by God in the heart, and the only baptism that

---

33. Gibson, "Fathers of Faith," 28.

means anything is that which follows a confession of faith, signifying union with Christ. Salvation is only found in the new covenant, and all within this covenant are in union with Christ, having a circumcised heart of flesh, and having been born of the Spirit. From the least to the greatest, all in this covenant know know the Lord, and the only access is through repentance and faith in the Christ, the one and only mediator.

One needs to realize that far from the new covenant being the last administration of the covenant of grace, it was actually in force before either the Abrahamic or Mosaic covenants, and is itself the only covenant of grace. Covenant duality exists not, as the paedobaptists maintain, in there being different categories within the covenant of grace, with its visible and invisible church. But, rather, as I keep saying, of there being two covenants, namely, the old covenant that Israel was placed under that was, as we will see, a reiteration of the conditional covenant of works, and the new covenant, that is unconditional and can only be entered through faith in the Messiah.

10

The Mosaic Covenant

QUESTIONS ABOUND WHENEVER THE Mosaic covenant is discussed, for example, does the law now make salvation dependent on our obedience? Does the law set aside the promise? Was this covenant of grace or of works? etc. Perhaps nothing has generated more confusion in the church. Jonathan Edwards noted that "there is perhaps no part of divinity attended with so much intricacy, and wherein orthodox divines do so much differ as stating the precise agreement and difference between the two dispensations of Moses and Christ"[1] According to the puritan Anthony Burgess:

> In expressing this covenant there is a difference among the Learned: some make the Law a covenant of works, and upon that ground it is abrogated: others call it a subservient covenant to the covenant of grace, and make it occasionally, as it were, introduced, to put more luster and splendour upon grace: Others call it a mixt covenant of works and grace; but it is hardly to be understood as possible, much lesse as true. I therefore think that opinion true . . . that the Law given by Moses was a Covenant of Grace.[2]

Israel was chosen solely on account of God's grace to be the conduit through which the Christ would come forth. As the apostle said, it was "from their race, according to the flesh, is the Christ" (Rom 9:5). The nation was especially blessed of God because of its exposure to the promises, as Paul tells us, "to them belong the adoption, the glory, the covenants, and the giving of the law, the worship and the promises"(Rom 9:4).

Because of the explicit revelation of the commandments upon the two tablets of stone at Sinai, one must not think that these commandments were not operational in the Abrahamic covenant. Abraham was well aware of

---

1. Edwards, *Works of President Edwards*, 160.
2. Burgess, *Vindiciae Legis*, 39.

God's law and taught such to his children. As the Lord reminded him, "For I have chosen him that he may command his children and his household after him to keep the way of the LORD by doing righteousness and justice" (Gen 18:19). Scripture tells us that blessings would come through Abraham "because he obeyed my voice, and kept my charge, my commandments, my statutes and my laws" (Gen 26:5). What we witness in the Mosaic covenant is a part fulfillment and also a renewal of the Abrahamic conditional covenant, with a more explicit manifestation of the law.

I have said that the Sinaitic covenant was of the same substance as the covenant established with Abraham. In Deut 5:3, however, we read that "Not with our fathers did the LORD make this covenant, but with us, who are all of us here alive today. How do we explain this? The answer lies in the conditionality of both covenants. This verse is alluding to specific temporal blessings and condemnations that were precluded from the Abrahamic covenant. The Sinaitic covenant, though a different covenant, builds upon that made with Abraham. While Abraham was aware of God's moral law, there was not a separate covenant made with him that specifically alluded to an obedience to this law as a condition for temporal blessings. The conditional side of the Abrahamic covenant concerned circumcision. Essentially then, in calling these covenants the same, I am emphasizing the fact that both were conditional upon obedience, and both spoke of temporal things that served to typify the eternal realities of the new covenant.

The major error made by the paedobaptists is their assumption that the Israel that was taken out of Egypt in the exodus was a spiritually redeemed people; that God was their God and they were his people. Imagine that I buy a house for a couple and place them in the house solely as a result of my free grace. I then say to them, "Keep the house tidy and make sure it is decorated and I will consider you to be true friends. If, however, you do not do this I will throw you out on the street." They agree to my terms, stating that they will do all that is required. If one year later I return to the house and find it looking like a pig-sty, the persons will not be my true friends and I will be justified in throwing them out onto the street. They will have clearly broken the terms of the covenant that I made with them. The paedobaptist mistake is one of presumption. To use the illustration, they are presuming that the couple had already completed my instructions just because they have occupied the house. Israel in the old covenant was very much like the couple in the illustration. For carnal Israel to become God's people it had to be obedient, "Now, therefore, if you will indeed obey my voice and keep my covenant, you shall be my treasured possession among the peoples" (Ex 19:5). They were told that if they were obedient they would be unto God "a kingdom of priests, and a holy nation" (v.6). I am sure that many read this verse without noticing the all-important word, "if", and tend to overlook the fact that to become God's people obedience to the covenantal stipulations was essential. The nation was not, as many claim, to keep the law out of gratitude for having become God's people, but as the requirement to become his people. Israel after the flesh, however, would never keep God's law. As Joshua stated shortly before his death, knowing Israel's sinful disposition, "You are not able to serve the LORD: for he is a holy God; he is a jealous God; he will not forgive your transgressions or your sins" (Joshua 24:19). Joshua clearly understood fallen human nature and the infinite holiness and justice of God. There was, however, one who would come from the loins of Abraham, a second Adam, who would keep God's statutes; fulfilling the conditions of the covenant that the first Adam broke. Consequently, because of his obedience, the words of Peter can only be addressed to those Israelites who believed in the promise about the approaching Christ, this is because they are themselves deemed to have been obedient on account of their position in Christ. They became, in the words of Peter, "a chosen generation, a royal priesthood, a holy nation, a people for his own possession" (1 Pet 2:9).

We see the same thing in one of the great promises running through the Old Testament, namely, that God will be a God to those who obey him: Gen 17:7; Ex 6:7; Jere 7:23, 31, 11:4, 30:22, Ezek 11:20 etc. Usually, when this promise is declared the condition of obedience is present. In Jeremiah we read, "But this thing commanded I them, saying, Obey my voice, and I will be your God, and you shall be my people: and walk you in all the ways that I have commanded you, that it may be well unto you" (Jere 7:23). Again, we find the same thing in Ezekiel, "That they may walk in my statutes, and keep mine ordinances, and do them, and I will be their God (Ezek 11:20). With perfect obedience being the condition it is only those who provide this who can then be considered the true people of God. This obedience has been provided in Christ, and it is in virtue of the believer's union with him that he too can be deemed to have provided this necessary obedience, hence God is truly his God and he is part of God's people.

The Law's Threefold Nature

The law that came through Moses was of a threefold nature,[3] consisting of civil or judicial, sacrificial and the moral law. The civil side included a wide variety of laws, ranging from the maintenance of proper hygiene

3. Although this has been questioned in recent years, for example, by New Covenant Theology, it is transparent to me that these three aspects of law are to be gleaned from the Torah.

(Deut.23:14) to the lending of money (Deut.23:19). According to Berkhof, the civil law was "simply the application of the principles of the moral law to the social and civic life of the people in all its ramifications."[4] In other words, it was the positive application or expression of the moral law in everyday behavior. Perhaps the most important function of the various elements of civil law was, to quote Peter Masters:

> A message or sermon from God. They were partly intended to be a standard of righteousness unattainable by sinful human beings, in order to discourage and dismay their pride and self-confidence. Let us not forget that these sundry laws were given as part of a package which if perfectly observed by the people as a whole, would have secured the rewards of righteousness for their whole nation-but these proved utterly impossible.[5]

As with the moral law, the ought do not imply the can. What the people were commanded to do and what they did do were two entirely different things.

The sacrificial law with its priesthood and bloody offerings was typical of the offering that would be made by the Messiah himself, the great archetype. Calvin asks the question, "For what is more vain or absurd than for men to offer a loathsome stench from the fat of cattle in order to reconcile themselves to God? Or have recourse to the sprinkling of water and blood to cleanse away their filth?" In answering this he states that "the whole cultus of the law taken literally and not as shadows and figures corresponding to the truth, will be utterly ridiculous."[6]

The sacrifices were essentially the gospel in drama. They served as "a copy and shadow of the heavenly things" (Heb 8:5). All the saints of God who have ever walked the earth have been purified in virtue of what God had determined to do in his Son. The Mosiac ministrations were but earthly types of the grand work of Christ. The efficacy they possessed amounted to only the "purification of the flesh," however, that to which they pointed could "purify our conscience from dead works to serve the living God" (Heb 9:13–14).

The moral law consisted of the Ten Commandments or the Decalogue. When the law is referred to in the New Testament, often it is only this aspect of the law that is meant (Rom 7:7–12, 13:8–12). It is generally agreed that whilst the civil and sacrificial laws ceased with their fulfillment in Christ, the moral law is of eternal relevance. One cannot imagine a situation in

---

4. Berkhof, *Systematic Theology*, 298.

5. Masters, *World Domination*, 31.

6. Calvin, *Institutes*, IV, XVI, 26.

which these commandments would not be relevant, for example, "You shall not covet" or "You shall have no other gods before me." It stands to reason then, if the Christian is to be an imitator of Christ, the one who lived a life in perfect conformity to the law, then we should consider the law to be relevant because we are being conformed to the image of him who perfectly kept it.

The importance of understanding the nature of the Sinaitic covenant and its relationship to the new covenant cannot be overstated. One can readily accede to the words of John Owen, "Here ariseth a difference of no small importance, namely, whether there are indeed two distinct covenants, as to the essence and substance of them, or only different administrations of the same covenant."[7]

Israel's Plight

The problem for Israel after the flesh was that it misunderstood the essential nature of the law, making it an end in itself rather than a means to an end. Israel failed to understand the true spiritual nature of what the law required. Many in Israel were like Paul prior to his conversion, namely, confident and self-assured in their own abilities. In his letter to the Romans, the apostle showed his concern for his people: "I have great sorrow and unceasing anguish in my heart" (Rom 9:2). Yes, Israel "have a zeal for God, but not according to knowledge" (Rom 10:2). They failed to realize that "cursed is everyone who does not abide by all the things written in the book of the law, and do them" (Gal 3:10). They remained ignorant of God's righteousness that had been set before them in the promise and sought to establish a righteousness of their own (Rom 10:3). The awful thing is they believed their own righteousness to be enough, not realizing that "whoever keeps the whole law but fails in one point has become accountable for all of it" (James 2:10).

About Israel's plight Paul tells us, "The Gentiles who did not pursue righteousness have attained it, that is, a righteousness that is by faith; but that Israel who pursued it by law that would lead to righteousness did not succeed in reaching that law. Why? Because they did not pursue it by faith, but as if it were by works" (Rom 9:30–32). This is exactly what we see today in other religions and in the cults. It is in Christianity alone where all true believers can say with the apostle, "Indeed, I count everything as loss because of the surpassing worth of knowing Christ Jesus my Lord. For his sake I have suffered the loss of all things and count them as rubbish, in order that I may gain Christ and be found in him, not having a righteousness of my

7. Owen, *Works*, 6, 69.

own that comes from the law, but that which comes through faith in Christ, the righteousness from God that depends on faith" (Phil 3:8–9). This is the very thing that man in sin, puffed up with pride, cannot accept. In his pride, he feels he must complete some work or other. Christian salvation insists on the emptying of pride and the acknowledgment that one must rely completely on the works of another. For all those Israelites who did look to the promise in faith, Christ became the "end of the law of righteousness"(Rom 10:4). His righteousness became theirs, and they, like Abraham, rejoiced to see Christ's day, and through faith in the promise they saw it and rejoiced (John 8:56). For those who relied on their own obedience, the very law they held in such esteem served only to condemn them.

Republication of Covenant of Works

Opinions differ even among paedobaptists as to the purpose of the Mosaic covenant. Of course, many do believe the law to be another administration of the covenant of grace, others, however, believe it to be a republication of the covenant of works. For example, Samuel Petto, John Owen, Thomas Goodwin, Hermon Witsius, Charles Hodge, Meredith Kline and the authors of the recently published work, *The Law is not of Faith,* to name but a few. They see the Mosaic law as standing apart from the covenant of grace, maintaining it to be essentially a regurgitation of the covenant of works. Herman Witsius states that "we more especially remark, that, when the law was given from Mount Sinai or Horeb, there was a repetition of the covenant of works."[8] Thomas Goodwin referred to it as "a promulgation of the covenant of nature made with Adam in paradise."[9] John Owen certainly did not consider the law as just another administration of the covenant of grace:

> If reconciliation and salvation by Christ were to be obtained not only under the old covenant but by virtue thereof, then it must be the same substance as the new. But this is not so; for no reconciliation or salvation could be obtained by virtue of the old covenant, or the administration of it.[10]

Rather, he saw it to be "but the covenant of works revived."[11] Owen's contemporary, Samuel Petto, was of the same opinion, believing "we must

---

8. Witsius, *Economy of the Covenants,* 2, 183.

9. Goodwin, *Work of the Holy Ghost,* 353.

10. Owen, *Works,* 6, 77.

11. Ibid., 78.

grant two distinct covenants rather than a twofold administration of the same covenant."[12]

The major difference between these paedobaptists and the Reformed Baptist position is that whilst *all* paedobaptists believe the Abrahamic covenant to be one of grace, Reformed Baptists, at least the position put forward here, believe *both* the Abrahamic and Mosaic covenants to be conditional, distinct from the unconditional covenant of grace. What Johnson calls "the fatal flaw"[13] lies not in the paedobaptist understanding of the Mosaic covenant, but in the way it assumes the Abrahamic covenant to be one of grace. We believe the Mosaic covenant to be essentially a revival, reiteration or republication of the covenant of works, with one vital caveat—there can be no possibility of any spiritual life resulting from man's obedience. It is a covenant now only unto death. It did not abrogate the penalty imposed on our first parents, or alter the demands of the original covenant of works, but rather served to spell out the fact that there can be no salvation without both a perfect obedience and punishment for transgressions. This is why it can be called "a ministry of death" (2 Cor 3:7). It *"revived the sanction of the first covenant*, in the curse or sentence of death which it denounced against all transgressions,"[14] and in so doing it was subservient to the new covenant, leading people, through the despair it engendered, to the promised new covenant in Christ. To quote William Pemble:

> The Law differs from it selfe, (sic) in that use which it had before, and which it hath since the Fall . . . It was given to Adam for this end, to bring himselfe to life . . . But unto the fallen, although the Band of Obedience doe remaine (sic): yet the End thereof (viz.). Justification and life by it, is now abolished by the promise.[15]

As with the paedobaptists, there is no consensus of opinion regarding the purpose of the Sinaitic covenant among Reformed Baptists. According to Earl Blackburn, "To believe that the Sinaitic Covenant to be a republication of the Covenant of Works or an absolute type of covenant of works is to back pedal in grace and create potential 'dance partners' that are theologically dangerous."[16] He then goes on to quote nine arguments put forward by the Puritan Samuel Bolton. Some of these are worth mentioning because

---

12. Ibid., 76

13. Johnson, *The Fatal Flaw*, 121.

14. Ibid., 77.

15. Pemble, *Vindiciae Fidei*, 140.

16. Blackburn, "Covenant Theology Simplified," 44.

not only are they somewhat ambiguous, but they serve as a backdrop enabling one to explicate the Reformed Baptist position. Argument six states:

> (6) *If it were God's purpose to give life and salvation to the lost sons of men by a covenant of grace, then He never set up the law as a covenant of works for that end.*

Bolton is, of course, correct in saying that the law was not set up to achieve "life and Salvation," this, however, does not mean that there was not a covenant of works unto death. Bolton seems to be of the opinion that to say the Mosaic law was a reiteration of the original covenant is to imply that it could hold out the possibility of life if sinful man should provide the necessary obedience. This is to misunderstand our position. The law reminded Israel of its position under the original covenant of works unto death, and, it was also a separate covenant of works with promises and threatenings of an earthly nature. For example, if it did speak of life it was not spiritual and eternal life, but a long and healthy earthly life, along with the other blessings we read about in, for example, Lev 26, Deut 28 etc. The law was not designed as a way for man to save himself but pointed to the fact that unless a perfect obedience was provided there can be no possibility of God's blessings, least of all the salvation of the soul. We can say that the law came in beside the promise of the new covenant of grace in order to manifest human inability so that the sons of men might look to the promised Messiah and be saved. The fact that one side would find the covenantal conditions impossible to keep did not invalidate the covenant.

In his seventh argument, Bolton states:

> (7) *If the law were a covenant of works, then the Jews were under a different covenant from us, and so none were saved.*

The Jews were indeed under a different covenant from us. This is why the Scriptures speak of the need for the new covenant (Heb 8:8). The Israelites were under the conditional old covenant that promised temporal blessings. None were saved by virtue of this covenant. Salvation, not in the earthly typical sense that God graciously provided when he led the people out of Egypt, but in the true spiritual sense was only through the new covenant in the completed future work of Christ. It was not those Israelites who had undergone a physical circumcision only, but they who had experienced a circumcision of the heart who were counted as God's true people. Of course, Bolton, being a paedobaptist saw the entire nation as constituting a people in the one covenant of grace. They were not. Unless they looked to the promise and became participants of the new covenant, they would remain under the original covenant of works and the law's condemnation.

To maintain that "none were saved" is to miss the essential point. Yes, none were saved by the old covenant. Many were, however, saved because the old covenant served its purpose in leading one to the promise that resides in the new covenant in Christ.

Finally, let me just quote argument nine:

> (9) *It could never suit with God's heart to sinners to give a covenant of works after the fall; because man could do nothing; he was dead and powerless.*[17]

This again is exactly why God gave a covenant of works. It was to spell out to man the fact that he was dead and powerless. What do Bolton, and Blackburn think God was talking about when he said to the people: "And if you faithfully obey the voice of the LORD your God, being careful to do all his commandments . . . " (Deut 28:1)? This covenant acted like a mirror in which Israel might see its true self. It was imposed by God because of her transgressions. The law of the old covenant killed in order that man might look to the promise and find life. Blackburn, however, is correct when he later states that the law was "conditional in the form of works only in regard to possession of external blessings in the land and in its reminder of needed repentance from sin."[18]

Reformed Baptist, Walter Chantry, in a chapter of his book entitled, "A Corrective to Perverted Views of Scripture," informs us, "it is plain from the beginning that the Hebrews were not called upon to keep the law in order to gain God's favor. He had already redeemed them."[19] It was indeed true that the Hebrews had been redeemed in that God had rescued them from their captivity in Egypt solely on account of his grace, this was, however, not a spiritual redemption from sin. Only those who embraced the promise would have known this. And, while Sinai in its typical function may have promised earthly blessings, it was made plain that obedience was the prerequisite:

> If you walk in my statutes and observe my commandments and do them, then I will give you your rains in their season, and the land shall yield its increase, and the trees of the field shall yield their fruit . . . I will give you peace in the land, you shall lie down, and none shall make you afraid. (Lev. 26:3–13)

This is clearly suggestive of a people being called upon to keep the law so as to merit God's favor. That they were not able to do so only served

17. Ibid., 44–5.

18. Ibid., 45.

19. Chantry, *Covenant of Works and Grace.*

to remind them of the sanctions of the original covenant of works that all unsaved humanity is under.

It is no good Chantry saying that "they were to keep his commandments in gratitude for what the Lord had already done for them."[20] This is not what Scripture tells us, for example, Exodus 19:5 and Deuteronomy 28–31. Chantry, and many others also, seems to be saying that Israel was to keep the law in the same way that a Christian is to do so, as a consequence of having been saved. This, however, is not comparing like with like. The Christian is one who has been spiritually redeemed, while Israel, as a nation, was not. The nation knew only a temporal type of redemption that was but a type of the antitype, namely, the redemption that is in Christ. The Lord had indeed done much for Israel, but this mundane redemption did not provide them with the wherewithal to keep God's commandments.

According to Chantry, "it would be monstrous and nearly blasphemous to suggest that the Lord came to fallen, corrupt, and helpless sinful man and seriously proposed that he seek restoration to life, knowledge, righteousness, and communion with God by his own means and works."[21] He fails to appreciate that one is not suggesting this, far from it. The republication of the covenant of works did not promise man the salvation of his soul upon his obedience, but, as already said, spoke of temporal conditional blessings, e.g., land, peace, and longevity etc. It was "a compact promising to Israel certain outward and national blessings on the condition of their rendering to God a general outward obedience to his law."[22] This reiteration of the covenant of works was essentially an external, mundane type that was designed to convey truths relating to man's spiritual condition. It spoke of earthly things to highlight and magnify man's inability to attain them so that he might in his subsequent despair be encouraged to consider the remedy for his spiritual malady in the promised Messiah. Why should it be monstrous for God to use a covenant of works, in which mundane things were spoken of, to make Israel aware of its true condition, showing that "all who rely on the law are under a curse" (Gal 3:10)? Is it not only through the knowledge of this that the people will seek to attain those spiritual blessings that are in Christ?

Chantry tells us that "every biblical covenant after the Fall is revealed by God as a form of the Covenant of Grace," and that "never did the Lord give a covenant of works to sinners as a way of blessing!"[23] The old covenant,

20. Ibid.
21. Ibid.
22. Pink, *The Divine Covenants*, 107.
23. Chantry, *Covenant of Works and Grace*.

however, was not a covenant of grace, salvific grace is only to be found in the new covenant, which as we have already seen, is the only covenant of grace. In the Sinaitic covenant, with its impossible demands, God was communicating to man the simple truth—if he cannot keep the covenant so as to merit blessings of an earthly nature, then how much less can he keep the covenant so as to secure spiritual eternal blessings. Being under the original covenant of works, as we all are, the republication of this law served to stir up sin, to expose it for what it is, thus making man aware of his sickness unto death so that he might look to the promised physician of his soul and be saved.

The Mosaic covenant could never be a covenant unto spiritual life. As we have seen, originally the law was a covenant unto life. There was the possibility of Adam keeping it so as to secure eternal blessings. In this sense Sinai could never be a covenant of works, to quote Herman Witsius:

> The Covenant made with Israel at Mount Sinai was not formally the covenant of works, 1st. Because it cannot be renewed with the sinner, in such a sense as to say, if, for the future, thou shalt perfect to perform every instance of obedience, thou shalt be justified by that, according to the covenant of works. For, by this, the pardon of former sins would be presupposed, which the covenant of works excludes.[24]

Sinai was then a separate covenant from the original covenant of works. It could never be a replacement of the latter because of the Fall. It was, however, a covenant of works of sorts, in that it faintly mirrored the original. It was a type of the original, but it did not serve as a replacement:

> God had before given the covenant of works, of perfect obedience, unto all mankind, in the law of creation. But this covenant at Sinai did not abrogate or disannul that covenant nor in any way fulfill it. And the reason is this, because it was never intended to come in the place or room thereof, as a covenant, containing the entire rule of all the faith and obedience of the whole church. God did not intend in it to abrogate the covenant of works, and to substitute this in place thereof; yea, in sundry things it re-enforced, established and confirmed that covenant.[25]

The true people of God, those circumcised of heart, the spiritual Israel, consisted not of those who kept the Mosaic law, but of those who believed in the one who would keep the original covenant of works, that covenant

24. Witsius, *Economy of the Covenants*, 184.
25. Owen, *Works*, 6, 77.

of which Sinai was but a type that spoke of temporal things so as to cause sinners to look to the eternal blessings found only in the new covenant. To quote Owen:

> This covenant, thus made with these ends and promises did never save nor condemn any man eternally. All that lived under the administration of it did attain eternal life or perished forever, but not by virtue of this covenant as formally such. It did, indeed, revive the commanding power and sanction of the first covenant of works; and in that respect as the apostle speaks, was the "ministry of condemnation" . . . And on the other hand, it directed also to the promise, which was the instrument of life and salvation to all that did believe. But as to what it had of its own, it was confined to things temporal. Believers were saved under it but not by virtue of it. Sinners perished eternally under it, but by the curse of the original law of works.[26]

Those saints who lived before the incarnation knew that through the Sinaitic covenant there was no possibility of salvation. They, like their father, Abraham, put their faith in God's promised Messiah whom they saw from afar, and in so doing became recipients of new covenant blessings. As John Owen commented, "the actual exhibition of Christ in the flesh belonged unto the promise of making a new covenant; for without it, it could not have been made. This was the desire of all the faithful from the foundation of the world; this they longed for, and fervently prayed for continually. And the prospect of it was the sole ground of their joy and consolation, 'Abraham saw his day, and rejoiced.'"[27]

Calvin believed the Mosaic covenant to be one of grace, and this view, to quote Ferguson, "received mature expression in the *Westminster Confession*."[28] The Larger Catechism states, in answer to the question: How was the covenant of grace administered during the Old Testament period?

> The covenant of grace was administered under the Old Testament, by promises, prophecies, sacrifices, circumcision, the Passover, and other types of ordinances, which all fore-signify Christ then to come, and were for that time sufficient to build up the elect in faith in the promised Messiah, by whom they then had full remission of sin, and eternal salvation.[29]

---

26. Coxe, "A Discourse of the Covenants," 197–98.

27. Owen, *Works*, 6, 114.

28. Ferguson, *John Owen on the Christian Life*, 28.

29. Westminster Confession of Faith, Larger Catechism Q&A 34, 144.

I don't think any Reformed Baptist would disagree with this, the paedo-baptist Achilles heel is its failure to recognize, or to downplay, the conditional nature of the Mosaic covenant. Also, and perhaps more importantly, the fact that it does not consider Old Testament believers to have been members of the new covenant. Yes, it correctly maintains that all the saints had new hearts (Ezek 36:26) and full remission of sin (Jer 31:34). It, however, omits to state that they possessed these blessings because they were in the new covenant. I say this simply because these blessings are only associated with the new covenant, a covenant that according to paedobaptists, did not become operative until the New Testament. Of course, the standard response is to say that Old Testament believers were in the covenant of grace, only a different administration of it from the new covenant. This is not, however, what Scripture tells us, furthermore, it should be borne in mind that the term "covenant of grace" is not Scriptural.

We see the same ambiguity with Charles Hodge. One feels that he has placed himself in an ambivalent position. On the one hand, Hodge acknowledges that the Mosaic covenant is one of works, "the law of Moses was in the first place a re-enactment of the covenant of works,"[30] while on the other hand he is, because of his paedobaptist predisposition, compelled to see it as a covenant of grace. He acknowledges the distinctions between the law and the spirit in that, "The one was external, the other spiritual; one was outward, the other an inward power. In the one covenant, the law was written on stone, in the other on the heart."[31] However, as with other paedobaptists, he appears to apply the spirit that gives life to a time following Christ's completed work, "it is plain that by the New Covenant the apostle means the gospel as distinguished from the law,—Christian as distinguished from the Mosaic dispensation."[32] This leaves Hodge having to explain how Old Testament saints could have been in possession of that "inward power" with the law "on the heart" while being outside the new covenant. This is why the Paedobaptist paradigm is forced to speak of multiple dispensations of the covenant of grace rather than acknowledges the new covenant to be the only covenant of grace.

The apostle Paul tells us that he is one of the "ministers of a new covenant, not of the letter but of the Spirit. For the letter kills, but the Spirit gives life" (2 Cor 3:6). The contrast made here should not be taken to imply a chronological distinction as if the "spirit" that "gives life" was somehow not operative before Christ's arrival in the flesh. Rather, Paul is recognizing

30. Hodge, *I and II Corinthians*, 433.

31. Ibid., 432.

32. Ibid., 431,

a qualitative distinction because now the gospel has been fully revealed in the completed work of Christ. He is not suggesting that the gospel or "spirit" only became operative after the law of Moses had ceased to apply. Both the law and the gospel coexisted in the Old Testament, the law on tablets of stone from the time of Moses. The gospel was there in the many types and shadows and in the prophetic utterances. Those who placed their faith in this gospel became members of the new covenant, not in virtue of the multitude of animal sacrifices, but of the blood of Christ.

A Law Unto Condemnation

The old covenant presented Israel with a promise suspended upon a condition. God promised to be faithful to all those who kept his commandments (Ex 19:6–6, Deut 7:9, 28:1). He was putting before the people an offer of life and death. The promises made to Israel could be realized if only it would remain faithful to the Lord. As the Lord himself stated, "I call heaven and earth to witness against you today, that I have set before you life and death, blessings and curse. Therefore choose life, that you and your offspring may live, loving the LORD your God, obeying his voice and holding fast to him, for he is your life and length of days, that you may dwell in the land that the LORD swore to your fathers, to Abraham, to Isaac, and to Jacob, to give them" (Deut 30:19–20).

According to Arthur Pink, the obedience God demanded from the nation was less severe than that which he demanded from the individual. He stated that this was because "nations as such have only a temporal existence; therefore they must be rewarded or punished in this present world, or not at all. This being so, the kind of obedience required from them is lower than from individuals."[33] This is questionable, and whilst it would be nice to spend time exploring this, the important thing to bear in mind is that the conditional Mosaic law, with its this-worldly blessings and punishments, typified the position of the individual as he stood under the original covenant of works. Temporal punishment was itself a type of that eternal punishment that awaits all those who find themselves under the law, whilst the blessings were a type of those blessings that belonged to all who placed their hope in the promised Messiah.

The problem for Israel, as we have seen, was that the "ought" did not imply the "can." These people were "dead in their trespasses and sins" (Eph 2:1). They were in the kingdom of darkness, living in the realm of the old man in the first Adam. The obedience the law demanded was far beyond

---

33. Pink, *Divine Covenants*, 109.

their capabilities, not only in regard to their meriting mundane blessings, but more importantly, spiritual blessings. The apostle tells us that "by the works of the law no human being will be justified in his sight, since through the law comes the knowledge of sin" (Rom 3:20).

At Sinai Israel was presented with what was essentially, to quote John Owen:

> A divine summary of the law written in the heart of man at his creation. And in this, the dreadful manner of its delivery or promulgation with its writings in tables of stone, is also to be considered; for in them the picture of that first covenant, with its inexorableness as to perfect obedience was represented'.[34]

In this the law served as a yardstick, enabling the people to see just how far short they fell in regard to its demands. Paul tells us that "the law came in to increase the trespass" (Rom 5:20), and that the work of the law "brings wrath, but where there is no law there is no transgression (Rom 4:15). Here Paul is not saying that without the law sin does not exist, rather, he is showing that it is the law's function to make us conscious of our sin. To make sin abound in our consciousness. It is only then that we realize the wrath of God is set against us because we have broken his law. It is only in the realization of this that we will look to the salvation that the Lord has provided in his Messiah. Perhaps the best example of the law at work in the life of the individual is in Romans 7:7–12 where the apostle considers how the law worked in his own soul:

> What then shall we say? That the law is sin?
> By no means! Yet if it had not been for the law,
> I would not have known sin. For I would not
> have known what it is to covet if the law
> had not said, 'You shall not covet.' But sin seizing
> the opportunity through the commandment
> produced in me all kinds of covetousness. For
> apart from the law, sin lies dead. I was once alive
> apart from the law, but when the commandment
> came, sin came alive and I died. The very commandment
> that promised life proved to be death to me . . .

Initially, Paul believed himself to be a keeper of the law. He was, however, only keeping the law by way of externals and believed himself to be

34. Owen, *Works*, 22:77.

alive unto God. Eventually, through the work of the Spirit, he saw beyond the letter of the law. In his case, this was particularly so in regard to the 10th commandment, "You shall not covet" (Exod 20:17). Coming to such a spiritual understanding of this commandment he realized that he was completely incapable of keeping it. The law "by presenting the perfect standard of duty, which cannot be seen without awakening the sense of obligation to be conformed to it, while it imparts no disposition or power to obey it, it exasperates the soul and thus again brings forth fruit unto death."[35] The apostle instead of believing himself alive to God came to the realization that he was like a dead man, totally incapable of doing anything acceptable to God.

By making people aware of their sin the Mosaic law:

> Declared the impossibility of obtaining reconciliation and peace with God any other way but by the promise. For representing the commands of the covenant of works requiring perfect, sinless obedience, under the penalty of the curse, it convinced men that this was no way for sinners to seek life and salvation by. And herewith it so urged the consciences of men, that they could have no rest nor peace in themselves but what the promise would afford them, whereunto they saw the necessity of betaking themselves.[36]

One is reminded of the words of Jesus, "Those who are well have no need of a physician, but those who are sick. I came not to call the righteous, but sinners." (Mark 2:17). The law can stop the boastful mouth of sinful man and hold before the sinner's eyes the true state of his accounts with the holy God. In the words of Francis Roberts, the law serves "to seal up condemnation by convincing all men of sin."[37]

One might ask: Why did God make a covenant based on conditions he knew the people would be incapable of keeping? Since the Fall all humanity has been under a curse, however, in spite of this, all are still responsible for their own actions. The law can do nothing to help, and man's responsibility has not diminished, to quote William Pemble, "though strength to obey be lost: yet the obligation to obedience remains. We are no more discharged from our duties because we have no strength to *doe* [sic] it, than a debtor is quitted of his Bands because he wants money to make payment."[38] Fallen humanity has great belief in its own ability, so much so that it will refuse any offer of help. Before man will seek help he must first be set a task that he

---

35. Hodge, *I and II Corinthians*, 432.

36. Owen, *The Works*, 22, 79.

37. Roberts, "God's Covenants," 157

38. Pemble, *Vindiciae Fide*, 91.

cannot achieve. It is only then, when he becomes aware of his inability that he, like the apostle, will seek help. The law was God's instrument to make man aware of his inability.

Recently a work was published entitled *Merit and Moses*.[39] It was a response to Meredith Kline's republication paradigm and the book referred to earlier, *The Law is Not of Faith*. While both these works are by Presbyterians, they differ in that the latter supports the contention that the law was a reiteration of the earlier covenant of works, that under Moses it was essentially a covenant unto death. *Merit and Moses, on the other hand,* seeks to refute the idea that Sinai was such a republication. Essentially it amounts to nothing more than a regurgitation of the standard Presbyterian contention that the law, the old covenant, is another administration of the covenant of grace. It seeks to do this not so much from Scripture, but from the Westminster Confession.

The contributers of the book employ somewhat specious arguments in an attempt to undermine the the "Republication Paradigm." One of the book's commendations is by Richard B. Gaffin. He tells us that, "This volume addresses a relatively recent appearance of the view that the Mosaic covenant embodies a republication of the covenant of works, a view that in its distinctive emphasis is arguably without precedent in the history of Reformed theology." This is simply untrue. The contributors of *The Law is not of Faith* were not putting forward a novel position. They were rather simply restating what was believed by men like Herman Witsius, John Owen and Samuel Petto, Nehemiah Coxe, etc.

We are told that "the Confession affirms that the Mosaic covenant is, in essence, a covenant of grace, it implies that it cannot in any way be in substance a covenant of works."[40] As already said, the book does not quote Scripture but simply defends the Westminster Confession. It must be said that while the Confession might well affirm this, Scriptures certainly do not.

We are told that:

> The obligations imposed upon Israel in the Ten Commandments do not function in any way as a covenant of works in which their obedience would merit blessings. Rather, it functions solely as a rule of life informing them of the proper expressions of their faith—reverent thankful obedience for God's gracious redemption.[41]

39. Elam, et al., *Merit and Moses*.
40. Ibid., 92.
41. Ibid., 93.

If this were the case then presumably the Commandments would be for the minority within the nation who constituted spiritual Israel, those whose hearts of stone had been replaced with hearts of flesh. For only these have faith and are able to show true reverence. The alternative would be to suggest that the exodus redemption equated with spiritual redemption and that the entire nation was saved.

In an attempt to explain the conditional passages, for example, Leviticus 26 and Deuteronomy 28, the writers quote Patrick Ramsey, believing his comments to be "helpful."

> The curses ("threatenings") of the Mosaic Law teach the regenerate what temporal afflictions they may expect when they sin while the blessings ("promises") instruct them concerning the benefits they may expect when they obey. Saving faith "trembles" at these curses and "embraces" the blessings for "this life, and that which is to come." To establish a connection between obedience and blessing and disobedience and cursing is for many—notably antinomians—to establish in some sense a covenant of works. The divines were certainly aware of this possible misunderstanding. After all, they debated this issue for years. Consequently, they made it explicitly clear that such a connection does not in any form or fashion indicate that man is under a covenant of works.[42]

The "divines" alluded to were clearly those Presbyterians who put together the Westminster Confession. They are clearly failing make the distinction we saw earlier between the old covenant that was a conditional covenant of works, which while reiterating the demands of the original covenant, could now, because of the flesh's weakness, only condemn, and the new covenant revealed in the promise. They also seem not to appreciate the old covenant's mundane nature, with its temporal promises, and the fact that the new covenant, the covenant of grace, stands apart from this. Instead, the two covenants are conflated. Another problem with this understanding is the same as we saw earlier, the regenerate made up only a small percentage of the nation. The "threatenings" became a reality for Israel not because there was a remnant of faithful servants, like the seven thousand who had not bowed the knee to Baal (1 Kgs 19:18, Rom 11:4), but because the majority turned their backs on the Lord and ran after other gods. So whilst the blessings of the life to come were secure for the true Israel, the same cannot be said about temporal blessings.

42. Ibid., 95.

The faithful servants of God within the nation went into exile along with the nation because the "promises" and "cursings" applied to Israel as a whole.

Ramsay is applying the conditional element of the covenant only to believers, to the "regenerate" where the temporal blessings enjoyed are the result of their obeying the Lord. This simply does not ring true. All too often the people of God suffered unjustly at the hands of the ungodly. This is why the saints looked for but did "not receive the things promised, having seen them and greeted them from afar, and having acknowledged that they were strangers and exiles on the earth" (Heb 11:13). Both the original covenant of works and its republication demands perfect obedience. In its typological function, the revival of the covenant under Moses reveals to man, to the nation, on the mundane, temporal level what the original covenant does at the spiritual level.

In *Merit and Moses* there are some rather bizarre statements, for example:

> The basic problem centers on how the same obedience of an Israelite in the Republication Paradigm could function on one level to merit a reward (apart from grace) and at the same time on another level to be rewarded by grace alone. This dual role of good works leads to a dualism in God's people—a kind of spiritual "schizophrenia" in the every day life of the believer.[43]

This is designed to confuse rather than clarify. The apostle has made it perfectly clear that dualism existed within the nation, between Abraham's physical and spiritual posterity. There were two kinds of Jew. Abraham's carnal children stood under the written code, condemned by the law, whereas his spiritual children, through faith in the "seed" had been declared righteous, having experienced circumcision of the heart by the Spirit of God. The "schizophrenic" scare arises from a faulty hermeneutic. It is the result of placing Israel after the flesh in the covenant of grace, and then applying what belongs to spiritual Israel to Abraham's natural seed.

The law too can be viewed on two levels, at least in regard to man's experience of it. On the one hand, there is the law that because of human inability and sin can only condemn; it is unto death. On the other hand, there is the law unto life because its requirements have been met in the work of the second Adam. So we see the consequences of the first Adam's sin and the meritorious righteousness of God in the second Adam. Again there are two types of Israelite. The carnal Israelite for whom the law was a terror unto death, and the Israelite who had received the new birth, for whom the law held no terror because of his position in Christ. We are still commanded to

43. Ibid., 126.

keep God's law, and it is only by trying to do so that one becomes, as we saw in the case of the apostle, aware of one's inability to do so. We see the same principle at work in Christ's earthly ministry, in the case of the rich young man (Matt 19:16–22; Mark 10:17–31). Hodge comments that "Our Lord assured the young man who came to Him for instruction that if he kept the commandments he should live."[44] No one would suggest that Christ believed this was a possibility. Had the man applied himself to keeping the law he would have quickly realized the futility of his endeavor and returned to Christ for salvation. None would argue, at least from the Reformed Baptist perspective, that the man, "put forth any exercise or perform any act in such a way as to merit the approbation of God."[45] Rather, the approbation of God has been secured by Christ, and his people consists of those deemed to have fulfilled the law because they are in Christ. It is these who constitute the true Israel of God. Dualism is Scriptural and it most certainly does not lead to "a kind of spiritual schizophrenia."

As with the young man who sought instruction from Christ, there was never any possibility of Israel keeping the commandments. In the midst of the nation's calamity, however, God would raise up prophets who not only reminded Israel of the law's demands, and the punishment due to those who kept it not, but also, in the depth of the nation's despair, pointed to the promise, so that the people might believe like their father Abraham and thereby receive the righteousness of another. So we see the function of the law that came through Moses, and the grace that came through Jesus Christ (John 1:17).

Merit and Moses goes further, to the point of accusing those who accept the Republication Paradigm of undermining Christ's perfect obedience:

> In the Republication Paradigm, God's "simple justice" does not require Christ's obedience to be perfect by *definition*. Simple justice would instruct Israel to consider their sin-tainted works as meritorious and deserving of reward on the basis of God's covenant word. Someone may ask the Israelite under the Republication Paradigm, "How can you a sinful creature, perform imperfect works that are meritorious? How are they deserving of blessing from a perfectly holy and righteous God?" The answer would be according to "simple justice." It doesn't matter that my works are tainted with sin. God did not require perfection in the covenant made at Sinai for me to merit temporal blessings and retain my life in the promised land. I have simply obeyed God's covenant stipulations (albeit, imperfectly), and no—according to "simple

44. Hodge, *Systematic Theology*, 2:375.
45. Ibid., 2:263.

justice"—he owns me the reward he promised . . . If their imperfect obedience can be constituted as the meritorious ground of
reward, where then do we find the ground for the necessity of the
absolute perfect obedience of Christ to merit salvation.[46]

As Reformed Baptists, we completely reject this idea of "simple justice."
And, what's more, this was not emphasized in *TLNF*. To talk about two types
of justice in regard to God is something entirely foreign to our paradigm, and
the Scriptures. The Lord always demands perfect obedience. He demanded
no less from Israel. God is holy, and he demanded that the nation be too.
Indeed, this is what he demands of all humanity. There is no such thing as
second best when it comes to God's justice. As God said to Abraham, "walk
before me, and be blameless" (Gen 17:1), so he says to Israel, "You shall be
holy, for I the LORD your God am holy" (Lev 19:2), "You shall be blameless
before the LORD your God" (Deut 18:13). Far from taking away from the
need for Christ to provide a perfect righteousness, the revival of the covenant
of works points to its necessity, because it so clearly reveals the inability of the
sinner and the perfect standard required by a holy God. In the case of Israel,
while the blessings were couched in a language the people could understand,
namely, with land, crops, and longevity etc., this did not imply that God demanded anything less than perfect obedience. The law has never changed, it
has always demanded the same perfect righteousness.

Those who argue for two levels of obedience perhaps do so because of
those Old Testament allusions to those who were obedient to the Lord. For
example, in Judges, we read, "They soon turned aside from their fathers, who
obeyed the commandments of the LORD" (Judg 2:17). In addressing this the
essential principle of interpretation must be borne in mind, namely, that God
does not contradict himself. As we saw earlier, there is none that can keep the
law except Christ, "no-one will be declared righteous in his sight by observing
the law" (Rom 3:20). The simple truth is that we have all sinned and continue
to fall short of God's glory (Rom 3:23). Those texts that speak of fallen man's
obedience must not be taken as referring to obedience to the Moral Law or
the Ten Commandments, because no fallen being can provide this. Such texts
are rather, speaking of an obedience in the performance of the Mosaic rituals.
Such an obedience, however, did not merit God's favor, indeed, many of those
who provided such an obedience were still in their sins, and any blessing received were unmerited and was but a type of the free unmerited blessings
available to all who put their faith in the promises of God.

In the introduction to *Merit and Moses*, we are told that: "Ironically,
the republication teaching, which was intended to preserve and protect

46. Ibid., 114.

the doctrine of justification, may (when consistently worked out) actually undercut this doctrine—the very doctrine by which the church stands or falls." This is, again, simply scaremongering. The truth is quite the opposite. As said above, the republication serves to make the sinner aware of his dire position, realizing that the perfect obedience the law demands is to be found elsewhere. John Owen did not employ the word 'republication' but rather 'revival'. This amounts to the same thing. One only needs to read what he says about Justification by faith[47] to realize that far from undercutting this doctrine, the republication of the law serves to magnify it. Because sin is brought to the fore by the law, one is enabled to see something of the radical nature of justification, this is because to see something of the nature of unrighteousness is to all the more appreciate the righteousness that comes through Christ.

Galatians 3:16–18

Having said that the covenant made with Abraham was not a covenant of grace, it is necessary to examine some verses in Paul's letter to the Galatians. Verses that according to some, prove the contrary, in particular, 3:16–18, where we read:

> Now the promises were made to Abraham, and to his offspring. It does not say "And to offsprings," referring to many, but referring to one. "And to your offspring," who is Christ. This is what I mean: the law which came 430 years afterward does not annul a covenant previously ratified by God, so as to make the promise void. For if the inheritance comes by the law, it no longer comes by promise, but God gave it to Abraham by promise.

We have alluded to the fact that some paedobaptists, whilst believing the Mosaic covenant to be one of works, still, nevertheless, believe the Abrahamic covenant to be an administration of the covenant of grace. Indeed, this understanding of the Abrahamic covenant appears to be the view of all paedobaptists, and, dare I say, of many who call themselves "Reformed Baptist". Do these verses prove their case? Was the apostle here stating that the "covenant previously ratified by God" was a covenant of grace? Is Paul making a comparison between the law given through Moses, the legal side, and the covenant of grace established with Abraham? An affirmative answer would undermine the Reformed Baptist position here put forward.

---

47. Owen, *Works*, vol. 5.

One of the authors of *The Law is Not of Faith*, David Gordon, concerning these verses in Galatians, states that "Paul did not conceive these two covenants as similar in kind, but rather as dissimilar in kind: one is characteristically promissory; the other is characteristically legal."[48] The question is: Was the apostle in verse 17 calling the Abrahamic covenant a covenant of grace, whilst maintaining the Mosaic covenant to be of works? Should this be the case it might then be argued that as children were circumcised and made members of the Abrahamic covenant of grace so they ought to be baptized and become members of the new covenant of grace, for, after all, are they not in substance one and the same?

Gordon disagrees with John Murray's comments regarding the Abrahamic and Mosaic covenants:

> What needs to be emphasized now is that the Mosaic covenant in respect of the condition of obedience is not in a different category from the Abrahamic. It is too frequently assumed that the conditions prescribed in connection with the Mosaic covenant place the Mosaic dispensation in a totally different category as respects grace, on the one hand, and the demand or obligation, on the other. In reality there is nothing that is principally different in the necessity of keeping the covenant and of the obedience to God's voice, which proceeds form the Mosaic covenant, from that which in involved in the keeping required in the Abrahamic.[49]

Murray was, like Gordon, a paedobaptist, and whilst his covenant theology differs markedly from the Reformed Baptist position put forward here, the latter would agree with what Murray says regarding the similarities between the two covenants. Both covenants are concerned with the necessity of obedience and are therefore conditional. Gordon, on the other hand, seeks to show that these two covenants are distinct, that they are founded on different conditions, namely faith and law. This interpretation is, however, fundamentally flawed in that it is missing the essential point in what Paul is saying. In this passage the apostle is not so much concerned with safeguarding the covenant, but, rather, the promise of what Abraham had believed prior to any covenant being established with him. While there were, of course, administrative differences between the Abrahamic and Mosaic covenants, they were, nevertheless, both based on the need for obedience. The apostle is saying that although the Mosaic covenant came in later, it, like the Abrahamic covenant, did not make void or in any way affect the promise

---

48. Gordon, "Abraham and Sinai," 250.
49. Murray, *Covenant of Grace*, 22.

previously given concerning the new covenant of grace. Both covenants are subservient to the promise and essentially serve as conduits through which the promise will come to its fruition in the incarnation of the Son of God.

Gordon makes the somewhat bizarre statement, using the sub-heading: "The Abrahamic Covenant Justifies; The Siniatic Covenant Does Not."[50] He erroneously identifies the Abrahamic covenant itself with the promise as if they are one and the same. They are not. It is only the new covenant in Christ that justifies. The Abrahamic covenant never justified anyone. Gordon is confusing the promise of the new covenant made to Abraham by which he was credited with righteousness, with the conditional covenant that was made with him about twenty-five years later. In Gal 3:17 Paul is essentially saying that far from removing the earlier covenant, the Sinai covenant builds upon it, supplements it. That it too, far from changing the promise, points towards it, safeguards it. One must draw a distinction between the covenant and the promise. Although the old covenant points toward the promise it should not be identified with the promise.

There is another way of looking at these verses. Again, one that draws a distinction between the new covenant by which Abraham received grace, and the conditional covenant later established with him. When in v.17 Paul speaks of a covenant "previously ratified by God" he has in mind Genesis 15. It is this covenant that is different from the covenant of circumcision we read about in Genesis 17, and the Sinaitic covenant that came 430 years later. The covenant referred to in chapter 15 is the future new covenant. This covenant was unconditional, and although we know that any conditions were later fulfilled by Christ, in chapter 15 no conditions are listed in regard to Israel. The entire chapter is about that which will occur in the future irrespective of Israel's obedience. This includes those blessings given to Abraham's natural seeds or "offsprings", for example, the land of Canaan, and of course, the promise concerning the "offspring", who is the Messiah. The former serving as an unconditional type to the latter's antitype. The covenant guarantee was the Lord himself passing between the dismembered sacrifice. So essentially, whilst the new covenant is revealed, its ratification will be in the future, and it is this the Lord is guaranteeing by the sacrifice made. So although this is called a covenant, it is essentially a covenant of guarantee because it concerns God's promise and not fallen man's obedience. At the time it may not have not have been ratified by the shed blood of Christ, but in another sense it was ratified because God himself had promised it by passing himself between the dismembered sacrifice which marked his solemn declaration

---

50. Gordon, "Abraham and Sinai," 248.

concerning the covenant's future consummation. It was this promise that Abraham believed, by which he was accounted righteous (Rom 4:3).

A Nation Set Apart

Israel was a privileged nation, "You only have I known of all the families of the earth" (Amos 3:2). God chose this people, not because of anything that they had done (Deut 7:7), nor because they possessed any special traits. Israel was to be the cradle of the Messiah, and because of this God hedged the nation about with his law. The main reasons for this, as well as pointing to the promise was to ensure the genealogical line and to restrain sin until the promise reached fruition in the work of Christ.

Israel was to be a holy and sanctified people. This essentially meant that the nation was to be set apart for God's purposes. The sign of circumcision in the male reproductive organ set the nation apart, and to keep the people pure, to protect the line, intermarrying with people of other nations was forbidden. The civil and sacrificial laws served to fence the nation off from its neighbors, acting as a "dividing wall of hostility" (Eph 2:14). To quote Johnson, "the law helped distinguish Israel from other ethnic groups. For instance, many of the ceremonial and judicial laws . . . were designed, not only to make a clear distinction between Jews and Gentiles but also to keep them separated. The various ceremonial washings, dietary laws, holy days, and other such regulations fenced off Israel from the rest of the world."[51] The law, to quote Arthur Pink, was "needed because of their transgressions. The children of Israel were so intractable and perverse, so prone to depart from God, that without such a divinely provided hedge, they would have lost their national identity, mixing themselves with the surrounding nations and becoming sunk in their idolatrous ways."[52]

Within Israel the punishment for many sins was immediate. For example, in Leviticus 12:20 we are told that the man who commits adultery is to be stoned to death. In the case of the Amalekites, the Lord ordered Saul to, "Now go and strike Amalek and devote to destruction all that they have. Do not spare them, but kill both man and woman, child and infant, ox and sheep, camel and donkey" (1 Sam 15:3). The immediacy and severity of the punishment might seem harsh to many today, it was nevertheless vital for maintaining the purity of the nation. The punishment was a deterrent, serving to restrain sin within the nation and it also revealed the heinous nature of sin in the eyes of a holy God.

51. Johnson, *Fatal Flaw,* 143.

52. Pink, *Divine Covenants,* 111.

Many Christians today have a somewhat illogical view in regard to the harshness of Old Testament justice, and there are passages they choose to avoid. These are often the same people who believe in the final judgment, where God will judge the living and the dead; where many souls will spend eternity in hell. What we see in the Old Testament is what one might call accelerated justice. It is God's judgment brought forward in order the safeguard the promised "seed" of Abraham.

What About Those Earthly Promises?

The old covenant performed a typological function about which Jonathan Edwards could write:

> That nation [Israel] was a typical nation. There was then literally a land, which was a type, of heaven, the true dwelling place of God; and an external city, which was a type of the spiritual city of God; an external temple of God which was a type of His spiritual temple So there was a external people and a family of God, by carnal generation, which was a type of His spiritual progeny. And the covenant by which they were made the people of God, was a type of the covenant of grace; and so is sometimes represented as a marriage covenant.[53]

The worldly promises and institutions were all part and parcel of the conditional covenant made with both Abraham and Moses. The covenant was a type which mirrored the antitype in Christ, as Renihan reminds us, "every single element of the Mosaic economy typologically revealed and set before the eyes of the Jews the covenant of grace wherein true righteousness, true forgiveness of sins, and true holiness could be found."[54] The covenant required acts of obedience but it did not provide the means, "it delivered the Israelites out of captivity in the land of Egypt (physical picture), but it did not deliver them from bondage to their own sinful natures."[55]

When the Israelites were in Egypt they suffered terribly under the Pharaoh. He believed they were becoming too numerous. They were therefore forced to build the cities of Pithom and Rameses. We are told that the taskmasters "made their lives bitter with hard service, in mortar and brick, and in all kinds of work in the field. In all their work they ruthlessly made

---

53. Edwards, *Works of President Edwards*, 463.
54. Renihan, "Reformed Baptist Covenant Theology," 481
55. Hicks, "John Owen on the Mosaic Covenant," 188.

them work as slaves" kinds of work in the fields; in all their hard labour the Egyptians used them ruthlessly" (Exod 1:14).

The people found themselves in an impossible position, forced to do work that was too hard for them. God intervened on the people's behalf. He raised up his servant, Moses, from among their own people. On the night of their escape from Egyptian bondage, each family was told to take a lamb without blemish, sacrifice it and daub the blood on the doorposts (Exod 12:21–23). When the LORD went through the land, taking the firstborn of the Egyptians he would see the blood and "passover" the house.

We are all familiar with this story, but how many stop to consider how the LORD redeemed this people and yet led them from one type of bondage into another? Their new taskmaster was the law, and a merciless taskmaster it was, to quote Gordon:

> The Sinaitic covenant administration was no bargain for sinners, and I pity all the poor Israelites who suffered under its administration, just as I understand perfectly well why seventy three (nearly half) of their psalms were laments. I would have resisted this covenant also, had I been there, because such a legal covenant, whose conditions require strict obedience (and threaten severe curse sanctions), is bound to fail if one of the parties to it is a sinful people.[56]

As with their ordeal in Egypt, the people would find the demands of this new taskmaster impossible. The load was too heavy for them. However, as God raised up Moses to redeem Israel from Egypt, so he would raise up another servant, who would redeem his people from the bondage of the law. A servant who would say, "Come unto me, all ye that labour and are heavy laden, and I will give you rest. Take my yoke upon you, and learn of me; for I am meek and lowly in heart, and ye shall find rest unto your souls. For my yoke is easy, and my burden is light" (Matt 11:28–30). As Israel under the old covenant was delivered in the physical exodus, only into a bondage to the law that they found insufferable, so in the new covenant the true Israel of God is delivered through the new exodus in Christ, only this time into a place where it can rest from all its works (Heb 4:13). So, yes, the law came through Moses, but grace and truth have come through Jesus Christ. As the first redemption was made possible by a miracle in the parting of the Red Sea, so Christ's redemption would be made possible by a miracle, where the Lord himself, became man and dwelt among us. Jesus then becomes our true Passover. He is the sacrificial lamb of God, whose blood is a propitiation for everyone who believes the promise.

56. Gordon, "Abraham and Sinai," 251.

It may well be asked: What exactly did the Old Testament saint see? Did he really see past the types to the Christ beyond? There is much that God has not revealed to us about the way his Spirit opened the eyes of the unbeliever in times of old. For example, Christ said that Abraham saw his day and rejoiced (John 8:56). When we read the accounts in Genesis we struggle to see this. This is because it was the Spirit of God communicating Christ. The various ceremonies associated with the Mosaic covenant typified, "Christ's person, offices, and benefits . . . the very great number of rites was like a vail (sic) by which the naked simplicity of the ancient promise was very much clouded . . . the greatest part of the Israelites cleaved to the ceremonies themselves, sought for justification and expiation of sin in them, and did not penetrate into the spiritual mysteries which were his under the vail (sic)."[57] It was only those who had been made alive by the Spirit of God, whose eyes were opened to turn to the Lord who had the veil removed (2 Cor 3:16) by the Spirit of God and were, therefore, enabled to see beyond to the glories of the Christ.

Both dispensationalists and premillennialists live in the expectation of seeing the earthly promises associated with the old covenant fulfilled in the millennium, or thousand year reign we read about in Revelation 20:6–7. This is said to be prior to there being a new heavens and a new earth. It is a view that fails to distinguish between those promises that only applied to the physical Israel that were entirely dependent on an impossible obedience, and those applicable only to spiritual Israel in Christ. Mixing up the old and new covenants, they apply those blessings that were conditional under the old covenant to the new covenant and vice versa.

The premillennialist looks for a this-worldly fulfillment of much Old Testament prophecy. They take, for example, Jeremiah's words and apply them to a millennial kingdom:

> Now therefore thus says the Lord, the God of Israel, concerning this city of which you say, "It is given into the hand of the king of Babylon by sword by famine and by pestilence." Behold, I will gather them from all the countries to which to which I drove them in my anger and my wrath and in great indignation. I will bring them back to this place, and I will make them dwell in safety. And they shall be my people, and I will be their God. I will give them one heart and one way, that they may fear me forever. (Jer 32:36ff)

Such promises, however, could never come to fruition for Abraham's natural seed because of their unfaithfulness. These promises, as applied to

---

57. Witsius, *Economy of the Covenants*, 365.

temporal Israel, were but types that spoke of spiritual antitypical realities in Christ. That these will come to fruition will be the result of the work of the Messiah who kept the mandate of the original covenant of works. They would never find their fulfillment in this fallen world, however, for all those who put their faith in Christ they are already a reality. Only believers are God's people and he is their God, and they dwell safely in Christ. These promises were expressed with references to earthly things in that these typified, be it ever so faintly, the nature of the indescribable blessings that belong those in Christ.

The paedobaptists tend to mix up the types with the substance. Reisinger is so right when he states that "we must remember that most of those redeemed people went to hell because they rejected the gospel."[58] Obviously, some may have been saved, but this was because they, like Abraham, believed in the promise. Reisinger states a fundamental truth that, all too often, paedobaptists tend to overlook, or deliberately ignore, "we must see that every single word like elect, chosen, loved, redeemer, son etc., describes Israel's relationship with God as a nation, having a totally different connotation when words are used of the church's relationship. One cannot mix spiritual and natural. *One cannot treat the type as the reality.*"[59]

Those who adopt the premillenial position are of the view that the Old Testament terrestrial promises will be realized in the 1000 year reign of Christ, a thousand years in which there will be peace and harmony upon this fallen earth. Wayne Gruden, in his *Systematic Theology* attempts to justify this position by referring to Isaiah 11:6–9 and 65:20. He states that "these passages seem to fit neither in the present age nor in the eternal state. These passages indicate some future stage in the history of redemption which is far greater than the present church age but which still does not see the removal of all sin and rebellion and death from the earth."[60] Isaiah prophesied that:

> The wolf shall dwell with the lamb,
> . . . the leopard shall lie down with the young goat,
> and the calf and the lion and the fattened calf together;
> and a little child shall lead them . . . (Isa 11:6)

> No more shall there be in it
> an infant that lives but a few days or an old man who
> does not fill out his days,

---

58. Italics added for emphasis. Reisinger, *Abraham's Four Seeds*, 30.

59. Ibid., 30.

60. Grudem, *Systematic Theology*, 1127.

for the young man shall die a hundred years old

and the sinner a hundred years old shall be accursed. (Isa 65:20)

Dispensationalism has been responsible for wrongly dividing the Word of God, failing to understand the essential unity of God's one covenant of grace, the new covenant. According to John Macarthur:

> Dispensationalism is a fundamentally correct system of understanding God's program through the ages. Its chief element is the recognition that God's plan for Israel is not superseded by or swallowed up in His program for the church. Israel and the church are separate entities, and God will restore national Israel under the earthly rule of Jesus the Messiah. I accept and affirm that tenet, because it emerges from a consistently literal interpretation of Scripture.[61]

What one believes about the end times is important here because it will affect the way we interpret these prophecies, and hence, where these promises fit into the covenants. Are these words to be understood as referring the some future millennial reign on this earth or can they best be understood as part and parcel of the conditional promises made to Israel? I would suggest the latter to be the case. If Israel faithfully obeyed the voice of the LORD their God and were careful to do all his commandments (Deut 28:1) then such manifold blessings of God would be showered upon them. MacArthur, it appears, fails to distinguish between those earthly blessings promised to carnal Israel upon the condition of her obedience, promises that would not come to fruition because of her disobedience, and those applicable only to spiritual Israel on account of Christ's righteousness.

In regard to Grudem's position, one must ask whether the prophecies in question referred to the millennium reign of Christ or are concerned with a time when this sinful earth has been replaced by a new earth and a new heavens.

It appears to me the blessings alluded to in these two Isaiah passages go beyond anything that was promised to carnal Israel upon her obedience. Rather, they are associated with another covenant, one based on Christ's obedience to the original covenant of works. In Isaiah 11 we are presented with what Leupold calls an "arrangement by pairs—one formally wild, one tame."[62] Those parts of nature that were traditionally hostile, depicting a nature "red in tooth and claw" are brought back into something reminiscent of the peace and harmony that existed before Adam's fall. Not only will this

---

61. MacArthur, *Gospel According to Jesus*, 40.

62. Leupold, *Exposition of Isaiah*, 221.

occur among the animals but any fear they may have had of man will cease to exist, so much so that even a defenseless "a little child shall lead them." It will be a time, to quote Leupold, when "every discordant note, every element of danger and disaster has been extracted."[63] What one is witnessing here has nothing to do with the Millennium, but, rather, that transformation of nature that will occur, as John informs us, "when there is a new heaven and a new earth" (Rev 21:1).

In Isaiah 65:17 we are told that the prophecy speaks of the very future age later referred to by John:

> For behold, I create new heavens
>   and a new earth,
> and the former things shall not be remembered
>   or come into mind.

Everything alluded to in this chapter of Isaiah must be viewed against this. All that is to occur must fit into the context of the new heaven and earth. This is, no doubt, the very passage Peter had in mind when he spoke about the passing away of this sinful world, looking is expectation to that which is to come, where we "are waiting for new heavens and a new earth in which righteousness dwells" (2 Pet 3:13). Is this not "the assurance of things hoped for, the conviction of things not seen" (Heb 11:1). It is unto this new world that Old Testament believers lived in anticipation of, in the knowledge that they "were strangers and exiles on this earth" (Heb 11:13).

Grudem, to shore up his argument that Isaiah 65 is referring to a Millennium Age, makes mention of the reference to death, "for the child shall die a hundred years old." In the new earth there will be no death, so why, we may ask, does the prophet refer to it here when speaking of the "new heavens and a new earth"? Often, when things spiritual and eternal are spoken of, the language used is couched in the language of the ideals of our temporary earthly existence. Also, as Leupold reminds us, "the truth concerning the eternal blessedness of God's children was, in the providence of God, but slowly revealed."[64] The allusions to death and to one living to be a hundred years should not be taken literally, but essentially as metaphorical, employing types the people could readily understand. They were essentially things to which fallen humanity could relate. Because of their immaturity God spoke of life in his future kingdom in terms of an ideal in the present. In the words of Alec Motyer:

---

63. Ibid., 221.
64. Ibid., 367.

"Things that we have no real capacity to understand can be expressed only through things we know and experience. So it is that this present order of things death cuts life off before it has well begun or before it has fully matured. But it will not be so then. No infant will fail to enjoy life, nor an elderly person come short of total fulfilment. Indeed, one would be but a youth were one to die aged a hundred! This does not imply that death will still be present . . . but rather affirms over the whole of life, as we should now say from infancy to old age, the power of death will be destroyed"[65]

Today Israel has served its purpose and should no longer be seen as being a sanctified nation or people. The coming of Christ marked the end of the conditional covenant made with the physical Israel. Christians today must not look for the fulfillment of these prophecies in this fallen, sinful world, although, in their types, they do provide us with a glimpse of what the new world will be like. One can wholeheartedly concur with Grier's take on this:

The literalism which insists on the Old Testament prophecies being referred to Israel after the flesh, is utterly inconsistent with the universal New Testament application of the promises to the spiritual seed. The New Testament insists that he is not a Jew who is one outwardly (Rom.2:28,29), that they are not all Israel which are of Israel (Rom.9:6), that they that are Christ's are Abraham's spiritual seed (Gal.3:29), that the blessing of Abraham has come upon the Gentiles in Christ Jesus (Gal.3:14) and that there can be neither Jew not Gentile (Greek), for "ye are all one in Christ Jesus" (Gal.3:28). The literalism that waits still for Christ to take His seat on David's throne at Jerusalem is inconsistent with Peter's announcement that Christ has already taken His seat on David's throne at His resurrection. The literalism that looks for a restoration at the temple in Jerusalem, with all the nations coming to take part in its worship and its sacrifices for sin, is inconsistent with the New Testament's assertion that such worhsip and sacrifices has been "taken away" (Heb.10:8,9).[66]

Premillennialists clearly fail to distinguish between those promises that were conditional upon carnal Israel's obedience, and were only ever subject to the divine "No," and those that would find their "Yes" in Christ.

A correct understanding would entail believers realizing that in this fallen world they have "no lasting city," but are awaiting that "city that is to

---

65. Motyer, *The Prophecy of Isaiah*, 530.

66. Grier, *Momentous Event*, 50.

come" (Heb 13:14). In this world, we are as Peter says, "sojourners and exiles" (1 Pet 2:11), we wait for "an inheritance that is imperishable, undefiled and unfading, kept in heaven" (1 Pet 1:4). One that is ready to be revealed when there is a new heaven and a new earth. We "desire a better country, that is, a heavenly one," where God himself has prepared a city for us (Heb 11:16). Obviously, if Grudem's take on the verses alluded to in Isaiah was correct, these saints would have looked not to a heavenly country but to this one.

There are many other inconsistencies in the premillennial and dispensationalist understanding of Old Testament prophecy. I will, however, leave this topic with a number of questions:

- *Are we to believe that in the Millennium reign there will be peace and harmony within nature in this fallen world?*

- *Can we envisage Christ reigning over a world, on a secular throne, in which, although all will bend the knee to Christ, many will still be destined for the pit?*

- *Are we to expect a reinstallation of the Old Testament sacrificial system that has served its purpose and is now of little value because the substance has come?*

To answer these in the affirmative results from not only to misunderstanding the nature of God's covenants, but makes nonsense of the Word of God.

The Case of Sarah and Hagar

Tell me, you who desire to be under the law, do you not listen to the law? For it is written that Abraham had two sons, one by a slave woman and one by a free woman. But the son of the slave was born according to the flesh, while the son of the free woman was born through promise. Now this may be interpreted allegorically: these women are two covenants. One is from Mount Sinai, bearing children for slavery; she is Hagar. Now Hagar is Mount Sinai in Arabia; she corresponds to the present Jerusalem, for she is in slavery with her children. But the Jerusalem above is free, and she is our mother. For it is written, "Rejoice, O barren one who does not bear; break forth and cry aloud, you who are not in labor! For the children of the desolate one will be more than those of the one who has a husband." Now you, brothers, like Isaac, are children of promise. But just as at that time he who was born according to the flesh persecuted him who was born according to the Spirit, so also it is now. But

what does the Scripture say? "Cast out the slave woman and her
son, for the son of the slave woman shall not inherit with the son
of the free woman." So, brothers, we are not children of the slave
but of the free woman. (Gal 4:21–31)

In his letter to the Galatians the apostle expresses his concern because
they were reverting to the old covenant practice of circumcision, effectively
choosing bondage after they had been given their freedom in Christ. It was
a position similar to that which occurred when the Israelites were redeemed
from the bondage in Egypt; having been set free they yearned to return to
Egypt. The apostle seeks to show the sheer folly of going back to the law
from which they have been liberated. He reminds them that 'all who rely
on the works of the law are under a curse' (Gal 2:10), and that "if a law
had been given that could give life then righteousness would indeed be by
the law" (Gal 3:21). In spite of already having all in Christ, the Galatians
were in danger of turning "back again to the weak and worthless elementary
principles of the world" (Gal 4:9). Paul wants the Galatians to know that the
law has served its purpose and that to turn back to it is futile and the height
of stupidity. It is tantamount to denying the finished work of Christ. It was
with this in mind that Paul presented the Galatians with an allegory (Gal
4:21–31), in which he compares the old and new covenants.

In his allegory the apostle highlights the duality of the Lord's dealings
with Abraham. Paul shows that Abraham is both the father of the true Israel,
the children of promise who belong to the new covenant, and the heavenly
Jerusalem, and the father of carnal Israel, those who belong to that earthly
Jerusalem that stands condemned by Sinai.

Hagar and Sarah represent these two covenants. Hagar, the "bondwoman," represents that covenant that was established with Abraham and
later augmented at Mount Sinai. This is the covenant that gives birth to
bondage because it is of works not grace. The children of this covenant can
be said to represent present Jerusalem, namely, that which is under law, by
which it stands condemned. The earthly promises applied to this Jerusalem,
but because of its disobedience none would come to fruition. Entrance into
this Jerusalem is by natural birth, what Christ refers to as the first birth that
comes through water (John 3:5). It is to be born of the flesh, for "that which
is born of the flesh is flesh" (John 3:6).

Sarah, on the other hand, is the "free woman" whose child Isaac is born
of promise through the supernatural intervention of God. Sarah and Isaac
represents that Jerusalem that is from above. In this spiritual Jerusalem, because it is established in virtue of Christ's obedience, "all the promises of God
find their Yes in him" (2 Cor 1:20). Entrance into this Jerusalem is by the

miracle of the new birth. This Jerusalem is the kingdom of God, and not only must one be born of water, a natural birth, but born also from above, as Jesus reminded his hearers, "Truly, truly, I say to you, unless one is born of water and the Spirit, he cannot enter the kingdom of God" (John 3:5–6).

The Mosaic covenant was "the ministration of condemnation" (2 Cor 3:9), and the plight of all those who rely on this covenant will be that of Hagar and her son who were cast out, as the Scriptures tell us, "for the son of the bondwoman shall not be heir with the son of the free woman." It will be no good Israel professing to be the physical children of Abraham, boasting, "We are offspring of Abraham and have never been enslaved to anyone" (John 8:33); they are, however, like Hagar the servant, who did "not remain in the house forever"(John 8:35). It is only those in Christ, the true spiritual seed of Abraham, who are the sons of God, and like the Son, they shall remain forever in the house (John 8:35).

Paul's purpose in providing the allegory becomes clear in the first verse of chapter five: "Stand fast, therefore in the liberty by which Christ has made us free, and do not be entangled again with the yoke of bondage." The use of the word "therefore" tells us that he is referring back to what he has just said. He wants the Galatians to draw the obvious conclusion and see just how foolish is their yearning for the Mosaic law. Why when they have been set free would they want to become again entangled? He tells them, "if you accept circumcision, Christ will be of no advantage to you" (Gal 5:2). The rite pertained only to those under the law, and, as Paul says, "I testify again to every man who accepts circumcision that he is obligated to keep the whole law" (Gal 5:3). Why would they wish to be circumcised in their flesh when they are in possession of the very thing this rite typified, namely a circumcised heart? These Galatians had once been slaves, but now they were sons of God. Paul is eager for them to realize that, "if the Son sets you free, you will be free indeed" (John 8:36).

This allegory poses a significant problem for the paedobaptist paradigm. The apostle clearly refers to two separate covenants, namely, that of works associated with Mount Sinai, and the new covenant associated with promise. If there is, as the paedobaptists tell us, but one covenant with various administrations, the problem becomes obvious. In their determination to resist acknowledging a covenant of works from Mount Sinai and a separate promised new covenant of grace, they revert to saying that the apostle was here referring to a misunderstanding amongst the Judaizers. According to O. Palmer Robertson:

> Paul alludes to the understanding of the Mosaic law-covenant
> maintained by the contemporary Judaizers. The new covenant

obviously stands in sharpest contrast with the legalism of the Judaism current in Paul's day. But this misappropriation of the Mosaic law-covenant certainly cannot be equated with God's original intention in giving of the law. The Judaizers of Paul's day day were not correct in their understanding of the Mosaic law. The full force of the apostle's polemic is directed against their misunderstanding.[67]

Again, he tells us:

It must be stressed that the understanding of the Mosaic law which Paul is contending cannot be viewed as the divinely intended purpose of the giving of the law at Sinai. Even though the middle member of this first triad (Hagar-Sinai-Present Jerusalem) is identified as "Mount Sinai" (v.25), it does not represent the true purpose of Sinaitic law-giving.[68]

In one sense these Christians were wrong in that they were allowing certain Jewish believers to superimpose the law onto the Faith. This was because it had already served its purpose through condemnation unto salvation in Christ. They were not here, however, trying to justify themselves through works, but believing somehow the Mosaic law still applied to Christians. They were not wrong in believing in a conditional Mosaic covenant, but wrong in that they did not fully grasp the fact that now Christ had come the conditional covenant had finally come to an end, and that "Christ is the end of the law for righteousness to every one that believeth" (Rom 10:4). O. Palmer Robertson's objection seems to fly in the face of the unambiguous fact that the Old Testament teaches that the old covenant was conditional: Lev 18:5; Num 9:29, Deut 8:1; 28:1; 30:10, Ezek 20:11, 13. This was also Paul's understanding. He was under no illusions about the purpose of the Mosaic law. He does not refer to any false understanding, but rather, he goes straight to Moses, "For all who rely on works of the law are under a curse; for it is written, "Cursed be everyone who does not abide by all things written in the Book of the Law, and do them" (Gal 3:10). The law is not of faith (Gal 3:12), it was never meant to be. The apostle is contrasting the law given through Moses that led to bondage and condemnation and is associated with earthly Jerusalem and the promised new covenant that leads to freedom and righteousness, and is connected with that Jerusalem that is above, the heavenly city. If Paul was dealing here is a wrong application of the law then surely he would have made some reference to this, yet

---

67. Robertson, *Christ of the Covenants*, 60–61.
68. Ibid., 181.

he does not. Whilst Paul is against the way certain Judaizers were trying to transfer elements of the Mosaic law into the new covenant, namely circumcision, and thereby undermining the liberty that is found in Jesus Christ, he, however, nowhere attacks them for any misunderstanding of the Mosaic law they might have held. No, they correctly understood this, they did not, however, quite grasp the fact that it did not apply to the new covenant. One can do no better here than quote Jeffrey Johnson who informs us that Paul:

> Warns against transferring the necessity of circumcision under the old covenant over to the New Testament church. The Judaizers did not have a legalistic view of circumcision, for the Old Testament Scriptures read: "And the uncircumcised man child whose flesh of his foreskin is not circumcised, that soul shall be cut off from his people; he hath broken my covenant" (Gen17:14). This is not a wrong view of circumcision. Circumcision was necessary in the Old Testament to be among God's people. It is simply wrong to take this Old Testament necessity and apply it to the new covenant as the Judaizers were doing.[69]

So then, the fundamental purpose of Paul's allegory is to highlight the fact that there were two covenants, one that was established and the new covenant that was promised. Paul warns the Galatians of the dangers of confusing the two. He wants them to see that the Mosaic covenant has fulfilled its purpose in leading people to Christ and that its conditional aspect has now come to an end.

69. Johnson, *Fatal Flaw*, 91.

11

The Davidic Covenant

JUST A LITTLE NEEDS to be said about God's covenant with David. This covenant is essentially a continuation of the conditional Abrahamic and Mosaic covenants, only now the promise of the coming Messiah is becoming more specific. Earlier promises, as we approach the climax in the Savior's appearance, now become clearer and more focused. We see a narrowing down of the promise, for example, in Genesis 49:10 we read, "The sceptre shall not depart from Judah, nor the ruler's staff from between his feet." Yet the sceptre departed from David's kingdom and the staff did not remain between his feet. However, another would come forth from David's line whose throne *is* for ever and ever, and he holds a sceptre of righteousness; the sceptre of his kingdom (Heb 1:8).

As David lay dying, God promised that:

> When your days are fulfilled to walk with your fathers. I will raise up your offspring after you, one of your own sons, and I will establish his kingdom. He shall build a house for me, and I will establish his throne forever. I will be to him a father, and he shall be to me a son. I will not take my steadfast love from him, as I took it from him who was before you, but I will confirm him in my house and in my kingdom forever, and his throne shall be established forever. (1 Chron. 17:11–15.)

This prophecy is not to be associated with David's immediate son, Solomon, or with any sinful earthly king because, as in the case of Solomon, none could stay faithful to the Lord. Rather, this reference is about the king we read of at the beginning of Matthew's gospel, "The book of the genealogy of Jesus Christ, the son of David, the son of Abraham" (Matt 1:1). This king would be faithful to all the Lord required and his is an everlasting kingdom.

David committed great sin, yet he was forgiven because he, like Abraham, believed the promise, he believed "on him who justifies the ungodly," and his faith was "counted to him as righteousness" (Rom 4:5). David was of the natural seed of Abraham and was already circumcised in his flesh and under the Mosaic covenant. It was later when he came to faith that he was circumcised in his heart, and hence he became a true spiritual son of Abraham in the new covenant. Abraham was saved though he was without circumcision whilst David had been saved after he had been circumcised, hence, Paul could then declare Abraham to be "the father of all who believe without being circumcised, so that righteousness would be counted to them as well, and to make him the father of the circumcised who are not merely circumcised but who also walk in the footsteps of the faith that our father Abraham had before he was circumcised" (Rom 4:11–12). It is not then the physical cutting of the flesh that marks one's entry into God's kingdom, but that blessedness that comes from believing the promise.

God would greatly bless David's kingship, but this was not because David deserved such blessings. As God led the Israelites out of Egypt because of his unmerited favor, so he would bless David's reign. This grace was again a 'type' of the grace available for those who would believe in Christ. As Arthur Pink puts it, "like every similar transaction which occurred during the Old Testament era, it has certain typical aspects which were the figures of higher spiritual blessings."[1] By grace, God blessed Israel, placing them in Canaan, and by grace, God placed the monarchy under David's kingship. However, the continuation of each was dependent on the people's faithfulness to the law of Moses.

Like the covenant with Abraham and Moses, the Davidic covenant was not a covenant of grace, it was essentially a reiteration of the Mosaic covenant. Being conditional it showed the people that there could be no possibility of everlasting blessings if their obedience was the criterion. Although David was only too aware that the blessings he received where the result of God's unmerited favor, he was under no illusions that for these to continue the people would have to be obedient to the law of Moses:

> When David's time to die drew near, he commanded Solomon, his son, saying, "I am about to go the way of all the earth, be strong, and show yourself a man, and keep the charge of the LORD your God, walking in his ways, and keeping his statutes, his commandments, his rules, and his testimonies, as it is written in the law of Moses, that you may prosper in all that you do and wherever you turn. That the LORD may establish his word that he spoke concerning me, saying, "If your sons pay close attention to their way, to walk before me in faithfulness with all

---

1. Pink, *Divine Covenants*, 55.

their heart and with all their soul, you shall not lack a man on the throne of Israel. (1 Kgs 2:1–4).

As with many of the Old Testament prophecies, there is both a literal and a figurative aspect. Concerning David's son Solomon, we know that he built the temple as the prophecy foretold, "Solomon thy son shall build my house and my courts: For I have chosen him to be my son, and I will be his father" (1 Chr 28:6). This Scripture, however, would find its ultimate fulfillment in Christ, "I will be to him a father, and he shall be to me a son" (Heb 1:5). Solomon's sonship was conditional. Yes, he build the temple, but he ended up disobeying the Lord, "Therefore the LORD said to Solomon, 'Since this has been your practice and you have not kept my covenant and my statutes that I have commanded you, I will surely tear the kingdom from you and will give it to your servant" (1 Kgs 11:11). It was not long before Israel had no king upon her throne because of her sinfulness. This was never the case, however, for true Israel, for those who were in the new covenant. Christ is the true son of God, the one who has kept the eternal covenant, and his kingship is truly everlasting because it is based upon his perfect obedience.

From the standpoint of the prophecy then, there was a day coming when all the commands, from that covenant of which the Mosaic law was but a reflection, would be perfectly kept and a king would forever sit upon a throne, one of much greater significance than any earthly throne in this sinful world. Yes, David was a king, ruling over Israel, however, from his loins was to come forth one who was David's king. This was to fulfill the prophecy, "I will raise up your offspring after you, one of your own sons, and I will establish his kingdom" (1 Chron 17:11).

1 2

The New Covenant

THE PROPHETS JEREMIAH AND Ezekiel prophesied what are perhaps the two most quoted passages from the whole of Scripture concerning the new covenant.

> Behold, the days are coming, declares the Lord, when I will make a new covenant with the house of Israel and the house of Judah, not like the covenant that I made with their fathers on the day when I took them by the hand to bring them out of the land of Egypt, my covenant that they broke, though I was their husband, declares the Lord. For this is the covenant that I will make with the house of Israel after those days, declares the Lord: I will put my law within them, and I will write it on their hearts. And I will be their God, and they shall be my people. And no longer shall each one teach his neighbor and each his brother, saying, 'Know the Lord,' for they shall all know me, from the least of them to the greatest, declares the Lord. For I will forgive their iniquity, and I will remember their sin no more. (Jer 31:31ff)

> I will sprinkle clean water on you, and you shall be clean from all your uncleannesses, and from all your idols I will cleanse you. And I will give you a new heart, and a new spirit I will put within you. And I will remove the heart of stone from your flesh and give you a heart of flesh. And I will put my Spirit within you, and cause you to walk in my statutes and be careful to obey my rules. (Ezek 36:25–27)

As we have seen, it is the contention of paedobaptists that the new covenant, whilst being a new administration, left the substance of the one covenant of grace unchanged. Wellum tells us that the "paedobaptists consistently interpret the new covenant in terms of 'renewal', rather than 'replacement', or better 'fulfillment' categories. The new covenant, they maintain is 'new' because it expands the previous era, broadens its extent, yields greater blessings, but the basic continuity is still in place, particularly in regard to the nature of covenant continuity."[1] According to Randy Booth, "The transition from the old covenant is a smooth unfolding of God's redemptive plan—because the two covenants are organically connected—they are essentially one covenant of grace."[2] He goes on to state that, "The new covenant administration of the covenant of grace is new in the sense that it expands the covenant of grace. It broadens its extent and application . . . it leaves intact the fundamental elements of the original covenant of grace."[3] Again, Jonty Rhodes tells us that the word "new" in new covenant does not really mean new, but rather it implies "more the sense of 'renewed' or 'dramatically changed for the better.'"[4]

This, it seems to me, is to deny what the Scriptures teach. They clearly suggest that the new covenant is most definitely not an add-on, or an extension of the old covenant, but, rather, new in regard to its substance. The new covenant , as we have seen, is the only covenant of which Jesus is mediator, and it is clearly the only covenant sealed in his blood. In his last meal before his death, Jesus uttered the words, "This cup that is poured out for you is the new covenant in my blood" (Luke 22:20). Can there really be anywhere else one might go to find salvation? The paedobaptist is left having to explain how any could be saved apart from those blessings that are unique to the new covenant. They have to show how it was possible for Old Testament believers to have been in possession of God's "law in their inward parts," having "a heart of flesh." etc., without belonging to the new covenant. Their only alternative is to maintain that these blessings were not available to those saints. If they argued that the various Old Testament covenants were designed to serve the new covenant and that the various types and shadows were a way of communicating the new covenant one would not have a problem, this, however, is not something they acknowledge. Of course, paedobaptists would have us believe that Old Testament believers were beneficiaries of the same blessings because they looked forward to the promise's fulfillment from the perspective of another covenantal administration of the so-called covenant of grace, not specifically the new covenant. They are not prepared to say that Old Testament believers were saved because they were

---

1. Wellum, "Relationship between the Covenants," 138.

2. Booth, *Children of Promise*, 195–96.

3. Ibid., 65.

4. Rhodes, *Covenants Made Simple*, 95–96.

participants in the new covenant on account of their having believed the promise.

The Reformed Baptist paradigm, as alluded to earlier, believes entrance into the new covenant to be a reality before Christ's completed work. The new covenant, in regard to its blessings, was before the old covenant. After the making of the old covenant, the old ran parallel to the promise of the new covenant. The conditional and the unconditional covenants co-existed, they were juxtaposed. The Old Testament saint was externally required to follow the Sinaitic requirements because as a Jew he came under its remit, however, at the same time he was also in receipt of new covenant blessings procured in the future work of Christ. So we see the letter that kills and the Spirit that gives life (2 Cor 3:6).

Some paedobaptists, for example, R. L. Pratt, in a determined attempt to escape the inevitable conclusion that these blessings apply only to the new covenant, attempts to locate them at the end of time, when there will be the consummation of all things.

> We can have confidence that after Christ returns in glory, every-one in the new creation will have the law of God written upon their hearts . . . In this sense, we expect Jeremiah's prophecy to find complete fulfillment when Christ returns At the pres-ent time, however, this expectation is only partially fulfilled . . . Until the consummation, the new covenant will continue to be a mixture of true believers and sanctified unbelievers.[5]

He maintains that while we presently see is a mixed church, there is nevertheless a day approaching when this will no longer be the case and all those in the new covenant will know the Lord. It's a case of "now, but not yet" Pratt tells us that, "We must approach Jeremiah 31:31–34 as we approach all prophecies regarding the restoration after exile: with the understanding that the restoration of the kingdom and the renewal of the covenant will not be complete until Jesus returns."[6]

The writer to the Hebrews, however, did not see the fulfillment of the new covenant laying somewhere in the future (Heb 8:7–13). The old covenant had passed, "it has been made obsolete because of the new covenant" (v.13). It, therefore, stands to reason that the blessings associated with the new cov-enant were now fully made manifest. Yes, it is correct to say that the believer will not be fully conformed to the image of Christ until the consummation, it

---

5. Pratt, "Infant Baptism," 171.

6. Ibid., 169.

is, however, most certainly wrong to think that the blessings have not always been applicable to the people of God.

Jeremiah's prophecy unambiguously demonstrates that the new covenant will not be like the old covenant that the people broke (Jer 31:32). In the third chapter of his second letter to the church at Corinth, the apostle speaks of the new covenant as being the antithesis of the old. The old was concerned with things of the flesh, the new covenant is by the Holy Spirit (v.3,6,8). The old was temporary in nature, as it was designed to be, whereas the new covenant is permanent (vv.3,7). The old could only condemn, being a "ministry of death," the new covenant, on the other hand, brings salvation v.7). The old was external, "carved in letters on stone" whereas the new covenant is written upon the heart of flesh (vv.2,3,7) The differences between these two covenants is well summed up in the words of Leonard Verduin:

> The two covenants are radically different, and have to be contrasted by us because they are contrasted in Scripture. The one, the Mosaic covenant, was the covenant of the flesh, outward, a shadow, ineffective, condemning, killing, a covenant of death, a temporary covenant which was fulfilled by Christ and abolished because it was weak and useless. The other covenant, the new covenant, is superior in that it is spiritual, of the Spirit, inward, the reality, effective, it is saving and permanent.[7]

When the old covenant was read, as the apostle reminds us, the people were in darkness with a veil covering their hearts (2 Cor 3:15), and it is only in the new covenant in Christ that this veil is taken away, "when one turns to the Lord the veil is removed" (v.15). One could ask: If the veil is only removed by virtue of the new covenant that, according to paedobaptists, did not become operative until after Christ's work, did not Old Testament saints still have the veil over their hearts? Did they not still have hearts that were hardened? (2 Cor 3:14) When Paul speaks of the veil he is not here referring to the idea that Old Testament believers saw the promise, as it were from a distance, as if through a veil that is only taken away, giving them, as it were, a unobscured view, only when the promise comes to fruition in Christ. No, the apostle is speaking, rather, about believers and unbelievers. The veil represented the blindness of the unbeliever, a blindness that prevented him from seeing what lay behind the old covenant types and shadows. It is only by exercising faith in the Lord that the veil that blinds is removed. In other words, when they apprehended the spiritual realities that lay behind the old covenant paraphernalia. We see also that Paul contrasts the new with the old, and associates the new covenant with those "who turn to the Lord."

7. Verduin, *Reformers and Their Stepchildren*, 210.

This is nothing less than the prerequisite for being in the new covenant, and it indicates that the old covenant was not of grace; that those who remained in the old covenant stood outside of Christ, for clearly, they had not turned unto him. In the same vein, the apostle alludes to the old covenant as the letter that kills and the new covenant in terms of the Spirit that gives life (2 Cor 3:6). He is not here speaking of one covenant of grace, as the paedobaptists would have us believe. Such a view serves to make nonsense of Paul's argument. In 2 Corinthians 3, Paul is not comparing like with like, but rather contrasting two entirely different covenants, one conditional the other unconditional.

The blessings that Jeremiah and Ezekiel refer to clearly relate to the new covenant. As said above, paedobaptists, by applying the new covenant to a particular time frame, one that does not commence until post-Christ's resurrection must lead to the logical conclusion that God's people prior to that time stood outside new covenant blessings. This being the case these believers were then without that internal religion of the heart spoken of by the above prophets. The only way paedobaptists might circumvent this is to maintain that somehow these blessings were available outside of the new covenant. This is exactly what they appear to do in their insistence that the new is not really new, but rather just another installment of what was there before.

The Reformed Baptist position is not presented with this illogicality;we have no hesitation in applying new covenant blessings to Old Testament believers because they, like us were by faith in the promise, participants of the new covenant. As I have said previously, there has never been a believer in all of history who has not possessed a heart of flesh, a heart upon which the laws of God have been written on account of their being in the new covenant.

What we see in Rhodes, Booth, Hodge, Murray and other paedobaptists is essentially biblical eisegesis. This is, however, quite reasonable considering they imbibed what is the predominant covenantal understanding in Reformed circles. They, therefore, superimpose their preconceived ideas, derived from the Reformers and the Westminster Confession, onto Scripture in an attempt to shore up the case for infant baptism.

It is only those in the new covenant who can be said to have the Spirit of God within them, by which he is causing them to walk in his statutes and obey his rules (Exod 36:27). This is why the Psalmist could glory in the law of God, "Oh how I love your law! It is my meditation all the day" (Psalm 119:97). The Psalmist, like all within spiritual Israel, shared in the new covenant. This internal restoration of God's law is at the heart is our sanctification, and applied as much to Abraham as it did to the apostle Paul. The new covenant is everything the old was not, concerning this glorious new covenant in Christ one can do no better than quote the words of Robert Purnell:

> The new covenant is full of sure mercies and sweet promises that God will give a new heart, a heart to know him, and that he can write his law within us, put his fear into us, cause us to walk in his statutes, forgive us our iniquities, cleanse us from our filthiness, be our God and make us his people . . . It is a free covenant, a full and complete covenant, a sure and firm covenant, and everlasting covenant. . . . To close up all as to the nature of this covenant, let me tell you the main substance in these words: 'I will be their God and they shall be my people', but sprinkling with clean water, taking away the stony heart, and giving a heart of flesh, all these are nothing but the fruits of the covenant. So Christ is given for a covenant for his people; that is the new covenant takes its being from Christ to us. All mankind was in Adam, as all mankind was in Adam, in the loins of Adam, so Christ is the new covenant, and all the covenant is as it were in the loins of Christ, and springs to us out of him. In this sense he is the covenant undertaker, he is the covenant manager, he is the covenant dispenser. He does everything in the covenant . . . Hence Christ is also the mediator of the covenant . . . Christ is the covenant.[8]

True covenantal unity is found not in the paedobaptist attempt to reconcile the old and new covenants, but, rather, in the application new covenant to all believers. Salvation in both Testaments has only ever been by means of the new covenant, and it applies to one people, one church, members of one kingdom. In the age preceding the arrival of Christ, it was only the spiritual seed of Abraham for whom the promises found their fulfillment. God was their God and they were his people. The majority of the people knew only the old covenant, the "ministration of death" with its impossible conditions. No-one, however, can be in the new covenant without knowing the Lord. When the Lord said through Jeremiah that "they all shall know me," it needs to be emphasized that 'all' meant all without exception.

Paedobaptists appear to confound the old and new covenants, for example, Douglas Wilson draws a typically false inference when he says, "Some Old Covenant members were regenerate some were not. Some New Covenant members are regenerate, some are not."[9] In truth, however, all under the old covenant, if they are not in the new covenant, were unregenerate, while no new covenant members are unregenerate. None can be in the new

---

8. Purnell, *Little Cabinet*, 20–25.
9. Wilson, *To A Thousand Generations*, 34.

covenant without being born from above by the Spirit of God. There is no allowance in what Jeremiah and Ezekiel say for anything less.

The Lord told Jeremiah, "I will make with them an everlasting covenant, that I will not turn away from doing good to them. And I will put the fear of me in their hearts, that they may not turn from me" (Jere 32:40). Wilson and others would have us believe that somehow these words don't quite mean what they say. God unambiguously tells us that he will not turn away from those in this covenant. Now we know that in the old covenant God turned his face away from the people because of their disobedience. In the new covenant, not only will the Lord never turn his face away from his people, but God promises his people that they will never turn their face away from him. Why will this be the case? Because God will put his fear into their hearts. In the light of this, it is difficult to comprehend how one can believe that in this "everlasting covenant" there will be those who are unregenerate. This is impossible because God keeps his promises. Paedobaptists tell us that the child of believing parent(s) are *bonafide* members of the new covenant, yet, at a later date, the child may well choose to opt out of the covenant, becoming a covenant-breaker. So when God said he would not turn his face away he didn't quite mean it, and when he said he would put his fear into the hearts of those in the covenant so they would not forsake the Lord, again, he didn't quite mean "all." It appears that paedobaptist/Presbyerian thinking on this matter flies in the face of what the plain teaching of Scripture tells us.

Wilson, like other paedobaptists, is again failing to compare like with like. In Old Testament times the only covenant infants belonged to was earthly and temporal, unless, of course, they were born again. Infants of believing parents today are blessed or sanctified because they are brought up hearing the gospel in its fullness. It is the duty of the church to baptize, not infants, but only those who confess with their mouth that Jesus is Lord, ultimately, however, whether the person truly believes in his heart is something only the Lord can know. The old covenant applied to a stiff-necked people, who, whilst blessed in the revelation given to them, were ungrateful and prone to scorn the things of God. The new covenant is spiritual and eternal, consisting of a people who have become a new humanity in Christ. The problem for paedobaptists is that they have to allow unregenerate members to be in the new covenant to justify the fact that many baptized infants end up falling away. The Reformed Baptist position insists that the circumcised

Israelite was as much outside the covenant of grace as his pagan neighbor. The same can be said about the children of believers. Only this understanding avoids the theological pitfalls associated with paedobaptism and what can only be called the slippery slope to justification by works that we see in the Federal Vision.

The charge often leveled against us is that we make the new covenant less generous than the old covenant where infants are concerned. Murray asks the question, "Is there less efficacy, as far as infants are concerned, in the new covenant than there was in the old?"[10] It is said that we make infants, 'in the new dispensation more *inhabile* to the grace of God."[11] This inference is again based on the assumption that the infant under the old covenant was in the covenant of grace. Beeke and Lanning, following this line, commented, "But no matter how baptism is presented, one question the Baptists can never answer is this: How could a converted Jew regard the new covenant as a better covenant, if now his children were to be excluded from God's dealings with his people?"[12]

They equate the new covenant with the New Testament and appear to be of the understanding that the Baptist position implies that with its arrival any blessings the infant might have possessed will be lost. This is far from being the case. The children of believers today are far from being disadvantaged in comparison to their old Testament counterparts, indeed, the truth is quite the opposite. In the New Testament children have an exposure to the gospel in a manner that was not available under the old covenant. Under the old covenant children would have only viewed the promise from afar off, in types and shadows, however, now, in the New Testament, Christ crucified is preached in the full light of day. They can now be brought up receiving instruction in the Word with far greater clarity than was previously available. There is no longer the need for strict controls touching all parts of a person's world. Far from any blessings being lost, the children of believers now have something beyond comparison in an unfettered exposure to the full gospel message. The New Testament Jewish Christian who correctly understands the old covenant will rejoice in the fact that his children are no longer under a conditional type of the covenant of works. That the old covenant has served its purpose, with its types and shadows having given way to the reality in Christ.

Baptists are sometimes charged with failing to address Jeremiah 32:39, where we read: "I will give them one heart, and one way, that they may

---

10. Murray, *Christian Baptism*, 49.

11. Ibid., 49.

12. Beeke and Ray, "Unto You and to Your Children, 58.

fear me forever, *for the good of them and of their children.*" (Italics added) We are told that this text clearly shows that children of believers are in the covenant of grace. If this is indeed the case, then what would we expect to see. First, we would expect the child to fear the Lord, second, we would expect the Lord to never turn from the child (v.40), and, third, because the LORD will put his fear in the child's heart, we would expect the child to never turn from the Lord (v.40). Now we all know that this is not what happens. The fact is, many children of believers, who have been baptized, and told that they are in the covenant, end up turning away from the Lord. There are no 'ifs' or 'buts' in what Jeremiah tells us, which clearly indicates that the paedobaptist interpretation is wrong. It is far more likely that all that is meant by these verses is that the children of believers will have all the benefits alluded to above in their greater exposure to the means of grace. In the same way that Israel of old had many privileges (Rom.9:4). The message to the infant, however, is the same, repent and believe. Some might ask: What if the child dies in infancy? It really makes no difference, as Jewett tells us, "only a sacramentalist would question the child's safety in the event of death. If a child is brought up with Christian instruction until he is of an age to make a profession of faith, how can he be disadvantaged from his baptized counterpart?"[13] It is God who regenerates and he can regenerate the soul of the infant in exactly the same way as he regenerates the adult. Infant baptism makes not one jot of difference.

What Calvin says about the Anabaptists is akin to the criticisms that are leveled against Reformed Baptists. He employs the most extreme adjectives, perhaps because his argument is weak:

> They [by this he means the Anabaptists] depict the Jews to us as so carnal that they are more like beasts than men. A covenant with them would not go beyond the temporal life, and the promises given to them would rest in the present and physical benefits. If this doctrine should obtain, what would remain save that the Jewish nation was satiated for a time with God's benefits (as man fatten a herd of swine in a sty), only to perish in eternal destruction? For when we mention circumcision and the promises attached to it, they at once reply that circumcision was a sign and its promises were carnal.[14]

This is clearly a false depiction of our position, suggesting that we pay no heed to the spiritual in the Old Testament. According to Randy Booth, "the Old Testament continually drives home the importance of heartfelt

---

13. Jewett, *Infant Baptism*, 215.
14. Calvin, *Institutes*, IV, XVI, 11.

devotion to God and the necessity of the inward and individual aspects of redemption."[15] He said this as if to imply that the Reformed Baptist position somehow denies this "heartfelt devotion" to those who lived prior to Christ's coming. The truth is we could not agree more. Indeed, we would go so far as to say that the entire purpose of the Old Testament is to point people to the promise of Christ. The old covenant, as we have seen, made people aware of their sinful position and held up the promise of salvation in Christ, it did not, however, like the new covenant, have an efficacy unto salvation. One feels that the paedobaptists in their insistence that the old and new covenants are simply administrations of the one covenant of grace are trying to put a square peg into a round hole or pour new wine into old wineskins. They superimpose their assumptions of the new covenant, in regard to its being the last administration of the covenant of grace, onto the Baptist paradigm and then charge us with denying vital blessings to Old Testament believers.

Booth maintains that, "the new covenant, like the older covenants, addresses husbands, wives, children, slaves, households, the visible and local church, the state, crime, politics, economies, social ethics, labor, education, the nations, and even our eating and drinking."[16] He tells us that "the baptistic view of both history and the future is not supported by the Bible. Both the old and new covenants show concern for the internal and external aspects of people."[17] This is a classic straw-man argument, based on a complete misunderstanding of what we believe. One will look in vain in the New Testament to find any direct references to many of the things mentioned in Booth's list. What we find in the old covenant is essentially a theocracy on earth. Much of what Booth refers to in his somewhat exhaustive list, makes reference to the type and not the substance. Regarding "Crime, politics, economics" etc., these were implemented by God to maintain the security of the earthly Israel until the Messiah appeared. They were part and parcel of a theocracy that is no longer applicable. In the new covenant, we do not have the detailed instructions of the Mosaic economy. Booth might have simply said that the new covenant is concerned with both the internal and external aspects of the person. Internally, the believer will have a heart of flesh, externally, he will behave according to this new heart. Essentially, the new covenant concerns our standing before God, and our conformity to Jesus Christ, with our citizenship being in heaven, not upon a fallen earth. As far as society goes, the new covenant is about the spreading of the gospel and

15. Booth, *Children of the Promise,* 75.

16. Ibid., 81.

17. Ibid., 81.

extending the kingdom of God. Christian witness might serve to influence others and restrain sin in society, but this is as far as it goes. On this earth, the Christian knows that he is but a pilgrim, that he is in the world but not of it. In regard to Booth's comments, we have already seen the error made by the magisterial Reformers as they mixed secular politics with the things of the church. Moreover, to imply that the 'baptistic' position does not show concern for both the internal and external aspects of the person is simply untrue. We live in the new covenant, as the true people of God have always done. We acknowledge a Christ who is concerned with the whole person. And, as already said, we do not set our mind on the things of this world, but we recognize that "our citizenship is in heaven, and from it we await a Savior, the Lord Jesus Christ" (Phil 3:20).

Walter Chantry, a Reformed Baptist, in his book, *God's Righteous Kingdom*, again appears to be somewhat confused about the difference between the old and new covenant:

> Jeremiah had stressed this distinction between the covenants. The new covenant would be unlike the old covenant in that the Lord said, "I will put my law in their inward parts, and write it in their hearts" (31:33). Though his contrasts are not absolute, they are striking. But of course there was inward spiritual reality in the old. But in the Old Testament all that is spiritual is identified with a ponderous outward nation. In the New Testament all that is outward and visible is identified with a spiritual nation. God's kingdom has come with an inwardness and therefore an invisibility.[18]

The mistake he makes is to associate the carnal nation with the true spiritual Israel, to maintain that there were spiritual realities arising from out of the old covenant. He tells us "there was inward reality in the old" by which he means the old covenant. This, however, was not the case. Any "inward reality" only resulted from the Israelite being in the new covenant, even if outwardly he might at the same time have found himself under the rigmarole of the Mosaic covenant. In the Old Testament the true Israel, consisted only of those who like Abraham, embraced the promise, looked not to an earthly country, but a heavenly one (Heb 11:16). It is, therefore, most unlikely that they associated spiritual blessings with "a ponderous outward nation." Again, Chantry appears not to have drawn the correct conclusion in light of the fact that "not all who are descended from Israel belong to Israel" (Rom 9:6), and that only the 'children of the promise are counted as the seed'(Rom 9:8). These constitute the "remnant chosen by grace" (Rom

18. Chantry, *God's Righteous Kingdom*, 52.

11:5). Chantry also fails to acknowledge the radical nature of new covenant blessings, and, that its blessings were not only for New Testament believers but for every member of the church of God from the very first promise in Genesis.

Paedobaptist, Geoffrey Neill, in arguing the case for infant baptism, again appears to misunderstand the Baptist position. He tells us that "God's law, the transcript of his holiness, and his expectations for his people, was already on the hearts of his people, and so is not new in the new covenant."[19] We fully agree with him in the first part of this. The problem is that he assumes that one can become a recipient of such blessings while being outside of the new covenant. If, however, these blessing did not arise as a consequence of being in the new covenant, then they were certainly not the result of being in the old covenant. Why he thinks some Reformed Baptists limit the blessings of the new covenant to after the covenant's formal establishment in the blood of Christ is somewhat puzzling. He then quotes from Leon Morris and Philip Hughes, showing that he has completely misunderstood what they are saying. Morris said about the new covenant:

> The first point is that the new covenant is inward and dynamic: it is written on the hearts and minds of the people. A defect in the old had been its outwardness, It has divinely given laws, indeed; but it was written on tablets of stone (Ex.32:15–16). The people had not been able to live up to what they knew was the word of God. It remained external.[20]

Neill then goes on to quote Philip Hughes, stating that he "is similarly incorrect."[21]

> This new covenant, not like the covenant made with the people through Moses, would be of grace, not of works; radical, not external; everlasting, not temporary; meeting man's deepest need and transforming his whole being, because from the beginning to the end it would be the work, not of man, but of God himself. In other words, the law which formally was external and accusing now becomes internal, an element of the redeemed nature, and a delight to fulfil.[22]

---

19. Neill, "Newness of the New Covenant," 131.
20. Morris, "Hebrews," 78.
21. Neill, "Newness of the New Covenant," 134.
22. Hughes, "Hebrews," 300.

Neill maintains that for the above writers "the internal operations of divine grace were not present for the old covenant saint."[23] He clearly fails to appreciate that the new covenant was before and contiguous with the old covenant throughout the Old Testament period.

He is essentially 'missing the wood for the trees.' It is the same straw-man argument we saw earlier. A few lines later he adds: "The Bible militates against such ideas. Morris and Hughes assert that the law was not internal until the new covenant."[24] It is apparent that by new covenant he is referring to something that, again, did not become operative until after Christ's completed work. From this he then reaches the erroneous conclusion that the internal elements of the new covenant were foreign to those who lived before the first advent. No Baptist would deny these internal blessings to Old Testament believers, because, as I keep saying, they were, by believing the promise, in the new covenant.

I was somewhat surprised to learn that a similar position is taken by Gentry and Wellum in their mighty tome, *Kingdom through Covenant*. They again assume the new covenant and its blessings to be, from the Old Testament believer's position, something futuristic. They imply that those characteristics essential for salvation, namely, the full forgiveness of sins and "the law written upon the heart" will become a reality only after the formal ratification of the new covenant in the death of Christ.

> Under the new covenant all will know the Lord, not in a mediate sense but in an immediate fashion, and all will have the law written upon their hearts and will experience the full forgiveness of sins. In fact, it is these last two aspects of the new covenant which highlight the incredible change that is anticipated and that is now a reality in the church.[25]

Gentry and Wellum locate their particular take on the relationship between the old and new covenants within the context of "new covenant theology."[26] We will see later when examining the believer's union with Christ that new covenant theology draws what I would see as a unscriptural dichotomy between Old and New Testament saints. While they do not deny true believers in the Old Testament to have been regenerate, they do appear to reserve the above blessings to, from the perspective of the Old Testament believer, a futuristic age. An age when the entire new covenant community will participate in the blessings. The problem with this is the failure to rec-

23. Ibid., 134.
24. Ibid., 135.
25. Gentry and Wellum, *Kingdom through Covenant*, 649.
26. Ibid., 24.

ognize that none can be saved and not be "in Christ" and none can be "in Christ" and not be in receipt of these new covenant blessings.

We are told that:

> In the Old Testament, particularly under the old covenant, the forgiveness of sins is normally granted through the sacrificial system, however, the Old Testament believer, if spiritually perceptive, knew that this was not enough, as evidenced in the repetitive nature of the system. But we are told that in the new covenant, sin will be remembered no more (Jer 31:34) . . . In the context of verse 34, for God "not to remember means that no action will be taken in the new age against sin. In the end, to be under the terms of this covenant entails that one experience a full and complete forgiveness of sin. Ultimately, when other texts are considered, Jeremiah's anticipates a perfect unfettered fellowship of God's people with the Lord, a harmony restored between creation and God—where the dwelling of God is with men, and they will be his people and he will be their God.[27]

It is true to say that following the formal ratification of the new covenant believers were enabled to subjectively enter into what was already true of them positionally, however, all the blessings referred to above, far from being anticipated, were already theirs. No true believer was forgiven through the many animal sacrifices. These, rather, served the nation in terms of external forgiveness and their possession of the land etc. Spiritual Israel, however, was forgiven, was solely on account of the future work of Christ at Calvary. Jeremiah was not speaking to a people (spiritual Israel) for whom the blessings were something foreign, something that lay in the remote future, but, rather, of the formal establishment or consummation of the covenant whose blessings true believers were already in possession of. When Abraham had Christ's righteousness credited to him he was in receipt of "full and complete forgiveness" because he was in Christ, having been made to share in his legacy.

Herman Witsius, one of the fathers of Federal Theology, who whilst acknowledging Old Testament believers to be in receipt of these internal blessings, also believed this was the result of something other than the new covenant:

> In the same base manner, they [Witsius designates in a general way those who saw the discontinuity between the Old and New Covenants] make the writing on the heart, a blessing peculiar to the New Testament: because Heb. Viii. 10. it is said from Jer

---

27. Ibid., 650.

XXXi. 34. "for this is the covenant that I will make with the
house of Israel after those days, saith the Lord; I will put my
laws into their minds and write them in their hearts:" [. . .]
If these words be taken as they lie, it follows, that the ancient
believers, who lived before the times of the New Testament, did
not receive the law of God, nor delight in it but forgot it. But that
these things are most eminently false, appears from the example
of David alone: who . . . professes, that he received the law when
he says, Psal CXIX. "Thy word have I hid in my heart:" and adds
ver.16. I will delight myself in they statutes . . . How then is this a
blessing peculiar to the New Testament, in which David claims
an interest in.[28]

The problem is the same, he is again left having to explain how the
saints living in the Old Testament age could be partakers of the blessings
that Jeremiah and Ezekiel specifically associate with the new covenant.
From the paedobaptist perspective, it appears that there is no way of over-
coming this problem unless they follow the unscriptural path of making
these blessings applicable to those outside of the new covenant. This is
exactly what Witsius does by locating the source of the blessings received
in the covenant of grace rather than specifically in the new covenant.

Were joined to God by the covenant of grace which he had sol-
emnly renewed with Abraham. And from that covenant they
had every thing that the writing of the law on the heart comprises, and God himself for their God, that is, the fountain of
salvation."[29]

Salvation was then available to Old Testament believers because the
Abrahamic covenant was of grace. This leaves one asking why Jeremiah and
Ezekiel specifically applied the blessings to the new covenant. One should
carefully consider the words of John Owen, "I shall take it here for granted,
that no man was ever saved but by virtue of the new covenant and the mediation of Christ therein."[30]

This suggests something of the difficulty paedobaptists have in trying
to make their position fit with with the Scriptures. They end up doing a kind
of theological gymnastics in order to make the old covenant something
other than a ministry that can only condemn.

In applying these internal blessings to Old Testament saints it is important to remember that Christ's legacy and its administration is very

28. Witsius, *Economy of the Covenants Between God and Man*, 335.

29. Ibid., 336.

30. Owen, *Works*, 6, 70.

different from that one associates with a this-worldly testator. When men write a will it is necessary for the person to die before the will takes place, this is, however, not the case in regard to Christ. John Gill provides a vivid illustration that aptly applies to the way in which the saints of old enjoyed the blessings procured by Christ's future redemptive work:

> with respect to the wills of men, the legacies are not payable, nor estates bequeathed enjoyed, until the testator dies; but such is not only the certainty of Christ's death, and which with God was ever as if it was, but such is the virtue and efficacy of it, that it reaches backward to the beginning of the world . . . wherefore Old Testament saints not only received the promise of eternal inheritance, but enjoyed it before the death of Christ, though in virtue of it, for they are said to inherit the promises, that in the things promised, Heb. 9:15, and 7:12; but the death of Christ was necessary to confirm the covenant or testament, that the legatees might appear to have the legal right to that which was bequeathed them.[31]

The 1689 Baptist Confession states that "although the price of redemption was not actually paid by Christ until after His incarnation, yet the virtue, efficacy *[the certain effect or result]*, and benefit arising from His payment were communicated to the elect in all ages from the beginning of the world."[32] The line could have ended with the words, "by the new covenant." They who, like Abraham, looked forward to the promise received the inheritance even before the death of the testator. The promise was the mode of revelation, by believing the promise those living prior to Christ were granted access and made to share in the testator's legacy in the same way as believers today who look back to the testator's completed work. Pascal Denault states that "The Covenant of Grace was revealed progressively under the Old Covenant. The arrival of the New Covenant marks the full revelation of the Covenant of Grace which passes from the state of promise to the state of a covenant accomplished and sealed in the blood."[33] I would go further than this, maintaining that Old Testament believers, by believing in the promise were actually in the new covenant, although, as we will see, they were like children under age, being somewhat ignorant of exactly what this entailed. Having spoken with Denault, this is exactly what he too believes.

---

31. Gill, *Body of Divinity*, 1, 345.
32. *The Baptist Confession of Faith* 1689, 8:6.
33. Denault,. *Distinctiveness of Baptist Covenant Theology*, 77.

As previously mentioned, the Old Testament believer was in the somewhat peculiar position of finding himself under two covenants. He was under the Mosaic covenant and as such had to abide by its demands as far as was possible, he was, however, also a member of the new covenant. To quote Coxe:

> Despite their interest in the promise by faith, they were not freed from the yoke and discipline of Moses' law until Christ came. They were indeed children of Abraham on a spiritual account. By the grace of a free promise which the law could not disannul they were relieved from its rigor as to their spiritual and eternal state. But being children under age, the pedagogy they were under differed nothing from that of servants; nor could they be discharged of this school master before Christ came.[34]

It is similar to what believers experience in modern society, where, even though they are citizens of heaven, they are still expected to abide by the laws of the land. "The position of Old Testament believers was anomalous. They were in the new covenant and therefore delighted in God's law (Psa 119) but at the same time they were under its burden in the old covenant."[35]

34. Coxe, "Discourse of the Covenants," 110

35. Gay, *New Covenant Articles*, 1, 24.

The Believer's Union with Christ

AT THE VERY HEART of covenant theology is the believer's union with Christ. The covenant's purpose was that God might deliver his people from their plight in the first Adam into the glorious light of the everlasting covenant in Christ. It is because Christ has honored all of the covenantal obligations that, in him, God's church is being transformed into his image, in order "that he might present the church to himself in splendor, without spot or wrinkle or any such thing, that she might be holy and without blemish" (Eph 5:27).

Union with Christ is unquestionably the greatest and most glorious blessing the believer will ever receive because it is on account of this that all other blessings are made possible. As Owen reminds us, it is "the cause of all other graces that we are made partakers of; they are all communicated unto us by virtue of our union with Christ."[1] Without this union Christ remains alien to us, as John Calvin stated, "as long as Christ remains outside of us, and we are separated from him, all that he has suffered and done for the salvation of the human race remains useless and of no value to us."[2] Such is the glorious nature of this vital union with Christ that "our grace of union with Christ, our participation of him and his glorious nature, is our greatest exaltation, the greatest and most glorious grace we can be made partakers of in this world . . . This is honour and glory unparalleled."[3]

Understanding something of the nature and consequences of this mystical and indessoluble union is essential for the believer's assurance of salvation, and in providing him with the motivation for Christian living. As Lloyd-Jones put it, "There is nothing, in the whole range and realm of doctrine which if properly grasped and understood, gives greater assurance,

1. Owen, *Works*, 6, 150.
2. Calvin, *Institutes*, III, I, I.
3. Owen, *Works*, 6, 149.

greater comfort, and greater hope than this doctrine of our union with Christ."[4]

In the economy of redemption, before the world was, God the Father chose us in Christ (Eph 1:3). But it was at a particular moment in time that God applied salvation to us by calling us into fellowship with Christ (1 Cor 1:9). The apostle tells us we are in Christ, "who became to us wisdom from God, righteousness and sanctification and redemption" (1 Cor 1:30). Is it any wonder that Paul kept using the phrase 'in Christ'. He knew that everything is found in, and flows out of this vital spiritual union by which we have become one flesh with Christ. As the child in its mother's womb is joined to the mother by the umbilical cord, through which all that is necessary for life is provided, so the Christian is united to Christ by the Holy Spirit, the one who takes the things of Christ and applies them to him (John 16:14).

Christians can only begin to appreciate the liberty that is theirs in Christ when they begin to appreciate the nature of this union. It is only by understanding this teaching and applying it to ourselves in faith that we can count ourselves dead to sin and alive unto God in Christ (Rom 6:11); that we have died to the law through the body of Christ, and now we belong to God (Rom 7:4). The Christian is one who has been quite literally resurrected, made spiritually alive through regeneration into an unbreakable union with Christ. The Christian can say that he has been crucified with Christ. He no longer lives but Christ lives in him (Gal 2:20). This union is what gives Christians the assurance of the final resurrection in which Christ will renew their mortal bodies, their bodies of sin, so that they will be like his glorified body. The entire salvific enterprise is dependent on our union with him, as Owen reminds us, "our resurrection also depends on this union,-I mean, a blessed resurrection in joy unto light and life eternal; for this resurrection is nothing but the entire gathering up together of the whole body of Christ unto himself, whereof he gave us a pledge, example, and assurance in his own person."[5]

The purpose of Romans 6 is to inform believers of what they have become in Christ. Paul was responding to a question he anticipated people asking because of his description of grace in chapters three to five, "Now the law came in to increase the trespass, but where sin increased, grace abounded all the more" (5:20). They were reaching the erroneous conclusion that if grace abounds even more when the law exposes sin, one should continue to sin so that grace may abound even more. They were incapable of seeing that

---

4. Lloyd-Jones, *Romans*, 6, 30.

5. Owen, *Works*, 6, 151,

the Christian has entered into a new relationship with God, and has been given a nature that seeks not to sin but to please him.

Paul seeks to show that living in sin is impossible because the believer is spiritually, quite literally, dead to sin (Rom 6:2). It would not make sense for him to live any longer in that realm from which he has been removed by the Spirit of God. The believer was once in Adam (Rom 5:12–18), and he lived according to his sinful nature. He is now, however, in Christ, having a new spiritual nature, having become a new creation, a new humanity. His allegiances have changed. Where he once served sin he now serves Christ. Paul describes how the believer has become dead to sin and alive to Christ (Rom 6:3–10). He wants believers to know this so that they can apply it to themselves and live unto God (Rom 6:11). In the words of John Murray, believers need to realize that, "When a person dies he is no longer active in the sphere or realm to which he had died. His connection with that realm has been dissolved; he has no further communications with those who still live in that realm." [6] The old world has become an alien place for the Christian because he is aware that he is now a citizen of heaven (Phil 3:20).

Understanding this and applying it to ourselves is at the heart of our sanctification. It is the great motivator. We are to live in the realization of what we have become in Christ, seeking those things that are above, things that correspond to our new nature and position at the right hand of God in Christ (Col 3:2–4). The knowledge of our union serves to encourage believers to yield themselves to God "as those who have been brought from death to life," and employ their "members to God as instruments for righteousness" (Rom 6:13). We are to put on the new man and learn to jettison, to cast off the ways that were associated with the man we used to be. This is why Paul can tell believers to put off the old self and put on the new. In other words, they are to to live according to what they have become, and not according to what they used to be (Col 3:7–10).

The apostle employs the word 'baptism' (Rom 6:3–4) to refer to the work of the Spirit whereby we partake of Christ. It is important to remember that the text has nothing to do with the rite of baptism. The word is used here to denote the placement of the believer into Christ so that he can now fully identify with him. As a branch can be taken and engrafted into another tree to partake of its life-giving sap, so the Christian has been engrafted into Christ.

This is sometimes referred to as definitive sanctification. It is that once and for all separation of the believer from what he was in the first Adam, into what he has become in his union with Christ, the second Adam. To quote Lloyd-Jones, "we are saved by this tremendous action of God through the

6. Murray, *Collected Writings*, 2, 279.

Spirit, who takes us out of Adam, incorporates us, implants us, baptizes us into Christ. That is the thing that saves us, and it happens to all."[7] It is because we have been made spiritually alive and translated from the realm of sin, and placed into the realm of Christ "that we might understand the gifts bestowed on us by God" (1 Cor 2:12). The astounding fact is that God views us as he views Christ because we are in him, and now we have a relationship with him as one who has kept all of the covenantal requirements because Christ has kept them on our behalf. As Owen reminds us: "Because being in him, and members of him, we are accounted to have done, in him and with him, whatsoever he hath done for us: We are 'dead with him,' Romans 6:8; 'buried with him,' verse 4; 'risen with him,' Colossians 3:1."[8] The believer possesses all, and can say of himself, to quote Lloyd-Jones, "I am in Christ that I am in His death, in His resurrection, in His life, in everything that is His."[9]

In his letter to the Colossians, as in his letter to the Romans, Paul again tells the believers that they "having been buried with him in baptism, in which you were also raised with him through faith in the powerful working of God, who raised him from the dead" (Col 2:12). Again Paul is not referring to water baptism. Because the Christian is in Christ, God the Father deals with us as he does with the glorified Christ. God can have nothing against us because we have died and have risen again in Christ. It's as if the old humanity in the second Adam has been written off, it has already died by the law and one is now on the other side, so, as a wife is no longer subject to her dead husband, the believer is no longer subject the the law's condemnation. All our sins have been forgiven and we share in Christ's righteousness. The law can no longer touch us because it has done its worst to him. The apostle reminds us that death and sin have lost their hold on the believer, "O death, where is your victory? O death, where is your sting? The sting of death is sin, and the power of sin is the law" (1 Cor 15:55,56). We have "died to the law through the body of Christ," sin has lost its strength and death its sting. We now "belong to him who has been raised from the dead, in order that we may bear fruit for God" (Rom 7:4). None can bring a charge against us (Rom 8:33), and there can be "no condemnation for those who are Christ Jesus" (Rom 8:1).

Our union in terms of causal priority precedes our justification by faith, for to be justified we must be in union with Christ, and none can be in union with him and not be justified. The word 'imputed' is traditionally used to describe the way in which Christ's righteousness becomes ours and

7. Lloyd-Jones, *Romans*, 6, *The New Man*, 39.

8. Owen, *Works*, 6, 150.

9. Lloyd-Jones, *Romans*, 6, 41.

our sins are punished in him. This can be somewhat misleading because it gives the impression that something has been given to us while we remain separate from the giver; that whilst being apart from Christ, he has given one a gift. If one received a liver transplant, one would not say that the blood has been imputed to the liver, rather, the organ becomes a recipient of the blood's vital nutrients because it has become a part of the person's body. In a similar way, we should consider our union with Christ. As George Hunginser reminds us, commenting on John Owen's position, "Imputation is not an external legal transaction which was merely observed by the believer at a distance. It was a dynamic process intrinsic to the believer's union with Christ."[10] John Calvin, again, clearly expresses this essential truth, "We do not, therefore, contemplate him outside ourselves from afar in order that his righteousness may be imputed to us but because we put on Christ and are engrafted into his body-in short, because he deigns to make us one with him."[11] His righteousness is ours because we have, so to speak, been dipped or baptized into him; we have become part of his body. What he is we are. Justification must not be looked at as if separate from our union with Christ, rather, we are justified because we are in union with him. As Luther put it:

> But so far as justification is concerned, Christ and I must be so closely attached that He lives in me and I in Him . . . Because He lives in me, whatever grace, righteousness, life, peace, and salvation there is in me is all of Christ's; nevertheless it is mine as well, by the cementing and attachment that are through faith, by which we become one body in the Spirit.[12]

Justification is a pronouncement made by God that the sinner is deemed to be righteousness in his sight on account of his union with Christ. All that Christ achieved by his vicarious substitutionary perfect obedience and sacrificial death becomes the property of the sinner. The Believer's union with Christ is then, in the words of Owen, "the foundation of the imputation asserted."[13] When we consider the *ordo salutis*, or order of salvation, perhaps it is wrong to think in terms of one thing following another i.e., adoption following justification etc. While this can be done logically, however, when looked at chronologically, everything occurs immediately upon our being united to Christ. The act of faith cannot be divorced from this union, nor justification from the act of faith. When we are united to Christ we are united to all of him, and everything that is true of him in regard to what he achieved,

10. Hunsinger, "Justification and Mystical Union with Christ," 207.

11. Calvin. *Institutes* III. XI, 10.

12. Luther, *Galatians*, 168.

13. Owen, *Works*, 5, 208.

becomes true of us. This is why I emphasize the fact that union with Christ lies at the very heart of salvation for all of God's people, from the very beginning. To imagine that Abraham was justified by faith without being united to the person of Christ is to separate Christ's work from his person. One cannot share in one without the other. Union with Christ is everything, and perhaps, books on justification should focus more on the believer's union with Christ, something many fail to do. It would be true to say that the instant we are united to Christ, we are justified, sanctified and glorified. This, however, does not necessarily mean that the recipient is aware of all that has become true of him. All of the saints who lived prior to Christ's incarnation were as much united to Christ as their New Testament brothers. They too, possessed all in Christ, even though they did not possess the assurance of their position that we associate with New Testament believers.

The Christian needs to remember that although his spirit is alive because of Christ's work, the body is still dead because of sin (Rom 8:10). In the body we still have the vestiges of sin, the remnants of the old regime in Adam. This is why Paul refers to the warfare that is raging within himself, between his resurrected spirit and his unredeemed body. In his spirit, he rejoices in God's law, yet in his body he sees another law at work, a law more associated with the old kingdom from which he has been redeemed (Rom 7:22–24, Gal 5:17). In regard to his spirit the Christian has been, past tense, resurrected to newness of life, but his mortal body has yet to be redeemed. It must await the final resurrection, when Christ returns to "be glorified in his saints" (2 Thess 1:10). Then "this perishable body must put on the imperishable, and this mortal body must put on immortality" (1 Cor 15:53). In that day the saints will be at home in the body and present with their Lord. Throughout his earthly pilgrimage, the believer patiently awaits, and deeply yearns for his bodily redemption (Rom 8:23), for that time when his body will be like Christ's glorified body. As the apostle put it, "as is the man of heaven, so also are those who are of heaven" and "we shall also bear the image of the man of heaven" (1 Cor 15:48–49). In the meantime, having the earnest of the Spirit, the believer strives to put to death the sin that remains in his mortal body (Rom 6:11–16), and use its members for righteousness, so that "the righteous requirements of the law might be fulfilled in us" (Rom 8:4).

There are a number of erroneous views held by evangelicals concerning the believer's union with Christ. I was somewhat surprised to read in an

article by J.F. Walvoord in the *Evangelical Dictionary of Theology* that "Identification with Christ is accomplished by the baptism of the Holy Spirit, an
act of divine grace and power sometimes expressed as being baptized into
the body of Christ."[14] By "identification with Christ" Walvoord, is referring
to one's union with him. As we will see later, the baptism with the Spirit was
not bestowed upon the church until Pentecost. If it is this baptism that united the believer to Christ, what Walvoord has said it would be logical to infer
that the saints who lived before Pentecost had no identification or union
with Christ. As I have emphasized throughout, if they didn't have union
with Christ then they would have been in Adam, standing condemned under the covenant of works.

Robert Letham, when examining the believer's union with Christ in
Romans chapter 6 in his recent book *Union with Christ* appears to link such
union with the rite of water baptism. He tells us that "baptism is not seen as
a human work but as a sacrament ordained by Christ in which the grace of
the Holy Spirit is given to the people of God through faith"[15] (Rom 6:3–11),
and that, "All who have been baptized into Christ have been united with
him in his death and resurrection." Letham quotes (1 Cor 12:12–13), again
taking the baptism to refer to the sacrament. By doing this he appears to
infuse the sacrament with an unwarranted efficacy: "The Spirit works with
power in and through it," that's the rite of baptism, "but as always his work
is not to be reduced to some automatic process; there must be an answering faith."[16] Again, in regard to water baptism, he states that "we have been
baptized into Christ's death, and raised in newness of life,"[17] and that, "the
earthly, material sacraments are God's prescribed vehicle through which he
communicates his mercies to us by the Holy Spirit through faith."[18]

I had to do a second take on Letham's understanding of this. About
one's union with Christ Letham states:

> In our union with Christ we share in his death and resurrection;
> signed, sealed and exhibited in baptism . . . Paul develops this in
> a number of places. All who have been baptized into Christ have
> been united with him in his death and resurrection (Rom.6:3–
> 11). In baptism we were baptized into Christ, and so we put on
> Christ (Gal.3:27). This means that we are made part of his body,
> the church, formed by the Holy Spirit. The Spirit baptized us

14. Walvoord, "Identification with Christ," 588.

15. Letham, *Union with Christ*, 139

16. Ibid., 139.

17. Ibid., 139.

18. Ibid., 139.

into the church, which Paul regards as the same thing as being baptized into Christ. "For just as the body is one and has many members . . . So it is with Christ. For in one Spirit we were all baptized into one body . . . and all made to drink of one Spirit." Baptism comes first, the Holy Spirit efficaciously uniting us to Christ in and through it, and thereafter we drink the Spirit—a possible reference to the other sacrament of the Lord's Supper.[19]

Had Letham been referring to that baptism by which the Spirit engrafts one into Christ these words would be understandable, however, the last line in the above quotation tells us that he most certainly referring to the rite of baptism.

I believe Letham is mistaken in that he equates baptism in these texts to that rite performed by human hands. He assumes that the texts referred to are concerned with only water baptism, thereby implying that water baptism is essential for one to be united to Christ. In other words, for one to be saved it is necessary not only to believe in Christ but also to be baptized with water. Letham tries to avoid the charge that he is effectively denying *sola fide* by insisting that baptism should be seen as the work of God not man, "Baptism is not seen as a human work but as a sacrament ordained by Christ in which the grace of the Holy Spirit is given to God's people through faith."[20] This view is doctrinally wrong. First, all who believe have already been united with Christ, to quote Vos, "One is first united to Christ, the Mediator of the covenant, by a mystical union, which finds its conscious recognition in faith. By this union with Christ, all that is in Christ is simultaneously given."[21] Faith is the result of one's union with Christ, not the cause.

Second, Letham is essentially denying *sola fide* by insisting on faith plus the rite of baptism. Trying to deny this by viewing the rite of baptism as the work of God does not succeed. It still makes salvation dependent on human action. Water baptism has, however, never been the vehicle that unites the believer with Christ. Rather, water baptism takes place because one has already been united to him. The Spirit of God has united us to Christ and water baptism is the believer witnessing, declaring, and identifying with this. To maintain that the rite comes before our union is to put the proverbial cart before the horse. If the rite is so fundamentally important in regard to our union with Christ, it would be very unlikely that the apostle would have uttered the words: "For Christ did not send me to baptize but to preach the gospel" (1 Cor 1:17). If Letham's take on these verses is correct,

19. Ibid., 138–39.
20. Ibid., 139.
21. Vos, *Redemptive History*, 256.

God forbid that one should come to faith in Christ on one's own, without someone being available to carry out baptism. Such a person would then believe on Christ without being united with him. Letham has effectively presented one with a theological impossibility, at least for those who believe in total depravity. Lloyd-Jones stated that "The teaching of the New Testament is that people who are to be baptized are those who have already given evidence that they are regenerate; it is believers who are baptized in the New Testament."[22] And, obviously, to be regenerate is to have spiritual life and to be in union with Christ. There can be no such life outside of him. The Christian is one who, in the words of Jesus, "has eternal life. He does not come into judgment, but has passed from death to life" (John 5:24). Another problem with Letham's position (being a Presbyterian) lies in the fact that water baptism is carried out on children. He is then left having to accord to the baptized infant the blessing of union with Christ. As we have seen, many baptized infants later become apostate, hence Letham is effectively saying that one can be in union with Christ and yet lose one's salvation.

It is important when distinguishing between the two testaments that one does not conclude, as many have done, that the body of Christ one reads about in the New Testament did not also exist in the Old Testament. The "body" metaphor may not have been employed before the incarnation, but the truth revealed by its usage in the New Testament has always applied to the people of God. The church has always consisted of his body, and we become members of it by participating in his flesh and blood. No saint can have any life in him unless he is part of this body, unless, to put it metaphorically, the blood of Christ flows in his veins. It's another either/or situation. One is either of his body, sharing in his achievements or one is outside of him and still under the law's condemnation. Objectively speaking, the body of Christ is the same in both testaments. What did change in regard to New Testament believers was their understanding of what being part of the body of Christ entails. In the Old Testament, in speaking of the believer's perception of his position, one might say that the body of Christ existed in embryonic form; it was developing, like a Jewish male child under age, awaiting of bar mitzvah. The body of Christ was not declared to be of age, so to speak, until Pentecost. Its Bar Mitzvah was on that day when the Spirit of Christ declared the child to be of age.

In recent years we have witnessed the growing popularity of what has become known as New Covenant Theology. This appears to hold peculiar, and dare one say, aberrant views concerning the believer's union and participation in the body of Christ. Its adherents appear to be of the opinion that

22. Lloyd-Jones, *Romans*, 6, 31.

those saints who lived prior to Christ's work were not "in him" in the same way New Testament saints are. According to Gary Long, the people of God who lived prior to Christ did not constitute the church or body of Christ. He maintains that the church began its life only at Pentecost: "New Covenant Theology holds that it is the Pentecost event that inaugurates the formation of the church in the unfolding of redemptive history,"[23] and that it is this "that makes believers members of the corporate body of Christ, it is that which places the believer into that union with Christ."[24] Long approvingly quotes Richard Gaffin, "Pentecost is nothing less than the establishment of the church as the new covenant people of God, as the body of Christ."[25]

A question sometimes asked is how could Old Testament believers be considered part of the body of Christ and seated in heavenly places in him before Christ's birth? The answers provided by the adherents of New Covenant Theology are somewhat surprising. According to Long, and he states this in bold print, so I'll do the same, "**if the church, which is Christ's body, had existed in the OT, it would have been headless**."[26] He later goes on to say, "No believer before Pentecost is ever said to be in Christ, but since Pentecost every believer is now in Christ."[27] Such statements, I believe, are the result of a faulty hermeneutic, one that draws a false dichotomy between Old and New Testament believers. It is a position that fails to distinguish between metaphor and reality. Jesus told his followers that "unless you eat the flesh of the Son of Man and drink his blood, you have no life in you" (John 6:53). Because Jesus had not actually assumed flesh in the Old Testament it is assumed that eating his flesh and drinking his blood would have been impossible, but such an inference fails to realize the metaphorical nature of this language. The only conclusion one can draw from Long's understanding is that saints like Abraham etc., had no life in them because Jesus had at that time not appeared in the flesh.

Similar assertions are made by John G. Reisinger in *Abraham's Four Seeds*. Like Long, he appears to exclude Old Testament believers from both the body of Christ and the church. He informs us that "The inauguration of the New Testament made possible the creation of the Body of Christ, the New Man,"[28] and again, "The Body of Christ is a new creation brought into being by the personal advent of the Holy Spirit on the day of Pentecost,"

23. Long, *New Covenant Theology*, 72.

24. Ibid., 72.

25. Ibid., 73.

26. Ibid., 71.

27. Ibid., 75.

28. Reisinger, *Abraham's Four Seeds*, 105

and, "it came to pass in the fullness of time when the risen Christ formed the church. He formed it when he poured out the gift of the Holy Spirit through faith. As a result they are incorporated into Christ's spiritual body, the church, so now under the New Covenant all are one corporate body in spiritual union with the Son."[29]

For Reisinger, "The Body of Christ is a new entity on the earth," which only started at Pentecost. He later adds, "In no sense whatsoever does this mean that the believer living prior to Christ's coming was not saved and secure as we are, or that he was not saved in exactly as we are today."[30] This is clearly a contradiction-in-terms. Reisinger then presents a chart[31] in which he shows what he considers to be true of those who make up the body of Christ. This includes being circumcised "of the heart by the Holy Spirit," being "born after the Spirit," being "loved, chosen, redeemed and adopted as a spiritual family." He tells us that all of this began at Pentecost. This mix-up is the result of what we saw earlier, namely, the belief that the new covenant started only after Christ's shed blood and resurrection. From this one can logically conclude that all Old Testament saints were excluded from these blessings. One may then ask how exactly did Abraham come to be a partaker of Christ's righteousness if he was not a participator of what Christ's work achieved, in other words, "in Christ"?

It may be the case that Reisinger is thinking more along the lines of the believer's perception, of his subjective awareness of being in Christ rather than his actual objective position. For example, he tells us "it does mean his personal apprehension of his experience, cannot exceed the revelation or covenant under which he lived."[32] I fear, however, that he does not mean this, and that he holds a position similar to Gary Long. Reisinger, like Long, fails to see that the new covenant applied as much to Old Testament believers as to those living in the New Testament age. Yes, the believer may have entered into a new awareness of the reality of his standing or position in Christ at Pentecost, this in no way, however, affected the reality of his position, a reality that applied outside of his subjective awareness. All believers, in both Testaments, have been in Christ, members of his body.

McGovan in his recent book, *Adam, Christ and Covenant*, again provides a good example placing a wedge between Old and New Testament believers. Commenting on the new covenant says, "This speaks of the new relationship in which Christians stand with God, through Jesus Christ. We

---

29. Ibid., 77.
30. Ibid.,111.
31. Ibid., 114–15.
32. Ibid., 111.

are still related to God by faith, as were Abraham and Moses, but now by faith, we are united spiritually with Christ. We are new creatures, in a new covenant, having experienced a new birth, and nothing can remove us from our relationship with God."[33] From this it is clear that he is saying that Abraham and Moses were not spiritually united with Christ, he even appears to suggest that the new creation and new birth are applicable only to New Testament believers. If Abraham and Moses were not united with Christ, then we must ask who were they were united with? One would have to say that they were united with Adam with all that this entails, I say this because there is no third position, one is either in Adam or in Christ.

The church of Christ existed throughout the Old Testament period in the spiritual Israel. Their hearts were circumcised with the result that they put faith in the promise of him who was to come forth from the loins of Abraham. To quote Owen:

> Abraham, on account of his faith, and not of his separation according to the flesh, was the father of all that believe, and heir of the world. And in the covenant made with him, as to that which concerns, not the bringing forth of the promised Seed according to the flesh, but as unto faith therein, and in the work of redemption to be performed. Thereby, lays the foundation of the church in all ages. Wheresoever this covenant is, and withsoever it is established, with them is the church; unto whom all the promises and privileges of the church do belong, hence it was that at the coming of the Messiah there was not one church taken away, and another set up in the room thereof; but the church continued in the same, in those what ere the children of Abraham according to the faith. The Christian church is not another church, but the very same that was before the coming of Christ, having the same faith with it, and interested in the same covenant.[34]

The church comprises of all who share in the salvation secured by Christ, who eat his flesh, and drink his blood (John 6:53). All humanity is either under the first Adam, united to him, or else under Christ, the second Adam. To eat his body and drink his blood is metaphorical language for the believers union with Christ. It denotes the fact that believers are the recipients of the salvific blessings procured by Christ in the work he completed in his body of flesh. The righteousness that was credited to Abraham was nothing less than that obtained by Christ. One can say that Abraham was sharing in the work of Christ, or was metaphorically eating Christ's body

---

33. McGowan, *Adam, Christ and Covenant*, 155.
34. Owen, *Works*, 6, 123.

and drinking his blood. He was a member of Christ's body! If this be not true then Abraham could have had no life in him (John 6:53). One must not, as we see in the case of Long and Reisinger, limit the efficacy of Christ's work to after the redemptive event. There is clearly a failure to appreciate the retrospective application of Christ's work.

We again see this in the way they understand the nature of Christ's intercession. According to Long, if Christ was not actually seated at the right hand of God, in his glorified physical body, he could not make intercession for his people who lived prior to his ascension and session.

This is partly because, Long, like so many, has a faulty understanding of what Christ's intercession involves. It is important to understand that his intercession at the right hand of God does not consist in his making requests to his Father based on the day-to-day activity of saints on earth. Rather, it consists in Christ's appearing in the presence of God bearing the marks of his completed work in his glorified body. The very fact that he is there declaring that his work is finished is essentially what his intercession consists of. As Thomas Boston, reminds us, Jesus, "in his appearing in heaven in his people's nature, and on their account. After he had shed his precious blood on earth for the expiation of their sin, he rose again from the dead, and ascended into heaven as their Advocate and Intercessor, that by the virtue of his meritorious sacrifice, he might answer all the charges brought against them."[35] He does not need to ask his Father for anything because he has already secured all blessings for his people, and he has now sat the right hand of God interceding for us (Rom 8:34). The fact that Jesus is depicted as "seated" suggests that his work is finished.

How then does this apply to Old Testament believers? The answer is provided by John Owen:

> For all things of this nature that belong to it do arise and spring from the mediation of Christ, or his interposition on the behalf of sinners. Wherefore this took place from the giving of the first promise; the administration of the grace of this covenant did therein and then take its date. Howbeit the Lord Christ had not yet done that thereby it was solemnly to be confirmed, and that thereon all the virtue of it did depend.[36]

Since the beginning, all blessings, and this includes Christ's intercession, are in virtue of Christ's mediation. Old Testament believers, like us, benefited from the fact that Christ's intercession was in the mind of God and viewed as completed even before the literal event. The fact that Christ

35. Boston, *Beauties of Boston*, 214.
36. Owen, *Hebrews*, 3, 147.

would complete his work and that his work would be accepted by his Father was enough to ensure that the benefits resulting from it were applied to the people of God, this is why John tells us that he was "slain from the foundation of the world" (KJV, Rev 13:8). If one seeks a loan, one offers to pay the money back at some future time. The benefit of the loan is granted to the recipient before the price of the loan is paid. In a similar fashion, God bestows the work of Christ before the actual payment was made. In the Old Testament his work was revealed in the copies of the heavenly, however, "Christ has entered, not into holy places made with hands, which are copies of the true things, but into heaven itself, now to appear in the presence of God on our behalf" (Heb 9:24).

Hebrews 11:39–40 is a text that has perplexed many, and it is often seized upon to justify an unscriptural hiatus between Old and New Testament saints. The writer tells us: "And all these though commended through their faith, did not receive what was promised, since God had provided something better for us, that apart from us they should not be made perfect." From these words many have inferred that Old Testament believers were somehow imperfect until the ratification of the new covenant. The confusion generated by this text caused Owen to comment, "I cannot but marvel that so many have stumbled, as most have done, in the exposition of these words, and involved themselves in difficulties of their own devising."[37] Gary Long seems to associate "what was promised" with the New Testament believer being "in Christ." He tells us that, "No believer before Pentecost is ever said to be in Christ. But since Pentecost, every believer is now in Christ (1Cor12:13) including Old Testament believers who, because of redemption accomplished under the New Covenant, are now made perfect with the "something better of NT believers."[38] His understanding is the result of a misreading of not only this verse, but, as I have previously said, a failure to grasp the essential nature of the new covenant. It results in denying spiritual life to Old Testament believers. We must also avoid making the mistake which John Owen accuses the church of Rome of, namely, dividing Old and New Testament saints, believing that the former lay in "limbus, a subterraneous receptacle of souls, wherein they say the spirits under the Old Testament were detained until after the resurrection."[39] This view is not that different from that held by some evangelicals.

So what exactly is the writer saying in this verse? The subject matter of the letter should be one's guide here. It was the writer's intention to

---

37. Ibid., 118.
38. Long, *New Covenant Theology*, 75.
39. Owen, *Works*, 6, 215.

show the superiority of the new covenant over the old; the superiority of Christ's ministry over that of the Mosaic covenant. Throughout chapter eleven we are told about those saints who lived prior to the consummation of the new covenant. Old Testament believers saw the completed work of Christ from a distance through the limited light given to them. Christ told his disciples, "many prophets, and kings desired to see what you see, and did not see it, and to hear what you hear and did not hear it" (Luke 10:24). Looking through the mists of time, Peter tells us, "concerning this salvation, the prophets who prophesied about the grace that was to be yours searched and inquired carefully, inquiring what person or time the Spirit of Christ in them was indicating" (1 Pet 1:10–11). What was it that these saints did not receive? It seems clear that they did not live to see the literal fulfillment of what was promised, the fulfillment of that which they embraced by faith. They found themselves in the position of Simeon before he witnessed in his flesh the "consolation of Israel" (Luke 2:25–35). They then received not the manifestation of the thing promised, although they still received the blessings arising from the work of that which was promised. As Owen reminds us, "they enjoyed the benefits of it, even as we . . . Howbeit; they received it not as unto its actual accomplishment in the coming of Christ."[40] So they looked to a work yet to be enacted out in time.

John Owen asks a number of questions concerning these believers from which he anticipates a positive answer:

> For were not these things which they received not under the old testament? were not these things which were promised from the beginning; which were expected, longed for, and desired by all believers of old, who yet saw them from afar, though through faith they were saved by virtue of them? and are not these the things whereby the state-church of the gospel was perfected and consummated, the things alone whereby out state is better than theirs.[41]

Old Testament saints could not be made perfect by the paraphernalia associated with the old covenant, things that were simply a copy of the heavenly, the symbols not the substance. That they were made perfect was because they looked forward in faith to the completed work of Christ. The text is essentially saying that both Old and New Testament believers are made perfect by the same redemptive work: "They without us were not made perfect," no, of course not, because all the saints of God are made perfect only in Christ, because of his finished redemptive work.

40. Ibid., 215.
41. Ibid., 217.

Often, it is the language employed that serves to encourage a false dichotomy between Old and New Testament believers. According to Robert Letham, who is certainly not an advocate of New Covenant Theology, at Pentecost, "the Spirit would come to indwell believers and unit them to Christ."[42] He, approvingly quotes Robert Stedman, "the Lord Jesus Christ, by his Spirit, taketh possession of them, and dwelleth in them; and believers through faith of the operation of the Spirit take hold of Christ, and get into him, and so they are knit together and become one."[43] I am not saying that Letham does not believe that the Spirit was present in Old Testament believers and that they were united to Christ. I do maintain, however, that the language used in relation to Pentecost can give the wrong impression. The implication appears to be that Old Testament believers as well as not being united to Christ they did not have the Spirit indwelling them. This obviously leaves one wondering about the position of Old Testament believers, exactly where they fit into God's redemptive plan. For example, looking at Abraham's position again, when he saw Christ's day and rejoiced about it (John 8:56), was he not united to Christ made a participator in his body? If he wasn't, then where was he? Was he in some sort of limbo? No, of course not! Abraham, like all the saved, had been taken out of Adam's realm and placed into Christ, and, whilst he did not enjoy the knowledge of the fullness of the blessings that were his in Christ, he was, nevertheless in Christ as much as we are today.

Many Reformed Presbyterian churches, especially in North America, have in recent years been affected, or should one say, afflicted, by the so-called Federal Vision. Federal Vision, as the name implies, is concerned with a particular understanding of God's covenant(s). Federal Vision started with the teachings of Norman Shepherd, a Professor of Dogmatics at Westminster Theological Seminary in Philadelphia. Shepherd's work was made publically available in his book *The Call of Grace*, published in 2000. According to David Engelsma, "In the book, Shepherd openly and explicitly attacks all the doctrines of sovereign grace confessed by the Reformed churches . . . and in the *Westminster Confession* . . . although not at the heart of it, is the denial of justification by faith alone."[44]

Federal Vision has essentially amalgamated the grace and works principle of the Mosaic covenant and applied it to the new covenant. Paedobaptists have always struggled in regard to the works principle associated with the Mosaic covenant and it was perhaps inevitable that something like Federal Vision should appear. It essentially employs the Reformed Paedobaptist

---

42. Letham, *Union with Christ*, 48.

43. Ibid., 51.

44. Engelsma, *Federal Vision*, 17.

paradigm and takes the next logical step in its attempt to explain the faith/ works paradox.

Ironically, Federal Vision claims to be rooted in the teachings of the Reformers, and the Presbyterian confessions of faith. When one looks at exactly what the Westminster Confession says about the position of baptized children one can perhaps glean some understanding of where Federal Vision is coming from:

> Baptism is the sacrament of the New Testament, ordained by Jesus Christ, not only for the solemn admission for the party baptized into the visible Church; but also to be unto him a sign and seal of the covenant of grace, of his *ingrafting into Christ, of regeneration, of remission of sins, and of his giving up unto God, through Jesus Christ, to walk in newness of life.* Which sacrament is by Christ's own appointment, to be continued in His Church unto the end of the world.[45]

Regarding infant baptism, the Confession tells us that "the right use of this ordinance, the grace promised is not only offered, but really exhibited and conferred by the Holy Ghost."[46]

The same teaching is found in earlier confessions, for example, the Second Helvetic Confession of 1566. About the position of infants of believing parents we read:

> To be baptized in the name of Christ is to be enrolled, initiated and received into the covenant (of grace), into the family, and the inheritance of the sons of God ... Children of believers should be baptized; for to children belongs the kingdom of God: why then should not the sign of the covenant be given to them?[47]

My reason for these quotes is to show that Federal Vision is simply interpreting the evidence within its paedobaptist mindset. It maintains that infant baptism actually links the child to the saving grace of Christ, where the child is not only believed to be but actually is united to Christ. One cannot deny that Federal Vision is literally applying the words of the 1647 Westminster Confession, "the grace promised is not only offered but really exhibited and conferred by the Holy Ghost." This appears on the face of it to be very close to baptismal regeneration. What else can the words, 'really exhibited and conferred by the Holy Ghost' mean? Either the rite of baptism confers grace or it does not, and there's no getting away from the fact that

45. Italics added for emphasis. Westminster Confession of Faith, 28.1.

46. Ibid., 28, 6.

47. Second Helvetic Confession 1566, 20.

according to the Confession, a Confession revered by so many Paedobaptists, infant baptism appears to have a real saving efficacy.

What makes Federal Vision particularly pernicious is the way it appears to deny justification by faith alone. It applies the promise, "I will be your God and you will be my people" to every child of believing parents. Baptism is believed to be a pledge made to God that one will be faithful to the covenant's requirements. The child's continuance in the covenant is dependent on whether he/she exercises faith and performs certain works. It is then possible for the child to be in the covenant of grace, and actually "in Christ," and yet at a later stage to be out of this position, to be without Christ. Covenant union with Christ is then conditional and can be broken. Wilkins tells us that "union with Christ means all that is true of Christ is true of us." Douglas Wilson approvingly quotes Joel Garver, where Garver is trying to explain the difference between those infants who, although in the covenant, end up falling away, and those who persevere, "we should not try to drive a wedge between 'special' and 'covenantal' elections, for special election simply is covenantal election for those, who by God's sovereign electing grace, persevere. For those who fall away, covenantal election devolves into reprobation."[48] When he refers to election he means it in the sense of Ephesians 1:4. The falling away of these children in no way negates the fact that they were once in the covenant, and in actuality, and not in appearance only, united or married to Christ. However, because he did not continue in the faith all is lost. God has essentially divorced the individual. Not only was the infant once in Christ, but it was considered to be among the elect of God. Steve Wilkins, at the Knox Colloquium in 2003 stated that "the elect are those who are faithful in Christ Jesus. If they later reject the Savior, they are no longer elect and thus lose their elect standing. But their falling away doesn't negate the reality of their standing prior to their apostasy."[49] Wilkins again stated:

> Covenant, therefore, is a gracious relationship between God and every baptized child . . .
>
> To be in covenant is to have the treasures of God's mercy and grace and the love which he
>
> has for his own Son given to you, that is to every baptized child, including those who perish.
>
> But the covenant is not unconditional. It requires persevering faithfulness.[50]

48. Wilson, *Reformed Is Not Enough*, 140–41.
49. Wilkins, "Covenant, Baptism, and Salvation."
50. Ibid.

Let us just look at another quote to ensure that we are not misrepresenting Wilkins's position, "being in covenant with God means being in Christ, those who are in covenant have all spiritual blessings in the heavenly places. Union with Christ means all that is true of Christ is true of us."[51] Now, whilst the Reformed Baptist would say Amen to this, Wilkins then goes on to speak of such blessings being applicable to those who may eventually fall away, "They may enjoy for a season the blessings of the covenant, including the forgiveness of sins, adoption, possession of the kingdom, and sanctification, and yet apostatize and fall short of the grace of God."[52]

Wilkins, it appears, fails to realize the profound nature of the change that takes place when one is placed into Christ. As alluded to earlier, the "old man" the believer used to be when he was in Adam has ceased to exist; indeed, he has been crucified with Christ (Rom 6:6). The "new Man" is one who has been regenerated by God's Spirit, and he is now united to Christ and in the kingdom of God. There can be no going back to the man he used to be. To say that children share in these blessings and that they can later lose them because of what their parents believe seems to me to be the height of folly.

The apostle Paul commenced his letters by identifying those to whom the letter is addressed, for example, "To all those in Rome who are loved by God and called to be saints" (Rom 1:7), or "To the church of God that is in Corinth" (1 Cor 1:2). The traditional Presbyterian position has tended to differentiate between those in the visible church and those who are truly in Christ, the invisible church. This is not the view of Federal Vision. Wilkins is of the opinion that what Paul said to the church in regard to its position in Christ necessarily applied to every individual in the make-up of that church. Likewise, John Barach states, "The whole church is in Christ. They have been baptized into Christ. They have clothed themselves with Christ (Gal 3:27). Paul wants them to know that all these blessings he is praising God for are theirs in Christ."[53] This being the case, those who then fall away have the blessings withdrawn, so although they were "in Christ," they later, because of their failure to persevere become apostates. The apostle is not, however, saying that the blessings automatically apply to all, but to those whose faith is true. We all know that any can claim to be in Christ, the world is full of charlatans. Only God knows the heart. The true believer is confident that God, who has begun a good work in him, will bring it to its completion in Christ Jesus (Phil 1:6). Christ said himself that his sheep will listen to his

51. Ibid.

52. Ibid.

53. Barach, "Covenant and Election."

voice, they will not listen to the voice of another (John 10:4,5). One cannot be a true sheep of Christ one day and a suckling of Satan the next.

According to Wilkins:

> All in covenant are given all that is true of Christ. If they perse-
> vere in faith to the end, they enjoy all those mercies eternally. If
> they fall away in unbelief, they lose these blessings and receive
> greater condemnation than Sodom and Gomorrah. Covenant
> can be broken by unbelief and rebellion, but until it is, those in
> covenant with Him are His. If they do not persevere, they lose
> the blessings that were given to them.[54]

Here he is comparing the position of the person who is "in Christ" with that of Israel in Canaan. As Israel's continuation in the land was depen-dent on her continued obedience, so the believer's continuation "in Christ" is dependent on his obedience, "If they persevere in faith to the end, they enjoy all these mercies eternally. If they fall away in unbelief, they lose these blessings."[55] So one can be saved and yet lost, have all that belongs to Christ and, yet, see it all disappear because of disobedience. Wilkins would clearly suggest a positive answer to Paul's question to the Corinthians, "For who sees anything different in you? What do you have that you did not receive?" (1 Cor 4:7). According to Wilkins one could put one's hand up and say that his perseverance makes him differ from another. He is guilty of putting the cart before the horse. The believer does not continue in Christ because he perseveres, rather, he perseveres because he is in Christ. The true believer does not fail to persevere, he does not continue, indeed, cannot continue, to live in sin. This is an impossibility because, as Paul tells us, "What shall we say then? Are we to continue in sin that grace may abound? By no means! How can we who died to sin still live in it?" (Rom 6:1–2).

Engelsma's severe denunciation of Federal Vision is the result of its denial of justification by faith alone, "The Federal Vision is a heresy. It is a stubborn, persistent, deliberate departure from and denial of a cardinal truth of Scripture, as this truth is rightly and authoritatively summarized and systematized in the Reformed creeds."[56] I would not agree that it is a deliberate departure. Those who embrace it sincerely believe themselves to be faithful to Scripture, and faithfully applying the paedobaptist paradigm. Federal Vision is essentially an attempt to overcome what many paedobap-tists see as being a major weakness in their covenantal understanding. Rath-er than adopt the Reformed Baptist position, the men of the Federal Vision

---

54. Wilkins, "Covenant, Baptism, and Salvation."

55. Ibid.

56. Engelsma, *Federal Vision*, 18.

have developed yet another system in an effort to explain the relationship between grace and works. Unfortunately, however, far from providing an answer, it has generated further division within the ranks of fellow paedo-baptists, to the point where open hostility has resulted.

According to Wilson, the Reformed Baptists are faced with the same problem in that many of those who are baptized as adults also end up falling away. He is, however, not comparing like with like. Yes, of course, some will say that they are Christian, that they are in the new covenant when they are not. Even in the church, the wheat will grow with the tares. Only God can know who is truly in the covenant. It is the church's duty to baptize those who confess with their mouth that Jesus is Lord; whether they believe in their heart, is another matter. It is something only the Lord can know.

Federal Vision proponents also hold a view, similar to that of New Covenant Theology, that dates the church as the body of Christ from Pentecost. Steve Wilkins tells us that, "The Bible teaches us that baptism unites us to Christ and His body by the power of the Holy Spirit . . . Baptism is an act of God (through His ministers) which signifies and seals our initiation into the Triune communion."[57] He goes on to say that "at baptism we are clothed with Christ, united to Him and to His Church which is His body." Douglas Wilson even goes so far as to associate the baptism with the Spirit with regeneration. In trying to establish the relationship between water baptism and the Spirit, he tells us what he believes the baptism with the Spirit accomplishes. This is his answer: "it circumcises the heart by removing the body of fleshly skin. It places the individual in union with Christ in His death, burial, and resurrection. It washes away all his sins. In short, this true baptism is what makes a person regenerate."[58]

The above writers fail to appreciate the fact that believers have always been united to Christ, and as already said, are members of his body—the church. There is no salvation outside of him. To suggest that it is only after water baptism that one is clothed with Christ is preposterous, it is akin to baptismal regeneration. Christ is the true ark of God, and, as in the time of Noah, humanity was either inside the ark and saved, or outside the ark and under God's condemnation, likewise, one is either in Christ and saved or in Adam, and again, under God's condemnation. The only way into the true ark of God, which is Christ, has always been by the Spirit engrafting or inserting one into his body, where one can participate in the salvation his work procured. It is true that the metaphor has changed, the body of Christ metaphor was not used outside the New Testament, however, the substance

57. Wilkins, "Covenant, Baptism, and Salvation."
58. Wilson, *To A Thousand Generations*, 53.

of what the metaphor conveys has always been the same i.e., the people of God have always been in Christ, the second Adam.

1 4

New Covenant Breakers?

ACCORDING TO BOOTH, "THE Bible teaches that the people of God in the Old Testament and the people of God in the New Testament are one and the same people."[1] One cannot but wholeheartedly agree with this. Paedobaptists, however, go further in that they associate carnal Israel with the Old Testament people of God, believing the entire nation to have been in the covenant of grace.

Reformed Baptists consider it essential to distinguish between the two Israels', between the carnal and the spiritual, between those under law and those in the new covenant. The great promise, "I will be your God and you will be my people," is conditional. To have applied to carnal Israel it would be necessary for it to adhere to the covenantal conditions. "If you walk in my statutes and observe my commandments and do them" (Lev 26:3). God then goes on to tell them about the blessings that will be theirs if only they could keep the covenant. One such blessing is, "I will make my dwelling place among you and my soul shall not abhor you. And I will walk among you, and *will be your God, and you shall be my people*" (Lev 26:11–12). Israel was, however, disobedient, and it was because of this God said he would " bring a sword upon you, that shall execute vengeance for the covenant. And if you gather within your cities, I will send pestilence among you, and you shall be delivered into the hand of the enemy" (Lev 26:25). Israel never became God's people and he never became their God. In spite of this God continued to exhibit grace, and while this was not unto salvation, except for those who believed the promises, it nevertheless served as a type of salvific grace. God, by his grace, brought Israel, after forty years of wandering the desert, to the banks of the Jordan. He stopped the Jordan to allow the people to cross into Canaan. However, God made it clear to Israel that its continuance in the land was conditional by reminding the people of their side of the covenant

1. Booth, *Children of the Promise*, 73.

that was made under Moses. "Only be strong and very courageous, being careful to do according to all the law that Moses my servant commanded you. Do not turn from it to the right hand or to the left, that you may have good success wherever you go" (Joshua 1:7). It was, however, not long before Israel forgot the covenant, just as Joshua had predicted (Josh 24:19). In the time of Solomon God renewed his covenantal demands and shortly thereafter the nation again drifted away from him. In terms of the nation breaking the old covenant, this is something every single person did. It was for Israel, an unkeepable covenant. All were covenant breakers because of the weakness of the flesh, as Owen informs us, "what consisted the weakness of unprofitableness of the old covenant . . . Was it not this, because, by reason of sin, we were in no way able to fulfill the condition thereof, 'Do this and live?'"[2] We need to bear in mind the words of the apostle regarding the law, "by the deeds of the law shall no flesh be justified in his sight, for by the law comes the knowledge of sin" (Rom 3:20). This is why it is called a "ministry of death" (2 Cor 3:7). Where the old covenant, being a reiteration of the original covenant made with Adam, demanded obedience without providing one with the means to perform, the new covenant grants one a new heart upon which the law is inscribed. Again, to quote Owen, "one main difference of these two covenants,–that the Lord did in the old only require the condition; now, in the new, he will also effect it in all the federates to whom this covenant is extended. And if the Lord should only exact the obedience required in the covenant of us, and not work and effect it also in us, the new covenant would be a show to increase our misery, and not a serious imparting and communication of grace and mercy.[3] The new covenant can then never be broken because Christ has kept it, and the grace thereof is "imparted and communicated" to

One could perhaps understand the Reformed paedobaptists if they espoused Arminian theology. They don't. They hold firm to the Westminster Confession, which teaches the eternal security of the saints. What one finds peculiar about their position is the notion that the new covenant can be broken in the same way as the old covenant. That it is possible for one to be in the new covenant, and yet become an apostate. This in spite of the words spoken by Jeremiah telling us that the Lord will put fear into the hearts of his people so that they will not turn away (Jer 32:39).

We would charge the paedobaptists, as we saw earlier, of, to use the illustration Christ used, sewing a new cloth onto an old garment, or pouring new wine into old wineskins. By this I mean they take that which applied to

2. Owen, *Works*, 10, 237.

3. Ibid., 237.

the old covenant and seek to impose it on the new covenant, and again, they take from the new and impose it on the old covenant. For example, God's promise to be his people's God and they his children can only ever be realized in Christ, in the new covenant. Paedobaptists, however, take this and, not only apply it to those living under the old covenant, but to the children of believing parent(s) today. They also take the new wine, or the new cloth, which both represent the new covenant, and impose upon it the old covenant concept of being a covenant breaker. They are thereby essentially confusing the law that came through Moses with grace and truth that came through Jesus Christ (John 1:17).

The writer to the Hebrews tells us that the new covenant will not be "like the covenant that I made with their fathers on the day when I took them by the hand to bring them out of the land of Egypt, my covenant that they broke, though I was their husband, declares the Lord" (Heb 8:9). He is contrasting the Mosaic covenant with the new covenant. One of the important things about the old covenant was that it could be broken. If the new covenant could also be broken, then any contrast that this text makes becomes meaningless. This text alone should suffice to show that the new covenant is unbreakable.

Let us examine some of the texts that are employed to supposedly prove that new covenant believers can become covenant breakers. One of their most important texts is found in Hebrews 10:26–29:

> For if we go on sinning deliberately after receiving the knowledge of the truth, there no longer remains a sacrifice for sins, but a fearful expectation of judgment, and a fury of fire that will consume the adversaries. Anyone who has set aside the law of Moses dies without mercy on the evidence of two or three witnesses. How much worse punishment, do you think will be deserved by the one who has spurned the Son of God, and profaned the blood of the covenant by which he was sanctified and has outraged the Spirit of grace.

The paedobaptist applies this text to those infants of believing parents who have apostatized. They were at one time in the covenant of grace, recipients of covenantal blessings, yet they later decided to turn their backs on the Lord. I would suggest, however, that the writer is not saying this. The essential line seems to be, "For if we go on sinning deliberately after receiving the knowledge of the truth, there no longer a sacrifice for sins." Far from suggesting that the believer might fall away, the opposite is being stressed. These believers have witnessed the finished work of Christ, they have been cleansed by the shed blood of Christ. The writer is hypothetically saying that the salvation that is theirs in Christ is the only salvation there is. If they were to turn away, there would be no forgiveness for sins possible anywhere. He is effectively saying that there is "salvation in no one else, for there is no other name under heaven given among men by which we must be saved" (Acts 4:12). To use a simple illustration, imagine a person who is in love with life, standing on a railway platform. The train is approaching. She might say to herself, "if I jumped now that would be the end of me." Of course, she is not going to jump. She knows that if she were to jump her life would be forfeit and there would be no means available to bring it back. It seems to me that the writer in the passage is doing something similar. Because Christ's shed blood is the highest manifestation of God's love, if you have benefitted from this, and if (the hypothetical "if") it was possible for you to fall away, then there would be nothing else available.

Hebrews 6:4–6 is another text often cited:

> For it is impossible, in the case of those who have once been enlightened, who have tasted the heavenly gift, and shared in the Holy Spirit, and have tasted the goodness of the word of God and the powers of the age to come, and then have fallen away, to restore them again to repentance, since they are crucifying once again the Son of God to their own harm and holding him up to contempt.

This, it must be acknowledged, is a difficult text for both Baptists and paedobaptists. I am of the opinion that the same idea can be applied here as in Hebrews 10:26ff. Although the word "if" is not found in the Greek, the author still appears to be emphasizing the fact that there is no salvation outside of Christ. Of course, the paedobaptists apply this to infant baptism, to those who were once deemed to have been blessed in that they have tasted the heavenly gift because of their membership in the covenant of grace. Taking this line, however, they would have to be consistent by believing that should these infants later fall away, it would then be impossible to bring them back to repentance. Taking God at his word, it would then be a futile exercise to witness to apostates.

The text may be concerned with those hypocrites who share in the life of the church. They sit under the ministry of the Word, and some may even become preachers. In worship they may even experience a certain melting of the heart, yet all falls short of regeneration. Always, in the end they fall away, abandoning any allegiance they may have had to the Faith.

In John 15 Jesus compares himself to a vine with his disciples being the branches, "I am the vine and you are the branches" (v.5). Jesus states that those branches that do not bear fruit will be thrown into the fire (v.6). He tells his disciples, "Abide in me and I in you, as the branch cannot bear fruit by itself, unless it abides in the vine, neither can you unless you abide in me" (v.4). Douglas Wilson tells us: "There really are people who are really removed from the vine."[4] These are those children of believers who are considered to be in Christ, in union with him, who, unless they perform good works through a conscious decision to abide in Christ, will forfeit their position in Christ.

In regard to this "abiding" Wilson examines John 8:31–35:

> Then Jesus said to those Jews which believed on him, If ye continue in my word, then ye are my disciples indeed; And ye shall know the truth, and the truth shall make you free. They answered him, We be Abraham's seed, and were never in bondage to any man: how sayest thou, Ye shall be made free? Jesus answered them, Verily, verily, I say unto you, whosoever committeth sin is the servant of sin. And the servant abideth not in the house for ever, but the Son abideth for ever. . . . A slave does not abide in the house forever, but a son does. In other words, while a slave may make the house his temporary abode, he will be removed from it. He is not an heir, and will not be counted among the heirs. If the slave is confused he may think himself a son, but the day will come when his presumption is exposed for what it is. As Christ teaches us the nature of abiding and not abiding. The contrast is rather between abiding temporarily and abiding permanently.[5]

One can, of course, see where Wilson is going with this. Infants of believers may be considered as slaves, in the covenant of grace, but not regenerate. If they, however, "abide" in their position of union with Christ where they are branches attached to the vine they may then be considered not as slaves but as sons. They are then considered to be, at least until they bare fruit, temporary dwellers in the house. This then, so Wilson would have us believe, shows that the makeup of the church in the new covenant is mixed, with some becoming covenant breakers.

There is, however, a fundamental weakness with this position. Christ, in relating to a son and a slave is not suggesting that both are in union with him. Rather, he is contrasting the position of those Israelites who are the

4. Wilson, *To A Thousand Generations*, 85.
5. Ibid., 85–86.

fleshly offspring of Abraham, under the old covenant of bondage, with Abraham's true sons, those who like him exercise faith.

It is unlikely that John 15 has anything to do with the believer's actual position in Christ as regards his salvation. According to Lloyd-Jones, we are here "dealing with 'office', 'function', 'work' rather than with personal salvation."[6] It is about the importance of doing good works in and through Christ; about the true nature of presenting our "bodies a living sacrifice, holy, acceptable unto God" (Rom 12:1). Although the person's salvation is secure, the same cannot be said about the works he does. The apostle Paul alludes to the same thing, telling us that we must build upon a foundation that is Christ. "Now if anyone builds on the foundation with gold, silver, precious stones, wood, hay, straw—each one's work will become manifest, for the Day will disclose it, because it will be revealed by fire, and the fire will test what sort of work each one has done. If the work that anyone has built on the foundation survives, he will receive a reward. If anyone's work is burned up, he will suffer loss, though he himself will be saved, but only as through fire" (1 Cor 3:12–15). Jesus is then "addressing His disciples as the future teachers and preachers and establishers of churches . . . If that be the case then the statements in ch.15 about the branches being taken out of the tree and burned, must be interpreted exactly the same as the statements in 1 Cor 9:27 and the parallel in 1 Cor 3."[7] The vine is Christ, and it is necessary for the Christian to do all his works through him, fed by the vital, life-giving sap. Many of a believer's works are fit only for the fire because they are not done with the correct motive. Jesus is showing that we must always be mindful of our position in him.

If the paedobaptists are determined to apply this passage to infants, to say that they are in the vine and unless they abide in that position they will lose what is theirs, they will find themselves in a theologically untenable position. These branches are clearly part of the vine, and presumably, they would have produced fruit in the past, even if they are not doing so now. This, however, is something only the regenerate can do, and to produce anything acceptable to God it is necessary for one to be removed from one's natural position under Adam and placed into Jesus Christ. Either these infants are in Christ, and if they are they are there to stay, or else they are still in their sins and estranged from God, able to do nothing that is acceptable in his sight.

2 Peter 2:1 is another text used to supposedly show that it is possible to be in the new covenant and yet become an apostate. Peter tells us that "But

6. Lloyd-Jones, *Romans*, 8:17–39, 298.

7. Ibid., 298.

false prophets arose among the people, just as there will be false teachers among you, who will secretly bring in destructive heresies, even denying the Master who bought them." Paedobaptists read this text as if it is saying that these false prophets had been purchased by the shed blood of Christ, and, in spite of this, they ended up falling away. And, obviously, if it happened to them then it can certainly happen in today's church. Look at what Jonty Rhodes said about this text:

> Who is Peter talking about? We might initially be tempted to say simply "non Christians" After all, they are teachers of heresy that leads other people . . . to be destroyed by Jesus. But tucked away in the middle of the verse is that simple phrase: "denying the master who bought them." In some sense Jesus owns these people in a different way from the way he owns every other human being. Normally, the language of "buying" is linked to salvation, but we've seen already that Jesus never loses those who are genuinely saved. We therefore need a third category, between "pagan" and "real Christian," to account for these people.[8]

He concludes that humanity can be sub-divided into three categories, namely, "non-Christians, covenant-breakers, and covenant-keepers."[9] By "covenant-breakers" he presumably means those baptized children who fall away. One can immediately see the ambiguity in this conclusion because we are all covenant breakers; we were all under the original covenant of works. It would be more accurate to say that humanity can be placed into two categories, those who still stand condemned by the original covenant of works and those who are in the new covenant in Christ.

In reaching an understanding of this verse we must remember that Peter was the apostle to the Jews (Gal 2:8). As we all know from the New Testament, many Jews found themselves unwilling to relinquish belief in their special status as the covenant people of God. They could never forget the words in Deuteronomy about the God who had 'bought' them (KJV, Deut 32:6). Israel as a nation was purchased as a special people. God had redeemed them from the land of Egypt. He revealed his grace to them in delivering them and placing them in the land of Canaan. This, however, was not a spiritual redemption. As Adam in the garden was told to keep certain conditions, so too was carnal Israel, only where in the case of Adam there was the possibility of success, with Israel there was none. Peter reminds the church of the fact that in spite of God's deliverance from bondage, there were false prophets who served to lead the nation away from God. In these

---

8. Rhodes, *Covenants Made Simple*, 154.

9. Ibid., 154.

verses Peter is simply warning the church to be ever vigilant regarding false teachers, using Israelite history as an example.

Perhaps the best explanation of this verse has been provided by Wayne Grudem:

> "Is not he your father who bought you?" . . . Peter is drawing an analogy between the past false prophets who arose among the Jews and those who will be false teachers within the the churches to which he writes . . . In line with this clear reference to false prophets in the Old Testament, Peter also alludes to the fact that the rebellious Jews turned away from God who "bought" them out of Egypt in the exodus. From the time of the exodus onward, any Jewish person would have considered himself or herself one who was "bought" by God in the exodus and therefore a person of God's own possession. In this sense, the false teachers arising among the people were denying God their father, to whom they rightfully belonged. So the text means not that Christ redeemed these false prophets, but simply that they were rebellious Jewish people (or church attenders in the same position as rebellious Jews) who were rightly owned by God because they had been bought out of the land of Egypt (or their forefathers had), but they were ungrateful to him. Christ's specific work on the cross is not mentioned in this verse.[10]

There are other texts that could have been examined. The above, however, should suffice to show that in spite of the protestations of paedobaptists to the contrary, the new covenant in Christ cannot be broken. There has only ever been one salvation and this is found only in the new covenant of Jesus Christ, a covenant not ratified with the blood of animals, but with the blood of God's own Son. This is the only covenant in which the true people of God are to be found, where they can cry with the apostle:

> For I am sure that neither death, nor life, nor angels, nor principalities, nor things present, nor things to come, nor powers, nor height, nor depth, nor anything else in all creation, will be able to separate us from the love of God in Christ Jesus our Lord (Rom 8:38–39)

---

10. Grudem, *Systematic Theology,* 599–600.

15

The Significance of Pentecost

WHEN JESUS WAS WITH his disciples he promised them that after his earthly work the Holy Spirit was going to come and be with them, "Nevertheless I tell you the truth: it is to your advantage that I go away, for if I do not go away, the Counselor will not come to you; but if I go, I will send him to you" (John 16:7). Just prior to Jesus' ascension he told his disciples to stay in Jerusalem to await the Holy Spirit when they would receive power to be his witnesses to the entire world (Acts 1:4–7). John had baptized with water, they were now, however, going to be baptized with the Holy Spirit (Acts 1:5).

While Old Testament believers were excluded from this particular manifestation of the Spirit one must not think that they did not have the Holy Spirit. No one can be a believer and not have the Spirit. The apostle Paul tells us "anyone who does not have the Spirit of Christ does not belong to him" (Rom 8:9). When Paul said this he was not just referring to New Testament times. King David prayed beseeching God not to take his Holy Spirit from him (Psa 51:12). Indeed, John the Baptist was filled with the Holy Spirit even from his birth (Luke 1:15).

Pentecost is about the Spirit coming upon God's people in an unprecedented new dimension. Some seem to think that in the Old Testament the Spirit was with the saints but did not indwell them. This seems to be based on what Jesus said in John 7:39; and 14:17. About the latter, Sinclair Ferguson observed:

> What is in view is not so much a distinction between the Spirit being "with" believers in the old covenant, while he dwells "in" them in the new covenant, although that view has widespread support . . . He who was "with" them in Christ's presence would then be "in" them as the Spirit of the incarnate and exalted

Christ. The contrast is located not in the manner of his dwelling so much as in the capacity in which he indwells.[1]

The important difference between the Spirit in the Old and the New Testament is to be found not in any distinction concerned "with" or "in," but rather "in the capacity in which he dwells," in other words, in the manner of his indwelling. The Spirit has always been at work, regenerating the elect and uniting them to Christ. John Owen, in reference to King David in Psalm 51, states that "it is the Spirit and his presence unto sanctification, not with respect to prophecy or any other gift whatever, that he is treating of with God. All the graces of the Spirit being almost dead and buried in him, he cries aloud that He whose they are, and who alone is able to revive and quicken them, may not be taken from him."[2] One should then have no hesitation in maintaining that the Holy Spirit was resident in believers of old, for all men are either of the flesh or of the spirit, and all Old Testament believers were of the spirit, having been made alive by the Holy Spirit (Rom 8:6).

Something new and unprecedented occurred on the Day of Pentecost. A new blessing was bestowed upon the church and it is this blessing that distinguishes New Testament saints from their Old Testament counterparts. For the first time in history, God's people were to subjectively enter into their full rights as sons. This blessing was to vouchsafe to the believer the legacy secured by Christ in the ratification of the new covenant.

The peculiar manifestation of the Spirit at Pentecost provided believers with a new awareness of their position in Christ. They were to "understand the gifts bestowed on us by God" (1 Cor 2:12). These "things freely given" have always been the possession of the church in Christ, for example, Abraham was as much in Christ, a joint heir with Christ, and a recipient of the same salvific blessings as New Testament saints. Even though he saw the promise from afar and was a participator in the new covenant, having become a new creation in Christ with a heart of flesh upon which God's law was being written, he nevertheless lacked that subjective appreciation of his position. He lacked the awareness of what his position in Christ entailed. To use a simple analogy. Man's position in the universe following the discoveries of Copernicus and Galileo did not change, objectively it was exactly the same as before. What changed was not man's position, but, rather, his perception of his position. In like manner, it was the believer's perception of his position in Christ that changed at Pentecost. The Old Testament saint possessed all, yet did not know it. Like a child under age, the believer prior to Christ had not reached that age when he would, so to speak, be given the key to the door; when he

1. Ferguson, *Holy Spirit*, 68.
2. Owen, *Works*, 11, 331.

would in an experiential manner enter into what was already his. Old Testament believers needed to undergo tutelage by their father to prepare them for maturity. Maturity came at Pentecost and for the first time believers could experientially enter into the glorious riches that are theirs in Christ. While the believer was previously a son, he had not received the Spirit of adoption (Rom 8:15), as Paul reminds the Galatians, "But when the fullness of time had come, God sent forth his Son, born of a woman, born under Law, to redeem those who were under the Law, so that we might receive adoption as sons. And because you are sons, God sent the Spirit of his Son into our hearts, crying 'Abba Father'" (Gal 4:4–7). This involves the Holy Spirit bearing witness to the believer's spirit that he is truly a son of God (Rom 8:16). It serves as an earnest guaranteeing to the believer's heart the inheritance that is his in Christ (Eph 1:14).

We see something of this in Acts chapter nineteen with the believers at Ephesus. Paul enquired as to whether they had received the Holy Spirit when they believed, and they retorted that they had not even heard of the Spirit (Acts 19:2). Obviously they had the Spirit, otherwise, they would not have believed the message of John about the one who was to come (v.4). They where, however, missing the Pentecostal blessing. The same can be seen in the case of Apollos, "He had been instructed in the way of the Lord; and being fervent in spirit, he spoke and taught accurately the things concerning Jesus, though he knew only the baptism of John" (Acts 18:25). He was, nevertheless lacking something and it was necessary for Aquila and Priscilla to give him further instruction in order that he might understand the way of "God more accurately" (v.26).

These believers were typical of the Old Testament saints, who had not received the inner witness of the Spirit concerning all the riches that are theirs in Christ.

John Owen paints a vivid picture of believers before Pentecost who:

> Had their sight under the Old Testament, and the object was proposed to them, but at a great distance . . . When the traveler in his way on the downs and hills is encompassed with a thick mist and fog, though he be in his way, yet he is uncertain, and nothing is presented to him in its proper shape and distance; things near seem to be afar off, and things afar off to be near, and everything

has, though not false, yet an uncertain appearance. Let the sun break forth and scatter the mists and fogs that are about him, and immediately everything appears quite another shape to him, so as indeed, he is already to think he is not where he was. His way is plain, he is certain of it and the entire region about lies evident under his eye; yet there is no alteration made, but the removal of the mists and clouds that interrupted his sight.[3]

What Benjamin Warfield said about the Trinity in the Old Testament can equally be applied to the believer's knowledge of his position in Christ:

> The Old Testament may be likened to a chamber richly furnished but dimly lighted; the introduction of light brings into it nothing which was not there before; but it brings out into clearer view much of what is in it but was only dimly or even not at all conceived before.[4]

In the pre-Pentecostal days, the saints were, metaphorically speaking, in regard to their position in Christ, surrounded by "thick mists and fogs." Even Jesus' disciples were confused. Jesus had to tell them that the Spirit would later come and lead them into truth (John 16:12–13). The sun broke "forth and scattered the mists and fogs," and for the first time, the saints were given a new revelation of Christ's legacy.

Pentecost marked not the beginning of the church, as some would have us believe, but rather, marked the church having reached adulthood. Prior to this, the believer was treated like a child, one who was awaiting that day when he would enter into the fullness of his inheritance. According to Nehemiah Coxe, Old Testament believers were "children of God (though children under age they were subject to the pedagogy of the law, yet) as to their spiritual and eternal state, walked with God and found acceptance with him in the covenant of grace."[5] Pre-Pentecost believers were as fully in the covenant of grace, the new covenant in Christ, as we are today, but it was only at Pentecost they experienced the true liberty of the children of God. The church at Pentecost became aware of the testator's legacy in a way it had never done before.

The apostle equates what occurred at Pentecost with being "sealed with the promised Holy Spirit" (Eph 1:13). The "effects of this sealing are gracious operations of the Holy Spirit in and upon believers but the sealing

---

3. Owen, *Works*, 15, 72.

4. Warfield, *Biblical and Theological Studies*, 30.

5. Coxe, "Discourse Of The Covenants," 133.

is itself the communication of the Spirit to us."[6] To quote Ferguson, "The promises of God—the promises of grace in salvation—are sealed to us and we, correspondingly enter into the enjoyment of him. The objective produces the subjective."[7] It is this particular manifestation of the Spirit that seals to the believer the inheritance of Christ's legacy. The Spirit is himself the seal because, as the Spirit of Christ, he dwells in us as the guarantor of what is ours. The Spirit makes known to the believer "the mystery of his will, according to his purpose, which he set forth in Christ as a plan for the fullness of time, to unite all things in him, things in heaven and things on earth" (Eph 1:9–10), or as Paul tells tells the Colossians, "the mystery hidden for ages and generations, but now revealed to his saints" (Col 1:26).

The baptism with the Spirit can be likened to a son meeting his father in person, where previously he had only a photograph. Being in possession of only the photograph, the son knows the person to be his father, however, he lacks that intimacy that comes with meeting his father face-to-face, where he can receive a fatherly hug. Another illustration would be the child who might refer to his father in a rather formal manner as 'father' or 'sir', there is something of a sternness about it. The baptism instead allows for the child to refer to his father by the more intimate name of "daddy."

Jesus told his disciples that, "In that day you will know that I am in the Father, and you in me" (John 14:20). He was not suggesting that from a certain time they would come into unity with him, but rather, that they would come to know what is the true nature of their position in him. Essentially, the believer is enabled to enter into a new level of intimacy with his God. Believers will experience a particular manifestation of the love of God, "My Father will love him, and we shall come to him and make our home with him" (John 14:23). Baptism with the Spirit is the third and highest level of assurance a believer can have. In regard to the Pentecostal Spirit baptism, Lloyd-Jones tells us that this blessing "is a consciousness of the fact that we have been adopted into the family of God. A consciousness of it, and not merely a belief of the fact."It involves feelings, of course, it does. The child who only saw his father in a photograph and now meets him in the flesh experiences something that goes beyond mere knowledge.

In the previous version of this book, I was criticized for implying that what occurred at Pentecost amounted to no more than believers attaining a greater intellectual appreciation of their position in Christ. It was, however, not my intention to give this impression. Of course, Spirit baptism goes well beyond the realm of the intellect. It is not something that only affects the

6. Owen, *Works*, 4, 400.

7. Ferguson, *John Owen*, 122.

believer's knowledge of what and who he is in Christ, no, it goes much deeper. I would suggest that it involves the very thing that is missing in so many of our churches. Today many in the church possess an awful lot of knowledge, but there is a lack of that visceral assurance; the profound certainty and conviction that we find exhibited in Christ's post-Pentecost disciples. The world does not seek to know about the things of Christ because when it looks at us it sees something it does not want. We go about with long faces and bowed heads, instead of radiating the fire that Christ's early disciples exhibited. None could accuse us of being on fire for the Lord. We need to get away from the idea that the baptism of the Spirit something unfelt, something we simply accept by faith. Nothing could be further from the truth. Let us look at some of the examples employed by Lloyd-Jones as he sought to convey the experiential nature of this blessing. He gives a number of testimonies, but here let us look at just a couple of these. Thomas Goodwin, when expounding Ephesians 1:13 put it like this:

> There is a light that cometh and over-powereth a man's soul and assureth him that God is his, and he is God's, and that God loveth him from everlasting . . . It is a light beyond the light of ordinary faith . . . the next thing to heaven; you have no more, you can have no more, till you come thither . . . It is faith elevated and raised up above its ordinary rate, it is the electing love of God brought home to the soul.[8]

The second comes from Jonathan Edwards:

> Once, as I rode out into the woods for my health, in 1737, having alighted from my horse in a retired place as my manner commonly has been, to walk for divine contemplation and prayer, I had a view that for me was extraordinary, of the glory of the Son of God as Mediator between God and man, and His wonderful, great, full, pure and sweet grace and love, and meek and gentle condescension. This grace that appeared so calm and sweet appeared also great above the heavens. The Person of Christ appeared ineffably excellent, with an excellency great enough to swallow up all though and conception, which continued, as near as I can judge, about an hour; which kept me the greater part of time in a flood of tears, and weeping aloud. I felt an ardency of soul to be, what I know not otherwise how to express, emptied and annihilated; to lie in the dust and be full of Christ alone; to love Him with a holy and pure love; to trust Him; to live upon

---

8. Lloyd-Jones, *Ephesians* ch 1, 274–75.

Him; and to serve and follow Him; and to be perfectly sanctified and made pure with a divine and heavenly purity.[9]

These two examples should suffice to show that the baptism or sealing with the Spirit affects the whole man and not just his intellect.

We must avoid equating what happened at Pentecost, where the disciples were filled with the Spirit, with passages such as Ephesians 5:18, "And do not get drunk with wine, for that is debauchery, but be filled with the Spirit" (Eph 5:18). Confusion arises because the word "filled" is used at both Pentecost and in Ephesians 5:18. The meaning, however, is very different. At Pentecost the disciples were passive recipients. The Spirit was concerned with providing them with a new appreciation of their position in Christ. It is not a blessing that they are able to control. Paul commands the Ephesian Christians to ensure that their minds are filled with the things of God. It is something the believer can control. Perhaps the best way to understand what the apostle means here is to give a simple example. My son is into cycling in a big way. One might say that he breathes, eats, and sleeps cycling. Cycling fills his mind. This is what Paul is saying here, only instead of cycling, we are to speak to ourselves about God's word, to deliberately fill our hearts with the things pertaining to God, as Paul puts it, "addressing one another in psalms and hymns and spiritual songs, singing and making melody to the Lord with your heart" (Eph 5:19).

There is a marked degree of confusion about the nature of the Pentecostal blessing, and all too often it results in Old Testament saints being denied what was theirs in Christ. By examining what the blessings is not, and what it does not achieve one will be able to appreciate its significance all the more. For example, James M. Hamilton in his book entitled *God's Indwelling Presence* argues that whilst Old Testament saints were regenerate, they were, however, not indwelt by the Spirit, "whereas circumcision of the heart was possible for Jeremiah's contemporaries, writing the law on their hearts would await the inauguration of the new covenant . . . although the old covenant remnant was not indwelt by the Spirit . . . the old covenant remnant were regenerate."[10] He further tells us, "If the Spirit indwelt anything in the Old Testament, it was the temple made with hands, God's Spirit, like His Torah, was to reside in the temple."[11] Hamilton is here clearly confusing the two covenants. Yes, on occasions God's Spirit did make himself manifest in the tabernacle, and then later in the temple, however, like the rest of the Mosaic covenant, this was conditional on an obedience the people could not

9. Ibid., 276.

10. Hamilton, *God's Indwelling Presence*, 47.

11. Ibid., 47.

deliver. On those occasions when God did manifest himself it was purely the result of grace. As God had settled the nation in Canaan purely based on his grace, but made their continuance conditional, so God at times displayed his presence in the temple but again made his continuance dependent on the people's obedience to his law. God's true temple, that in which God's true people dwells, is not made with human hands. The type is only a faint reflection of the antitype. The earthly temple was part and parcel of that covenant that the people broke.

The Israelite who embraced the promise, who saw beyond the outward paraphernalia, those externals "that deal only with food and drink and various washings, regulations for the body imposed until the time of the reformation" (Heb 9:10), participated in the new covenant. The only covenant of grace, whose temple was the heart, from which the believer makes 'living sacrifices' (Rom 12:1). Hamilton suggests that Jeremiah's promise about the writing of God's laws on the heart was only for a time after Christ, when the Spirit would indwell the believer. He tells us that "the concerns of the Old Testament is with God's presence with the nation, not with individual members possessing the Spirit."[12]

Here again, he is confusing the conditional promise given to the nation with the new covenant in which there is salvation. The whole point of the Old Testament is concerned with directing individuals to the new covenant in Christ, that they, though living before its ratification in the death of the testator, might receive its blessings. Within the nation there existed the true people of God, the remnant. As I have kept emphasizing, all of these had experienced a new birth, knew justification by faith, and were being sanctified by the Spirit of God who indwelt them, in other words, they were all in Christ.

The Spirit was not with the nation because of its disobedience. As we have seen, the law given to the nation served to make manifest man's inability to meet its conditions that they might lay hold of the promise in Christ. Hamilton is confusing the means with the end and the type with the antitype. He appears to be saying that the Spirit dealt with those external things, things of the letter, rather than in the hearts of individual believers. He is essentially endowing the old covenant with an efficacy it never possessed, whilst, at the same time, denuding the new covenant of the benefits of Christ for the Old Testament believer.

In Hebrews 9:8 we are told that under the Old Testament the way into the most holy place had not been opened or made manifest. Many appeal to verses like this in an attempt to show that Old Testament saints had no access

12. Ibid., 25.

into the presence of God. They link verses like this to Spirit baptism, believing that it was this blessing enabled believers to have access to God that had previously been unavailable to them. The text, however, does not say this, as Owen puts it, "it is not that there was no entrance into the holiest of holies during that season," (the Old Testament), "but only that the way of it was not yet manifest."[13] In the formal consummation of the new covenant we see a public declaration of our access where "the curtain of the temple was torn in two, from top to bottom" (Matt 27:51). Old Testament believers could enter into the holiest place, and here one does not mean the type that the priest entered into but once a year. Although believers did not fully grasp the significance of this as did their New Testament counterparts, they did commune directly with God through Christ "although the whereby they did so was not yet openly declared, for they had but a shadow, or dark obscure representation of the good things to come."[14] In saying that the way had not yet been made manifest the writer essentially means that "there was not an 'open manifestation' of it."[15] Again, to quote Owen, the writer "does not say that there was no way then into the most holy place, none made, none provided, none made use of, but there was not an 'open Manifestation' of it."[16] What does this have to do with the baptism of the Spirit? It was at Pentecost that believers came to a realization of the liberty that was theirs in Christ. It was a liberty that provided them with a new boldness to come before the throne of God. As we saw earlier, Spirit baptism enabled the sons of God to experientially enter into the true nature of their sonship.

One question that has caused much controversy in today's church concerns whether the gift of the Holy Spirit is received at or subsequent to conversion. Many evangelicals are of the opinion that since Pentecost all believers, from the moment of conversion, are in receipt of this blessing. They use 1 Corinthians 12:13 as proof of this: "For in one Spirit we were all baptized into one body-Jews and Greeks, slaves and free-all were made to drink of one Spirit." The verse clearly does refer to all believers, but is it concerned with the baptism of the Spirit referred to by Jesus (Acts 1:5)?

According to John Stott, the Spirit in this verse "is the means of entry into the body of Christ."[17] Peter Masters tells us that "this verse shows very clearly that the baptism with the Spirit occurs at conversion . . . Every believer has been baptized (which means placed into), the body of Christ by

13. Owen, *Works*, 6, 238.

14. Ibid., 238.

15. Ibid., 240.

16. Ibid., 240.

17. Stott, *Baptism and Fullness*, 39.

the Holy Spirit. Obviously, it is at conversion that we enter the family, the body of Christ."[18] Edgar Andrews appears to take a similar position. He too insists that the blessing occurs at conversion, "baptism in the Spirit here refers to our initiation into the body of Christ, the church. It is universal among believers."[19] Packer and Stibbs maintain that "all who have come to faith since the day of Pentecost, without a single exception, have been 'baptized' by Him in the Spirit into the one body . . . the glorified Lord has sent His Spirit to indwell them."[20] According to Jonty Rhodes, 'there's only one body of Christ, the church. And there's only one way into that body: Spirit baptism. Therefore, whoever you are, you've been baptized with the Spirit."[21] J. D. Watson tells that "the Baptism with the Holy Spirit places us into the body of Christ. At one time we were in Adam, but now we are in Christ."[22] We see again this same teaching with Douglas Wilson, where he tells us that, "it is necessary to recall what this spiritual baptism of the Spirit accomplishes. It circumcises the heart by removing the body of fleshly sin. It places the individual into union with Christ in His death, burial, and resurrection. It washes his sins away. In short, this true baptism is what makes a person regenerate."[23] By the baptism of the Spirit, Watson and Wilson are clearly referring to what took place at Pentecost.

I have alluded to the above to show just how widespread this teaching is in evangelical circles. All of the above associate 1 Cor 12:13 with what occurred at Pentecost. This, however, is a grave mistake because it again places a wedge between Old and New Testament believers. To imply that union with Christ only began at Pentecost is tantamount to saying that Old Testament saints were either not united to him or that they could be saved outside of Christ. Such a possibility is unthinkable. If one was to accept Douglas Wilson's position one would have to draw the unscriptural conclusion that all who lived before Pentecost were uncircumcised of heart.

The only valid alternative, if one is determined to apply this verse to the baptism with the Spirit, is to see the baptism as more of a validation of a previously existing position in Christ. The baptism does not place one into the body of Christ, but, rather, in the words of Derek Prince, it "acknowledges and makes public and effectual our membership in the body, of which

18. Masters, *Only One Baptism*, 18.

19. Andrews, *Spirit Has Come*, 140.

20. Stibbs, *Spirit Within You*, 35.

21. Rhodes, *Covenants Made Simple*, 164.

22. Watson, *Salvation is of the Lord*, 236.

23. Wilson, *To A Thousand Generations*, 53.

we already have been a part."[24] So the believer was previously in Christ, but at Pentecost the Spirit sealed us by which Jesus "acknowledges the member as a part of His body."[25]

1 Corinthians 12:13, however, has nothing to do with the Pentecostal experience, but is, rather, concerned with the act of regeneration where the person is spiritually resurrected and placed into the sphere or realm of Christ. It concerns that work of the Spirit where the believer is taken out of Adam and placed into the the second Adam. About this text, Lloyd-Jones commented that we need to be "clear in our minds that he," the apostle, "is not dealing with experience, but status, condition, position. There are only two possibilities; we are either, every one of us, in Adam, or else we are in Christ. There is no middle position."[26] It is as a consequence of this the believer comes under the influence of the Holy Spirit and is made to drink of the Spirit of God.

Where the baptism that occurred at Pentecost is experimental, the baptism by which the Holy Spirit makes one a member of Christ's body is not. Whether one is looking at, say, Abraham, Enoch or the apostle Paul, all have been baptized by the Spirit into Christ's body, they have all been made beneficiaries of his saving work. Nevertheless, they were not all baptized with the Holy Spirit.

What then was the purpose of the peculiar Pentecostal blessing? It seems that Luke provides the answer. The disciples were not to go and immediately start witnessing but were instructed to wait in Jerusalem for the gift of the Holy Spirit. They were told that when he came they would "receive power when the Holy Spirit has come upon you, and you will be my witnesses in Jerusalem and in all Judea and Samaria, and to the end of the earth" (Acts 1:7–8). It seems clear that the gift of the Spirit was for witnessing. To provide the disciples with the power necessary to preach the gospel. It was the conviction and assurance provided by the Spirit that enabled them to witness so effectively.

At or After Conversion?

Whether the baptism with the Spirit has since Pentecost been given to all at their conversion, or can, in certain circumstances, be given subsequent to conversion is a subject that has generated much controversy. One thing does

24. Prince, *Baptism in the Holy Spirit*, 19.
25. Ibid., 20.
26. Lloyd-Jones, *Romans*, 6, *The New Man*, 39.

seem clear from reading the New Testament. When believers were baptized with the Holy Spirit and with fire, they knew all about it. It was experiential! Also, the baptism and the sealing appear to be closely related, for example, Paul tells the Ephesians that they had been "sealed with the promised Holy Spirit" (Eph 1:13). The promise referred to appears to be the same as that which Christ gave to his disciples just prior to his ascension. Watson tells us the "sealing has nothing to do with experience,"[27] and that it 'occurs at the moment of salvation.'[28] He accuses men such as the late Martyn Lloyd-Jones of allowing "mystical ideas about the sealing to violate the simple purpose of the act."[29] I am certain, however, that the disciples did not simply take it by faith. On the day of Pentecost the people thought the disciples were "full of new wine" (Acts 2:13). In other words, they exhibited the characteristics on someone slightly inebriated. And, of course, there must be a mystical dimension, for one is here speaking of the Spirit of the living God filling one's whole being. In Galatians 3:2 Paul asks the Christians: "Did you receive the Spirit by the works of the law or by hearing with faith?" (Gal 3:5). Martyn Lloyd-Jones asks a question that, I believe, clearly points to the baptism with the Spirit as being something experiential: "How can anyone answer this question if it is something outside the realm of experience? How can one know if he has received the Spirit if it is not something experimental?"[30] Again, if one unconsciously receives the blessing at conversion the very question would be superfluous.

Clearly, something new occurred at Pentecost, something that would substantially change the church of Christ. Something that would differentiate post-Pentecost believers from their Old Testament forbears. This being the case it is very difficult to maintain the blessing to be non-experiential. And, indeed, if this blessings is not experiential one is justified in asking the question: What do we have that makes us any different from Abraham, Isaac and Jacob etc? If we just accept the baptism of the Spirit by faith, just assume that it happens at conversion, then it appears the only thing that actually differentiates us is our clearer understanding of redemption; the fact that we have the New Testament and a greater intellectual appreciation of our position in Christ. The Christian Church has never before in its history possessed a greater intellectual understanding of the Faith, yet, that being said, it appears to me that far from having more, the church in certain parts of this world, and by this I mean the Western world, appears to have

27. Watson, *Salvation is of the Lord*, 239.

28. Ibid., 239.

29. Ibid., 239.

30. Lloyd-Jones, *Ephesians 1, God's Ultimate Purpose*, 271.

considerably less. Where is that inexpressible joy that is filled with the glory of God (1 Pet 1:8)? "The Christian is not meant to be a man who is just managing to hold on and who is miserable and unhappy, and forcing himself to do these things, dragging himself, as it were, to the house of God."[31] Yet this is just what appears to be happening . We speak of our orthodoxy, yet we seem, all too often, to be just going through the motions without that fire in our bones; without the excitation that should be the result of being in Christ. There appears to be something of a hiatus between that which we profess with our tongues and what we experience in our hearts.

Speaking from a Welsh perspective, one only needs to attend many of our churches to know that all is not right. One can legitimately ask the question: Have these people really been baptized with the Holy Spirit and with fire? Perhaps one of the most prominent symptoms that all is far from well is that instead of worshipping twice on a Sunday, it is becoming more common now for evangelical churches to have one meeting. Does it not stand to reason that if Christians were truly on fire for the things of God every opportunity would be taken to meet and worship together? It seems that we are witnessing the opposite of that which takes place when Christians are filled with the Spirit. To quote Lloyd-Jones, referring to what occurred in the New Testament church, he tells us that "when people are baptized with the Holy Spirit . . . they want to keep together, to get together as often as they can-they continued daily, steadfastly, talking about these things, singing together, praising God together. This was the thing that was first above everything else. Everything else came second."[32] This no longer seems to be a priority in the church.

Our pews are largely empty and the world outside treats our message with a cold indifference. In our superficial attempts to communicate, the church is allowing, in an unprecedented manner, cultural trends to change doctrine and practice. Perhaps nowhere is this more evident in evangelical churches than in the increasing tendency to include of women in the ministry, where they are allowed to have authority over men. The plain teaching of Scripture (1 Tim 2:11–14) is now being contradicted and reinterpreted so as not to offend the cultural fashions. The plain fact is we don't appear to have the necessary conviction, power, and boldness in our preaching and witness that we see in the New Testament.

This leads me to the conclusion that what is required is nothing less than the baptism with the Spirit! That in many, if not most, instances the blessing is most certainly not received at conversion. The church needs to

---

31. Lloyd-Jones, *Joy Unspeakable*, 102.
32. Ibid., 102.

pray for this, not, as an aside, but as its main priority. Nothing short of this is required, providing believers with not only the realization of what it means to be in Christ, but also the necessary power to turn the world upside down, to turn men and women from sin to that salvation that is to be found only in Christ Jesus.

16

Proof Texts for Infant Baptism?

BEFORE CONCLUDING, I WANT to examine some of the texts used by the paedobaptists that supposedly support infant baptism. I shall briefly examine four texts, namely, Acts 2:39, 1 Cor 7:14, household baptisms in the case of Lydia in Acts 16:14–15 and the Philippian Jailer in Acts 16:25–40, and, finally, Jesus' concern for "little children."

Perhaps the most frequently quoted verse supposedly proving infant baptism is Acts 2:39, where Peter on the day of Pentecost announced to the crowd, "For the promise is for you and for your children and for all who are far off, everyone whom the Lord our God calls to himself." According to Jewett, "this verse is frequently inscribed as a sort of paedobaptist motto at the beginning of books and pamphlets defending infant baptism."[1] However, the promise Peter was speaking of here was concerned with the baptism of the Spirit. Paedobaptist interpretations tend to omit what Peter said before mentioning the promise, "Repent and be baptized every one of you in the name of Jesus Christ for the forgiveness of your sins, and you will receive the gift of the Holy Spirit" (Acts 2:38). This verse is the qualifier. Yes, the promise is for their children; should they repent. Repentance comes before one can receive the gift. It is difficult to see how the paedobaptist can circumvent this.

The obvious interpretation of Peter's words is that the promise is both for Jews and Gentiles, "The promise is for you and your children." This simply means that it is applicable for present and future generations of Jews who believe and repent. "To all who are afar off," simply alludes to the Gentile world, as the apostle states in Ephesians concerning the Gentiles, "you who were once far off have been brought near by the blood of Christ" (Eph 2:13). If one paraphrased the text it would run as follows, "the promised Spirit of God is now for the whole world, and regarding the Jews, it is not only for

1. Jewett, *Infant Baptism*, 119.

present generations but for those in the future. It is also for those who thus far have been outside of the covenant, namely the Gentiles." It has nothing whatsoever to do with the baptism of infants.

Behind the paedobaptist insistence on Peter's words relating to one's literal children is again their refusal to acknowledge the new covenant as being radically different, rather than just a restatement of the old covenant. As we have seen, paedobaptists want the filial bonds of the old covenant to be imposed on the new. Yes, father and son were both in the old covenant, and all sons were circumcised, but it was a national covenant that only condemned. Both father and son, unless they believed the promises, were equally lost in sin. Beeke and Lanning ask the following question regarding the Jews who listened to Peter's words:

> Suppose that you were one of those Jews, who had grown up knowing all the privileges and encouragements of a God who says, "As the soul of the father, so also the soul of the son is mine" (Ezek 18:4). You are told that in Christ the covenant has been restated in a new and better way, but children are now left out of the picture. They are no longer included in the way that God deals with people. Would it not at least trouble you to think that God has made such as alteration in the way in which he offers his grace to men and women?[2]

They seem to be suggesting that the new covenant did not radically alter what was there before. One should remember that with the formal establishment of the new covenant, the old covenant, with all its paraphernalia came to an end. All that Israel after the flesh had known and boasted about was over. The covenant had not simply "been restated in a new and better way," but is an entirely new covenant. I don't see how the text from Ezekiel could support the paedobaptist case. Children were not in the covenant of grace then and they are not in the covenant of grace today, unless, of course, they undergo a new birth. It should also be noted that the souls of all men belong to the Lord. If, however, Beeke and Lanning mean that the soul belongs to the Lord in a new covenantal sense, then it is a somewhat precarious stance to take, for, according to them, many souls knew only the outward administration of the covenant rather than the inner substance, and were lost. One might wonder, therefore, if, perhaps, God has failed to safeguard such souls? That he who began a good work did not see it through to fruition.

2. Beeke, "Unto You And Your Children," 57.

Beeke and Lanning appear to be suggesting that Peter could not be referring to something that was radically new because the Jews would have taken umbrage:

> We have to remind ourselves that the multitude who heard Peter's sermon on Pentecost was Jewish. It included Jews from Palestine, proselytes . . . The Old Testament was all they had of the Holy Scriptures. As they listened to Peter preaching from those Scriptures . . . they could have understood his words in only one way—as a reference to the promise in God's covenant and the fact that that promise extended not only to believers but to their children as well.[3]

To suggest this is to turn a blind eye to the fact that already so much had changed. The Messiah the Jews expected was certainly not the one who had died upon a cross, and the kingdom they anticipated was not that borne reference to by Jesus. They had heard of Jesus' resurrection, and that there was to be a change of order. They, no doubt, were acquainted with Jeremiah's words, "I will make a new covenant with the house Israel and of Judah, not like the covenant I made with their fathers" (Jer 31:31). They were all aware that they were in the midst of radical change, so it seems unlikely that they would have protested at Peter's words, "the promise is for you and your children." Beeke and Lanning are using Old Testament passages concerning doctrines that were passing away to interpret something that will be of abiding significance in the church of God.

Presbyterians, in their desire to make the text conform to their paradigm, in the words of Jewett, "violate the elementary structure of the text. Whether we think of Peter's listeners or their children or those far removed from the immediate scene of the first-century kerygma, the point is that the promise is to all whom God shall call."[4] Howard Marshall's hits the nail on the head concerning this text:

> This phrase has sometimes been taken as a justification for infant baptism, but this is to press it unduly. If we are to link it with the context, we note that the prophecy in verse 17 thinks of children who are old enough to prophesy, and that verse 38 speaks of receiving forgiveness and the Spirit; in neither case are infants obviously involved. The point of the phrase is rather to express the unlimited mercy of God which embraces the hearers

---

3. Beeke, "Unto You And To Your Children," 57.

4. Jewett, *Infant Baptism*, 121.

and subsequent generations of their descendents, and in addition all that are afar off.[5]

Paul's first letter to the Corinthians, when dealing with the principles surrounding marriage provides advice on what the believer should do if he/she finds that the wife or husband is an unbeliever: "if any brother has a wife who is an unbeliever, and she consents to live with him, he should not divorce her" (1 Cor 7:12). The apostle's reason for this teaching has been used by the paedobaptists to justify baptizing infants:

> For the unbelieving husband is made holy because of his wife, and the unbelieving wife is made holy because of her husband. Otherwise your children would be unclean, but as it is they are holy. (1 Cor 7:15)

It is somewhat bizarre that they should use this text. If the child is holy and thus needs to be baptized, then can not the same be said about the Christian's unbelieving wife or husband? According to the text, they too are deemed to be holy or sanctified. According to Errol Hulse:

> To be born into a Christian family is to be born into an environment of blessing. To be born into or to be adopted into such a family is to be sanctified in the basic meaning of that term. To be sanctified simply means to be set aside or apart. Hence the unconverted partner in a marriage is set apart. He is sanctified in the sense that God takes into account the fact that he or she is joined in life to a believer. That does not mean that the person is holy in the converted sense. 1 Corinthians 7:14 expressly states the case of the unbelieving partners, "they are holy." Their lives are the very opposite of holiness. It is their position of being set apart that is acknowledge.[6]

The same applies to the children, they too are set apart. The text does not touch upon baptism, and to use the text to somehow justify infant baptism is to misuse Scripture to satisfy one's presuppositions. About this verse, R. Lenski, who is a paedobaptist, wrote, "Paul intimates nothing about in regard to the baptism of such children . . . The holiness which Paul here predicates regarding children has nothing to do with the sacrament."[7]

Much has been made of household baptisms. Paedobaptists insist that if the entire household was to be baptized, it must have contained children, and these too would have been baptized. Two texts frequently used concern

5. Marshall, *Acts*, 82.

6. Hulse, *Testimony of Baptism*, 121–22.

7. Lenski, *First and Second Epistles to the Corinthians*, 293.

the case of Lydia (Acts 16:14–15), and the Philippian Jailer (Acts 16:25–34). In both of these, there is a preaching of the Word preceding baptism. In Lydia's case we read that she was one of the people who heard Paul and Silas, and "the Lord opened her heart to pay attention to what was said by Paul"(v.14). We then read, 'after she was baptized, and her household as well" (v.15). If we apply Occam's Razor here, where the simplest explanation is usually the best, it would appear that Lydia's household also heard the message, believed, and was baptized. Even if there were infants present, the word household does not have to mean every single person. Jewett comments that

> Nothing in the passage implies that Lydia was a married woman with nursing children. For she travelled on business some 300 miles from her native city and felt the liberty as head of the house, to invite men into her home. Since Luke speaks of her household being baptized, and of the importunity with which she constrained the apostles to abide in her house, no mention being made of her husband, the most likely hypothesis is that she had no husband. In any event there must have been other adults in her household-domestics, friends, business associates-who were led by her example to confess their faith with her in baptism.[8]

Nothing can be inferred from the text about the baptism of infants.

The case of the Philippian Jailer is similar, however, the preaching about Christ is even more pronounced:

> And the jailer called for lights and rushed in, and trembling with fear he fell down before Paul and Silas. Then he brought them out and said, "Sirs, what must I do to be saved?" And they said, "Believe in the Lord Jesus, and you will be saved, you and your household." And they spoke the word of the Lord to him and to all who were in his house. And he took them the same hour of the night and washed their wounds; and he was baptized at once, he and all his family. Then he brought them up into his house and set food before them. And he rejoiced along with his entire household that he had believed in God (Acts 16:29–34).

From this, we can see that their baptism was subsequent to their faith in Christ. According to Marcel, "it is only the head of the family who manifests repentance and confesses his faith,"[9] in the case of the Philippian Jailer,

8. Jewett, *Infant Baptism*, 49.
9. Marcel, *Biblical Doctrine of Infant Baptism*, 209.

only he became a Christian, the others in his household perhaps simply following his example in being baptized. We are, according to this kind of explanation, expected to believe that whilst the "household" did not actually believe, they still rejoiced on account of the head of the household believing. This, however, makes little sense. If they did not believe they must have rejected the gospel message. They were still in their sins and at enmity with God. Can one then honestly say that such persons would have rejoiced because another had believed the gospel?

If one allows the text to speak, instead of imposing upon it one's preconceived theology, what we see follows the same baptismal formula that we see in Acts 2:28; those who hear the gospel, believe the gospel and are baptized. Faith and repentance precede baptism. Instead of suggesting that it was only the Jailer who believed, one should notice that the entire household heard the gospel, "they spoke the word of the Lord to him *and to all who were in his house.*" Clearly, they believed and their baptism was a result of this. In chapter 16:34, we read, "And he rejoiced along with his entire household that he had believed in God." In other words, the jailer rejoiced because he had been saved, the household also rejoiced because they had likewise been saved. Any emphasis on the jailer is no doubt because he had control over the prisoners, and now he would treat them fairly and with respect. The text is most certainly not speaking about infants. No doubt, in the case of the Philippian Jailer, because of the time being the early hours of the morning, infants would have been tucked up in bed. Therefore, "Household" in all probability simply related to all those who had exercised faith in Christ.

The other so-called proof for infant baptism are those gospel references of Jesus blessing the little children (Matt 19:13–15; Mark 10:13–16; Luke 18:15–17). In Matthew we read:

> Then children were brought to him that he might lay his hands of them and pray. The disciples rebuked the people, but Jesus said, "Let the little children come come to me and do not hinder them, for to such belongs the kingdom of heaven."

This passage "has become dearer to paedobaptists than any other in Scripture."[10] Calvin, commenting on these verses, goes so far as to exclude the need for faith in children, as if they are in a special category:

> To exclude from the grace of redemption those who are of that age would be too cruel . . . [The Anabaptists] refuse baptism to infants, because infants are incapable of understanding that

---

10. Jewett, *Infant Baptism*, 55.

mystery which is denoted by it. We on the other hand, maintain that . . . it ought not to be denied to infants, whom God
adopts and washes with the blood of his Son. Their objection
that repentance and newness of life are also denoted by it, it is
easily answered. Infants are renewed by the Spirit of God, according to the capacity of their age . . Again, when they argue
that there is no other way in which we are reconciled to God,
and become heirs of adoption, than by faith, we admit this as
to adults, but, with respect to infants, this passage demonstrates
it to be false . . . But it is presumption and sacrilege to drive far
from the fold of Christ those whom he cherishes in his bosom.[11]

David Gibson tells us why this text is considered so important to
paedobaptists:

but its bearing lies in the fact that paedobaptists work from a
theology of *infants* before we develop a theology of infant *baptism*. Jesus does not say that the kingdom of heaven belongs to
those who are *like* little children; rather it belongs to 'such as
these' (v. 14). When Calvin argues, in discussion of this passage,
that Christ came to enlarge not restrict the Father's mercy, he is
working from a covenantal frame of reference. A biblical theology of covenant charts the drama of exclusivity developing into
increasing inclusivity, as the gospel to Israel progresses towards
its intended fulfillment as the gospel to the nations. If children
were included in covenant promise in the OT, would we really
expect Jesus to exclude them as he comes to fulfill all that had
been promised?[12]

So, in other words, Gibson is acknowledging that it is an interpretation
determined entirely by their presuppositions. We have seen the old covenant was not of grace but of works, this being the case, the entire paedobaptist paradigm collapses like the proverbial house of cards because whilst
the children may have been in the old covenant, without faith, they were
certainly not in the new covenant.

Marcel, commenting on this passage makes a totally unwarranted assumption, "He could not have offered these children to God without giving
them purity . . . It follows then that they were regenerated by the Spirit of
God in the hope of salvation."[13] To maintain this goes against the whole tenor
of conservative evangelical theology. Quoting Calvin, Marcel tells us, "The

---

11. Calvin, *Harmony of the Evangelists*, 2:390–91.

12. Gibson, "Fathers of Faith," 25.

13. Ibid., 193.

children of believers are holy from the time of their birth, because before coming into the world they are adopted into the covenant of eternal life; and there is absolutely no other reason for receiving them into the Church except that already beforehand they belong to the body of Christ . . . It is necessary that the grace of adoption should precede baptism."[14] Such an assertion is, to say the least, extraordinary, especially when one considers the fact that so many children later fall away. By investing them with what can only belong to the true believer he is undermining the perseverance of the saints.

To talk about cruelty, as some do, is to play upon the emotions. Perhaps it would be crueler to see children of believers as being saved simply on account of what their parents believe, while the vast majority of children, whose parents believe not, are considered lost. Yes, in the Old Testament, when the parents ate sour grapes the children's teeth were set on edge (Jer 31:29) because they too lived in the nation whose prosperity depended on a collective obedience. Hence, the children living in the land would reap what their parents had sown. This, however, is not the case in the new covenant. Calvin makes mighty assumptions without stopping to question his own presuppositions.

One does wonder why this text is employed as a proof for infant baptism, for there is no mention of water. Spurgeon commented, "see that you read the word (about blessing the children) as it is written, and you will find no water in it, but Jesus only. Are the water and Christ the same thing? Nay, here is a wide difference, as wide as between Rome and Jerusalem . . . between false doctrine and the gospel of our Lord Jesus Christ."[15] Surely if Jesus believed in infant baptism these children would have been baptized, for clearly the rite had been brought in by this time; Jesus' own disciples had been baptized and they were baptizing others.

Jesus often taught his disciples important truths using everyday things, for example, a sower of seed, wheat, a vine etc. He is doing something similar here by comparing the innocent trust of a small child to that attitude Christians are to display. The most obvious interpretation of this text is that Jesus was demonstrating the need for a childlike faith. The point of the message has more to do with a characteristic displayed in the child's simple faith, namely, his willingness to trust than it has to do with the child himself. The child will believe whatever his father tells him. So Jesus' disciples must do the same in regard to their heavenly Father. One should, of course, consider the obvious, namely, "If therefore it was His [Jesus'] will that henceforth

14. Marcel, *Infant Baptism*, 199.
15. Spurgeon, "Children Brought to Christ," 57.

babies should be baptized, what better occasion than this to say so? Why did He not give His disciples a lesson by baptizing these babies [or having them baptized] there and then?"[16] It is clear that it wasn't his will, he didn't baptize babies and, therefore, neither should we.

16. Watson, *Should Babies Be Baptized?*, 27.

17

Conclusion

THERE IS SO MUCH more one could write about this vital doctrine. The above, however, should suffice to provide one with a flavor of the Reformed Baptist position. God is not a God of confusion but of order (1 Cor 14:33), and nowhere is this order revealed more clearly than in Baptist covenant theology. Since the Fall all humanity has been under God's curse and sentence of death. From shortly after the fall of the first man God's kingdom has been advancing, as men and woman have embraced the promised Messiah. All men sinned in Adam, and many are made alive in the second Adam. Prior to the Mosaic dispensation men and women were saved through faith in the promised Christ. This did not change at Sinai. To facilitate the Messiah's work God provided a particular nation with an explicit revelation of his righteous requirements in the Mosaic Law. The intention was not to provide an alternative way of salvation, but, rather, to, in the despair it generated, encourage fallen man to believe in the one remedy for sin, namely Jesus Christ; the one to both the law and the prophets bore witness.

Ultimately, excepting the covenant of redemption, there has only been two primary covenants, namely, the covenant of works that Adam broke and the new covenant in Christ. By birth, we are all under the first covenant. However, by a spiritual rebirth, many are under the new covenant because the second Adam has succeeded where the first failed. They have had their sins forgiven and have been pronounced righteous because Christ's righteousness has become theirs. Indeed, they are complete in him because they are part of the same mystical body, with all that belongs to Christ now belonging to them.

Throughout this work, I have sought to show that all the saved have been participants in the new covenant. In the Old Testament Christ was revealed through the promise; a promise that was ratified in his shed blood and resurrection from the dead. Even before this covenant's ratification men and woman, who believed, like Abraham, were included in the blessings of the new covenant.

It is usual for books, when examining the way covenantal blessings in the Old Testament were conveyed upon believers, to refer to the "covenant of grace." In this work, I have, on the whole, done the same. It is, however, something I have not been completely comfortable with. This is because the term is not employed in the Scriptures, and also, because no one has ever been saved but by the new covenant. It seems, therefore, more reasonable to say that all believers were members of the new covenant.

The Reformed Baptist covenantal paradigm displays unity in its simplicity. There is no duality within the new covenant. Entrance into God's salvation has always been the same, namely by exercising faith in Christ, be he promised to appear at some future time, or after his completed work. With God there is no favoritism, one child is not favored over another on the basis of what its parents may believe, except, of course, of finding itself in a privileged position in regard to the hearing of the gospel. Children of believers do not become members of the new covenant simply in virtue of being born into a certain family. God is Spirit and those who worship him do so in spirit and in truth (John 4:24). The only way into Christ is by the new birth, by becoming a new creation; having a new heart of flesh. The church of God is, and always has been, the body of Christ, and Christ as the head of his church is transforming it into the image of his glorified humanity. Unto him be the glory, both now and forever.

Bibliography

Andrews, Edgar. *The Spirit Has Come*. Darlington, UK: Evangelical Press, 1994.

Barach, John. "Covenant and Election." In *The Federal Vision*, edited by Steve Wilkins and Duane Garner. Monroe: Athanasius, 2004.

Barcellos, Richard. *Paedoism or Credoism*. Fullerton, CA: Reformed Baptist Publishers, 2000.

———., ed. *Recovering a Covenantal Heritage: Essays in Baptist Covenant Theology*. Palmdale, CA: Reformed Baptist Academic Press, 2014.

Bavinck, Herman. *Our Reasonable Faith*. Grand Rapids: Baker, 1977.

———. *Reformed Dogmatics* Vol. 3,. Grand Rapids: Baker, 2006.

Beale, G.K. *A New Testament Biblical Theology: The Unfolding of the Old Testament in the New*. Grand Rapids: Baker, 2011.

Beeke, Joel R., and Lanning B. Ray. "Unto You and Your Children." In *The Case For Covenantal Infant Baptism*, edited by Greg Strawbridge, 49–69. P&R: Phillipsburg, NJ, 2003.

Berkhof, Louis. *Systematic Theology*. Edinburgh: Banner of Truth Trust, 1979.

Blackburn, Earl. "Covenant Theology Simplified." In *Covenant Theology: A Baptist Distinctive*, edtied by Earl Blackburn, 17–61. Pelham, AL: Solid Ground Books, 2013.

Blamires, Harry. *Recovering The Christian Mind: Meeting the Challenge of Secularism*. Downers Grove, IL: InterVarsity, 1988.

Boettner, Loraine. *Studies in Theology*. Grand Rapids: Eerdmans, 1947.

Bolton, Samuel. *The True Bounds of Christian Freedom*. London: Banner of Truth Trust, 1964.

Booth, Robert R. *Children of Promise*. P&R: Phillipsburg, NJ, 1995.

Boston, Thomas. *The Beauties of Boston: A Selection of His Writings*. Inverness: Christian Focus, 1979.

Brown, Michael. *Christ And The Condition: The Covenant Theology of Samuel Petto [1624–1711]*. Grand Rapids: Reformation Heritage Books, 2012.

Buchanan, James. *The Doctrine of Justification by Faith*. Grand Rapids: Baker, 1955.

Bunyan, John. *Doctine of Law and Grace Unfolded*. http://www.chapellibrary.org/files/3913/7642/2845/bun-lawgrace.pdf.

Burgess, Anthony. *Vindiciae Legis*. London: James Young, 1646.

Calvin, John. *Commentary on a Harmony of the Evangelists, Matthew, Mark, and Luke*. Translated by William Pringle. Grand Rapids: Baker, 1996.

———. *Institutes of the Christian Religion*. Grand Rapids: Eerdmans, 1951.

Chantry, Walter J. "Baptism and Covenant Theology." In *Covenant Theology: A Baptist Distinctive*, edtied by Earl Blackburn, 125–36. Pelham, AL: Solid Ground Books, 2013.

———. *The Covenants of Works and of Grace*. Pensacola, FL: Chapel Library, 2014.

———. "The Covenants of Work" in *Covenant Theology: A Baptist Distinctive*, edited by Earl Blackburn, pp. 89–110. Pelham, AL: Solid Ground Books, 2013.

———. *God's Righteous Kingdom: Focusing on the Law's Connection with the Gospel*. Edinburgh: Banner of Truth, 1980.

———. "Imputation of Righteousness and Covenant Theology." http://www.chantry-sermons.com/imputation.htm.

Conner, Alan. *Covenant Children Today*. Palmdale, CA: Reformed Baptist Academic Press, 2007.

Coxe, Nehemiah. "The Discourse Of The Covenants That God Made With Men Before The Law." In *Covenant Theology From Adam to Christ*, edited by Ronald Miller, et al., 29–140. Palmdale, CA: Reformed Baptist Academic Press, 2005.

Crampton, Gary W. *From Paedobaptism to Credobaptism*. Owensboro, KY: Reformed Baptist Academic Press, 2010.

Dabney, Robert L. *Lectures in Systematic Theology*. Grand Rapids: Zondervan, 1972.

Denault, Pascal. "By Further Steps: A Seventeenth-Century Particular Baptist Covenant Theology." In *Recovering A Covenantal Heritage*, edited by Richard C. Barcellos, 71–108. Palmdale CA: Reformed Baptist Academic Press, 2014.

———. *The Distinctiveness of Baptist Covenant Theology*. Pelham, AL: Solid Ground 2013.

Downes, Martin. *Risking the Truth: Handling Error in the Church*. Fearn, Ross-shire: Christian Focus, 2009.

Edwards, Jonathan, *The Works of President Edwards*, Vol. 1. New York: Leavitt and Allan, 1856.

Elam, Andrew M., et al. *Merit and Moses: A Critique of the Klinean Doctrine of Republication,* Eugene, OR: Wipf & Stock, 2014.

Engelsma, David J. *Federal Vision: Heresy at Root*. Jenison, MI: Reformed Free Publishing Association, 2012.

Estelle, Bryan, et al., eds. *The Law Is Not Of Faith*. Phillipsburg, NJ: P&R, 2009.

Fesko J.V. "Calvin and Witsius on the Mosaic Covenant" in *The Law is not of Faith*, edited Bryan D. Estelle, J.V. Fesko, David Van Drunen. Phillipsburg, R&P, 2009.

Fisher, Edward, and Thomas Boston. *The Marrow of Modern Divinity*. Swengel, PA: Reiner Publications, 1978.

Ferguson, Sinclair B. *The Holy Spirit*. Downers Grove: InterVarsity 1996.

———. *John Owen: The Man and His Theology*. Phillipsburg, NJ: P&R, 2002.

———. *John Owen on the Christian Life*. Edinburgh: Banner of Truth, 1987.

Fowler, James A. "Old Testament Believers and New Testament Christians." http://www.christinyou.net/pages/otbntc.htm.

Gallant, Tim. *These Are Two Covenants: Reconsidering Paul on the Mosaic Law*. Grande Prairie, AB: Pactum Books, 2012.

Garcia, Brian. *Can I Get A Witness: How to Understand and Set Free Jehovah Witnesses*. USA: CreateSpace, 2013.

Gay, David H. J. *New Covenant Articles*. Vol. 1. England: Brachus, 2014.

———. *New Covenant Articles*. Vol. 3. England Brachus, 2015.

Gentry, Peter J., and Stephen J. Wellum. *Kingdom through Covenant*. Wheaton, IL: Crossway, 2012.

Gibson, David. "Fathers of Faith, My Fathers Now!" *Themelios* 40.1 (2015) 14–34.

Gill, John. *Gill's Body of Divinity*. Grand Rapids: Baker, 1978.

Golding, Peter. *Covenant Theology: The Key of Theology In Reformed Thought And Tradition*. Fearn, Ross-shire, Mentor, 2004.

Goodwin, Thomas. *The Work of the Holy Ghost in our Salvation*. Eureka, CA: Tanski, 1996.

Gordon, T. David. "Abraham and Sinai Contrasted in Galatians 3:6–14." In *The Law Is Not Of Faith*, edited by Bryan Estelle, et al., 240–58. Phillipsburg, NJ: P&R, 2009.

Grier, W. J. *The Momentous Event*. London: Banner of Truth, 1970.

Grudem, Wayne. *Systematic Theology*. Grand Rapids: Zondervan, 1994.

Haddleton, Don. "Evangelical Superficiality." http://www.evangelical-times.org/archive/item/139/Ecclesiological—amp—Pastoral/Evangelical-superficiality/.

Ham, Ken. *Understanding the Times*. Pensacola, FL: Chapel Library, 2010.

Hamer, Colin. *The Bridegroom Messiah*. London: Apostolic, 2018.

Hamilton Jr., James M. *God's Indwelling Presence*. Nashville: B&H Academic, 2006.

Hicks Jr., Thomas E. "John Owen on the Mosaic Covenant." In *Recovering a Covenantal Heritage: Essays in Baptist Covenant Theology*, edited by Richard Barcellos, 175–92. Palmdale, CA: Reformed Baptist Academic Press, 2014.

Hodge, A. A. "Baptism." http://www.the-highway.com/Baptism_Hodge.html.

———. *Evangelical Theology*. London: Banner of Truth, 1976.

Hodge, Charles. *Systematic Theology*. London: Nelson, 1872.

———. *A Commentary on I and II Corinthians*. London: Banner of Truth, 1974.

———. "The Church Membership of Infants." *Biblical Repository and Princeton Review*, 30.111 Article 7 (1858) 347–89.

Horton, Michael. *Introducing Covenant Theology*. Grand Rapids: Baker, 2009.

Hughes, Philip E. *A Commentary On the Epistle To The Hebrews*. Grand Rapids: Eerdmans, 1977.

Hulse, Errol. *The Testimony of Baptism*. Haywards Heath Sussex: Carey, 1982.

Hunsinger, George. "Justification and Mystical Union with Christ: Where Does Owen Stand?" In *The Ashgate Research Companion to John Owen's Theology*, edited by Kelly M. Kapic and Mark Jones, 199–214. Ashgate Research Companion. Burlington, VT: Ashgate, 2012.

Hunter, James D. *Evangelicalism: The Coming Generation*. Chicago: University of Chicago, 1987.

Jewett, Paul K. *Infant Baptism and the Covenant of Grace*. Grand Rapids: Eerdmans, 1980.

Johnson, Jeffrey D. *The Kingdom of God: A Baptist Expression Of Covenant and Biblical Theology*. Conway, AR: Free Grace, 2014

———. *The Fatal Flaw of the Theology Behind Infant Baptism*. Conway, AR: Free Grace, 2010.

Kingdon, David. *Children of Abraham*. Worthing, England: Carey Publications, 1973.

Lawrence, Henry. *Of Baptism*. London: Macock, 1659.

Lenski, R. C. H. *The Interpretation of Saint Pauls First and Second Epistles to the Corinthians*. Minneapolis, MN: Augsburg, 1937.

Letham, Robert. *Union with Christ in Scripture, History, and Theology*. Phillipsburg, NJ: P&R, 2011.

———. *The Work of Christ*. Downers Grove, IL: IVP, 1993.

Leupold, H.C. *Exposition of Isaiah*. Grand Rapids: Baker, 1968.

Lloyd-Jones, Martyn. *God's Ultimate Purpose: An Exposition of Ephesians One* Edinburgh: Banner of Truth, 1978.

———. *Joy Unspeakable*: Kingsway Publications, 1985.

———. *Romans, Exposition of Chapter* 2:1—3:20. Edinburgh, Banner of Truth, Edinburgh, 1989.

———. *Romans, Assurance, Exposition of Chapter 5*. Edinburgh, Banner of Truth 1976.

———. *Romans, The New Man: Exposition of Chapter 6*. Edinburgh, Banner of Truth, 1979.

———. *Romans, 8:17–39 The Final Perseverance of the Saints*. Edinburgh, The Banner of Truth, 1975.

Long, Gary D. *New Covenant Theology: Time For A More Accurate Way*. USA: Create Space, 2013.

Luther, Martin. *Lectures on Galatians 1–4*. Luther's Works, 55 Vols. Edited by Jaroslav Pelikan. St. Louis, MO: Concordia, 1968.

Lyman, Atwater H. "Children of the Covenant and Their Part in the Lord." *Biblical Repertory and Princeton Review*. Vol. XXXV, No. IV, (1863).

MacArthur, John. *The Gospel According to Jesus*. Grand Rapids: Zondervan, 2008.

Marcel, Pierre-Charles. *The Biblical Doctrine of Infant Baptism*. Cambridge: James Clark, 2002.

Marshall, I. Howard. *Acts: Tyndale New Testament Commentaries*. Downers Grove, IL: InterVarsity, 1980.

Martin, Hugh. *The Atonement*. London: Banner of Truth 2013.

Masters, Peter. *Only One Baptism Of The Holy Spirit*. London: Wakeman Trust, 1994.

———. *World Domination: The High Ambition of Reconstructionism*. London: Wakeman Trust, 1994.

Mauro, Philip. "Baptism, Place and Importance in Christianity." https://archive.org/stream/MauroPhilipBaptism/.

McGowan A. T. B. *Adam, Christ and Covenant*, London, Inter-Vasity Press, 2016.

McManigal, Daniel. *Encountering Christ in the Covenants*. Portland, OR: Monergism, 2013.

Mohler Jr., Albert R. *The Disappearance of God*. Colorado Springs: Multnomah Books, 2009.

Morris, Leon. "Hebrews." In *The Expositor's Bible Commentary: Hebrews through Revelation*, Vol. 12, edited by Frank E Gaebelein. Grand Rapids: Zondervan, 1981.

Motyer, J. Alec, *The Prophecy of Isaiah: An Introduction and Commentary*, Downers Grove: IVP, 1993.

Murray, John. *Christian Baptism*, Phillipsburg, NJ: P&R, 1980.

———. *Collected Writings of John Murray*, Vol. 2. Edinburgh: Banner of Truth, 1977.

———. *The Covenant of Grace: A Biblico-Theological Study*, London: Tyndale, 1954.

———. *The Epistle to the Romans*. London: Marshall, Morgan, and Scott, 1974.

———. *Redemption Accomplished and Applied*. Grand Rapids: Eerdmans, 1955.

Neill, Jeffrey D. "The Newness of the New Covenant." In *The Case For Covenantal Infant Baptism*, edited by Gregg Strawbridge, 127–55. Phillipsburg, NJ: P&R, 2003.

Owen, John.*The Death of Death in the Death of Christ*. Edinburgh: Banner of Truth, 1978.

———. *An Exposition of Hebrews*. 4 Vols. Indiana, Sovereign Grace, 1961.

———. "An Exposition of Hebrews 8:6–13." In *Covenant Theology From Adam to Christ*, edited by Ronald Miller, et al., 156–312. Palmdale, CA: Reformed Baptist Academic Press, 2005.

———. *The Works of John Owen*, 16 Vols. Edinburgh: Banner of Truth, 1968.

Pemble, William. *Vindiciae Fidei or A Treatise of Justification by Faith*. Oxford: John Lichfield, 1629.

Petersen, Rodney. "The Debate throughout Church History." In *Continuity and Discontinuity: Perspectives on the Relationship between the Old and New Testaments*, edited by John S. Feinberg, 17–34.Wheaton, IL: Crossway, 1988.

Pink, Arthur W. *The Divine Covenants*. Memphis, TN: Bottom of the Hill, 2011.

———. *The Doctrine of Salvation*. Grand Rapids: Baker, 1979.

Prager, Dennis. *A Civilization that Believes in Nothing*. The Door, Nov/Dec, 1990, 11–15.

Pratt, Richard L. "Infant Baptism in the New Covenant." In *The Case For Covenantal Infant Baptism*, edited by Gregg Strawbridge, 156–74. Phillipsburg, NJ: P&R, 2003.

Prince, Derek. *The Baptism in the Holy Spirit*. New Kensington, PA: Whitaker House, 1996.

Purnell, Robert. *A Little Cabinet Richly Stored with all Sorts of Heavenly Varieties and Soul-refining Influences, etc.* London, 1657.

Reisinger, John. *Abraham's Four Seeds*. Frederisk, MD: New Covenant Media, 1998.

Renihan, Samuel. "1689 Federalism Compared to 20th Century Reformed Baptists." https://www.youtube.com/watch?v=ZvPoAnMGuGE.

Renihan, James M., "Introduction" in *Recovering a Covenantal Heritage: Essays in Baptist Covenant Theology*, ed. Richard Barcellos, Palmdale, CA: Reformed Baptist Academic Press, 2014.

Renihan, Micah, and Samuel Renihan. "Reformed Baptist Covenant Theology and Biblical Theology." In *Recovering a Covenantal Heritage: Essays in Baptist Covenant Theology*, edited by Richard Barcellos, 475–506. Palmdale, CA: Reformed Baptist Academic Press, 2014.

Reymond L. Robert. *A New Systematic Theology of the Christian Faith*. Nashville: Thomas Nelson, 1998.

Rhodes, Jonty. *Covenants Made Simple*. Phillipsburg, NJ: P&R 2014.

Riggs, John W. *Baptism in the Reformed Tradition: A Historical and Practical Theology*. London: Westminster John Knox, 2002.

Roberts, Francis. "Of God's Covenants." In *Mysterium & Medulla Bibliorum the Mysterie and Marrow of the Bible*. Ann Arbor, MI: Text Creation Partnership, 2003–2009.

Robertson, O. Palmer. *The Christ of the Covenants*. Phillipsburg, NJ: P&R, 1980.

———. *The Israel of God*, Phillipsburg, NJ: P&R, 2012.

Schaff, Philip. *Creeds of the Evangelical Churches*. London: Hodder & Stoughton, 1878.

Schenck, Lewis B. *The Presbyterian Doctrine of the Children in the Covenant*. Phillipsburg, NJ: P&R, 2003.

Schrenk, Gottlob. *Gottesreich und Bund im älteren Protestantismus vornehmlich bei Johannes Cocceius*. Gutersloh: Bertelsmann, 1923.

Schulthess-Rechberg, Gustav von. *Luther, Zwingli und Calvin in ihren Ansichten über das Verhältnis von Staat und Kirche*. Aarau: Sauerländer, 1909.

Spilsbury, John. *A Treatise Concerning the Lawful Subject of Baptisme*. London: 1643.

Sproul R. C. *Everyone's A Theologian*. Orlando: Reformation Trust, 2014.

Spurgeon, Charles H. "Children Brought to Christ, and Not to the Font." http://www.
    spurgeon.org/sermons/0581.php.

Stibbs, A. M., and J. I. Packer. *The Spirit Within You*. Grand Rapids: Baker, 1979.

Stott, John. *Baptism and Fullness*, Leicester: InterVarsity, 1977.

Stott, John, and Alec Motyer. *The Anglican Evangelical Doctrine of Infant Baptism*.
    London: Latimer Trust, 2008.

Thomas, Geoffrey. "From A Welsh Revival To A Baptist Pulpit." In *Why I Am A Baptist*,
    edited by Tom J. Nettles and Russell D. Moore, 102–12. Nashville, TN: B&H, 2001.

Trueman, Carl R. *Reformation, Yesterday, Today and Tomorrow*. Ross-shire, Scotland:
    Christian Focus, 2011.

Ursinus, Zacharaias. *The Commentary of Dr. Zacharaias Ursinus on the Heidelberg
    Catechism*. Translated by Rev. G.W. Williard. Columbus: Scott and Bascom, 1851.

Verduin, Leonard. *The Reformers and Their Stepchildren*. Grand Rapids: Eerdmans,
    1964.

Vos, Geerhardus. *Redemptive History and Biblical Interpretation*. Phillipsburg, NJ: P&R,
    2001.

———. *Blue Banner of Faith and Life*. January–March Issue. Beaver Falls, PA: RPCNA,
    1959.

Walvoord, J. F. "Identification with Christ." In *Evangelical Dictionary of Theology* 2nd
    edition, edited by Walter A. Elwell, 588. Grand Rapids: Baker, 2001.

Ware, Bruce G. "Believer's Baptism View." In *Baptism: Three Views*, edited by David F.
    Wright, 19–50. Downers Grove, IL: IVP Academic, 2009.

Warfield, Benjamin B. *Biblical and Theological Studies*. Philadelphia: P&R, 1968.

———. "The Polemics of Infant Baptism." *The Presbyterian Quarterly* 8 (1899) 313–34.

Watson, J.D. *Salvation is of the Lord*. Meeker, CO: Sola Scriptura, 2015.

Watson T. E. *Should Babies Be Baptized?* Durham, UK: Evangelical Press & Services
    Limited, 2004.

Watson, Thomas. *A Body Of Divinity*. Edinburgh: Banner of Truth, 1978.

Wells F. David. *God in the Wasteland*, Grand Rapids: Eerdmans, 1994.

———. *No Place For Truth: or Whatever Happened to Evangelical Theology?*. Grand
    Rapids: Eerdmans, 1994.

Wellum J. Stephen. "Baptism and the Relationship between the Covenants." In *Believer's
    Baptism*, edited by Thomas R. Schreiner and Shawn D. Wright, 97–162. Nashville,
    TN: B&H Academic, 2006.

White, James R. "The Newness of the New Covenant Part 2." *Reformed Baptist
    Theological Review* 1:2 (2005) 144–52.

Wilkins, Steve. "Covenant, Baptism, and Salvation." In *The Federal Vision*, edited by
    Steve Wilkins and Duane Garner. Monroe: Athanasius, 2004.

Wilson, Douglas. *To A Thousand Generations*. Moscow, ID: Canon Press, 1996.

Witsius, Herman. *The Economy of the Covenants Between God and Man*, Vol.1.
    Escondido, CA: Den Dulk Christian Foundation, 2010.

Woolsey A. Andrew, "The Covenant in the Church Fathers," Haddington House
    Journal, 2003.

Wright, David. "Christian Baptism: Where Do We Go From Here?" *Evangelical
    Quarterly* 78 (2006) 163–69.

Confessions of Faith

The Baptist Confession of Faith of 1689. Updated English with notes and proof texts, Ch.8:6. London:The Wakeman.

Heidelberg Catechism: Method of Instruction in the Christian Religion,www.ccel.org/creeds/heidelberg-cat.html.

The Westminster Confession of Faith. The Publications Committee Of The Free Presbyterian Church Of Scotland. John G Eccles Printers Ltd. Inversness, 1976.

Printed in the USA
CPSIA information can be obtained
at www.ICGtesting.com
LVHW022036091223
766037LV00005B/462